Performance Information in the Public Sector

Governance and Public Management Series

Series edited by:

International Institute of Administrative Sciences, Belgium

Ken Kernaghan, Brock University, Canada; **Wim van de Donk**, Tilburg University, The Netherlands

Titles include:

Michiel S. De Vries, P. S. Reddy, M. Shamsul Haque (*editors*)
IMPROVING LOCAL GOVERNMENT
Outcomes of Comparative Research

Wouter Van Dooren and Steven Van de Walle (*editors*)
PERFORMANCE INFORMATION IN THE PUBLIC SECTOR
How it is Used

Governance and Public Management Series
Series Standing Order ISBN 978–0230–50655–8 (hardback) 978–0230–50656–5 (paperback)

You can receive future titles in this series as they are published by placing a standing order. Please contact your bookseller or, in case of difficulty, write to us at the address below with your name and address, the title of the series and the ISBN quoted above.

Customer Services Department, Macmillan Distribution Ltd, Houndmills, Basingstoke, Hampshire RG21 6XS, England

Performance Information in the Public Sector

How it is Used

Edited by

Wouter Van Dooren
Assistant Professor, Department of Political Science
University of Antwerp, Belgium

and

Steven Van de Walle
Associate Professor of Public Administration
Erasmus University Rotterdam, The Netherlands

First published 2008 by
PALGRAVE MACMILLAN

Palgrave Macmillan in the UK is an imprint of Macmillan Publishers Limited,
registered in England, company number 785998, of Houndmills, Basingstoke,
Hampshire RG21 6XS.

Palgrave Macmillan in the US is a division of St Martin's Press LLC,
175 Fifth Avenue, New York, NY 10010.

Palgrave Macmillan is the global academic imprint of the above companies
and has companies and representatives throughout the world.

Palgrave® and Macmillan® are registered trademarks in the United States,
the United Kingdom, Europe and other countries.

ISBN-13: 978-0-230-55197-8 hardback
ISBN-10: 0-230-55197-1   hardback

This book is printed on paper suitable for recycling and made from fully
managed and sustained forest sources. Logging, pulping and manufacturing
processes are expected to conform to the environmental regulations of the
country of origin.

A catalogue record for this book is available from the British Library.

Library of Congress Cataloging-in-Publication Data

    Performance information in the public sector / edited by
Wouter Van Dooren.
        p. cm.—(Governance and public management)
    Includes bibliographical references and index.
    ISBN 978-0-230-55197-8 (alk. paper)
        1. Government productivity – Evaluation. 2. Performance –
Management. 3. Public administration. I. Dooren, Wouter van.

JF1525.P67P473 2008
352.6'6—dc22   2008027560

10 9 8 7 6 5 4 3 2 1
17 16 15 14 13 12 11 10 09 08

Printed and bound in Great Britain by
CPI Antony Rowe, Chippenham and Eastbourne

Contents

Part II Politics and Society

List of Figures and Tables

Figures

Tables

List of Abbreviations

ACSP	Agency-School Collaboration Partnership
ASPA	American Society for Public Administration
CCRS	Citywide Citizen Response System
CIPA	Citizen-Initiated Performance Assessment
CLG	Communities and Local Government
DEFR	Department for Environment, Food and Rural Affairs
DOT	Department of Transportation
DWP	Department for Work and Pensions
EBP	Evidence-Based Policy
EGPA	European Group of Public Administration
FABRIC	Focused, Appropriate, Balanced, Robust, Integrated and Cost Effective
FCO	Foreign and Commonwealth Office
GAO	US General Accounting Office; since 2004 Government Accountability Office
GASB	Governmental Accounting Standards Board
GPRA	Government Performance and Results Act
GPEA	Government Policy Evaluation Act
GSB	Grotestedenbeleid (Dutch Urban Policy)
ICC	Interagency Coordinating Councils
ICMA	International City/County Management Association
ICT	Information and Communications Technology
IRS	Internal Revenue Service
KOSTRA	Kommune-Stat-Rapportering (Municipality-State-Reporting)
MBO	Management By Objectives
MBOR	Management By Objectives and Results
MRRS	Management Resources and Results Structure
NAO	National Audit Office
NHS	National Health Service
NPM	New Public Management
NYBMR	New York Bureau of Municipal Research
ODPM	Office of the Deputy Prime Minister
OECD	Organization for Economic Cooperation and Development
OLM	Organizational Learning Mechanisms

OMB	Office of Management and Budget
PAC	Public Accounts Committee
PASC	Public Administration Select Committee
PART	Performance Assessment Rating Tool
PBS	Portfolio Budget Statement
PI	Performance Indicator
PISA	Programme for International Student Assessment
PPBS	Planning Programming Budgeting System
PSA	Public Service Agreement
PUMA	Public Management Section, OECD
QUANGO	Quasi-Autonomous Non-Governmental Organization
RAE	Research Assessment Exercise
SMART	Specific, Measurable, Accurate, Realistic and Timely
VHA	Veterans Health Administration
VISN	Veterans Integrated Service Networks
ZBB	Zero-Based Budgeting

Notes on the Contributors

Maria P. Aristigueta is Professor and Director of the School of Urban Affairs and Public Policy of the University of Delaware (USA).

Jostein Askim (PhD) is Associate Professor at the Department of Political Science of the University of Oslo (Norway).

Geert Bouckaert is Professor and Director of the Public Management Institute of the Katholieke Universiteit Leuven (Belgium). He is also President of the European Group of Public Administration.

Dennis de Kool (PhD) is a Research Fellow at the Center for Public Innovation, Erasmus University Rotterdam (the Netherlands).

Patria de Lancer Julnes is associate professor and director of the doctor of public administration program in the School of Public Affairs at the University of Baltimore (USA).

Kathryn G. Denhardt is Professor at the School of Urban Affairs and Public Policy of the University of Delaware (USA).

John Halligan is Research Professor at the School of Business and Government of the University of Canberra (Australia).

Harry Hatry is a distinguished Fellow and Director of the Public Management Program at the Urban Institute (USA).

Alfred Tat-Kei Ho is Associate Professor at the School of Public and Environmental Affairs, Indiana University-Purdue University Indianapolis (USA).

Åge Johnsen is Professor at the Faculty of Social Sciences of the Oslo University College (Norway).

Carole Johnson is Lecturer at the Manchester Business School (UK) and Fellow with the Herbert Simon Institute (UK).

Per Lægreid is Professor at the Department of Administration and Organization Theory of the University of Bergen, and Senior Researcher at the Stein Rokkan Centre, University of Bergen (Norway).

Donald Moynihan is Associate Professor at the LaFollette School of Public Affairs of the University of Wisconsin – Madison (USA).

Zoe Radnor is Senior Lecturer at the Warwick Business School (UK).

Alasdair Roberts is the Rappaport Professor of Law and Public Policy at Suffolk University Law School (USA).

Paul G. Roness is Professor at the Department of Administration and Organization Theory of the University of Bergen (Norway).

Kristin Rubecksen is a PhD candidate at the Department of Administration and Organization Theory of the University of Bergen (Norway).

Colin Talbot is Professor at the Manchester Business School and Director of the Herbert Simon Institute (UK).

Steven Van de Walle is Associate Professor at the Department of Public Administration, Erasmus University Rotterdam (the Netherlands).

Wouter Van Dooren is Assistant Professor at the Department of Political Science of the University of Antwerp and Research Fellow at the Public Management Institute of the Katholieke Universiteit Leuven (Belgium).

Introduction: Using Public Sector Performance Information

Steven Van de Walle and Wouter Van Dooren

Use – a neglected issue in performance measurement research

Martha S. Feldman, a distinguished student of the role of information in organizations and in decision making starts her seminal book *Order without Design* by writing about her experiences undertaking fieldwork for a research project in the US Department of Energy:

> When I explained to the members of this office that I was interested in how the policy office produces information and how it was used, I was met time and again with the response that the information is not used.
>
> (Feldman, 1989: 1)

Does this reflect officials' cynicism, or does it really mean that information is not used in organizations, or should the notion of "use" be enriched to reflect its many dimensions and subtleties?

Although the practice of performance measurement is at least a century old, we witnessed a remarkable revival with the advent of New Public Management (NPM). Performance measurement is at the core of this doctrine, which propagated, amongst other things, managerial freedom based on output controls (Hood, 1991). In recent decades, performance measurement and NPM have become Siamese twins, both in thinking and in practice. There has been a growing disillusionment with NPM and this has reflected on performance measurement. The question then is: is there a future for performance measurement beyond NPM? The contributions in this volume seek the answer to this question in a redefinition of how performance information is used.

In decades of research on performance information in the public sector, it was often assumed that the mere availability of performance information would lead to its use by decision makers. While the production of performance information has received considerable attention in the public sector performance measurement and management literature, actual use of this information has traditionally not been very high on the research agenda. One reason for this neglect is that the use of performance information has long been considered as unproblematic in the performance measurement cycle. Another reason may be a cynical presumption that politicians don't use performance information; citizens don't understand it and don't bother about it; and that public managers don't trust it or don't take it seriously.

While the link between performance measurement and the use of this information in decision making is often assumed, actual use is often the weak spot in performance information systems. Much of the evidence on whether performance information is actually used in decision making is still rather anecdotal (de Lancer Julnes and Holzer, 2001), and opinion on whether performance measurement actually matters for decisions is divided (Askim, 2007a; Ho, 2006; Moynihan and Ingraham, 2004; Pollitt, 2006b).

Patterns of performance information use are different at the various stages of the decision-making process (Melkers and Willoughby, 2005). There are also important sectoral differences, meaning that performance information is more embedded in some policy sectors than in others (Askim, 2007a; Davies, Nutley and Smith, 2000; Van Dooren, 2004). Individual organizations have different organizational cultures, impacting on the use of performance information (Moynihan, 2005a: 204), and large differences exist between countries in patterns of use of performance information (Pollitt, 2005).

End-users: managers, politicians and citizens

In this volume, we focus on the "end-users" of the information generated by performance measurement systems: once the information exists, how is it then read, analyzed, and used in future decisions or in shaping public organizations? How does this information have an influence on organizational routines, on decisions, on the people in the organization, on the politicians steering these organizations, or on the citizens using the services of these organizations?

There are different types of end-users. There are managers and other public employees who make operational or strategic decisions. There are politicians who decide about budgets, who steer agencies, and who have to legitimize their policies. There are citizens who want to see how their taxes are being used, and who want to be informed about how the public services they use are performing.

Why use performance information?

In the rational decision-making model, the role of performance information is rather straightforward: Neat performance information contributes to the attainment of neatly defined organizational goals. The rational decision-making model fails to recognize that performance information may actually amplify ambiguity rather than reduce it. There is at the same time too much information creating overload and cognitive problems, and too little information to control all aspects of public services. As a result, the same information may lead to entirely different outcomes. Use (or indeed non-use) is not a linear process, and performance information systems may be more loosely coupled than their outward appearance suggests.

Performance measurement and management is in fact a very multi-faceted phenomenon. Use is therefore also quite diverse. Robert Behn (2003) listed eight different purposes of performance measurement (evaluate, control, budget, motivate, promote, celebrate, learn, improve), and each of these purposes has its own logic and determinants. An analysis of whether and how performance information is actually used in the public sector has to take the different types of use into account. When we analyze how performance information is used to improve front-line service delivery, we are in fact studying a phenomenon that is fundamentally different from a situation where performance information is used for advocacy or accountability purposes. Performance information and its use by public organizations, politicians and citizens can be studied as an instrument for service improvements. But it can also be studied as a symbol in the wider policy process or as a social phenomenon reflecting societal change.

Definitions of use

When policy makers say they "don't use" performance information, what does this, then, actually mean? Does it mean they generally do not sit down with a 200-page performance report and a cup of coffee? This is quite likely. Henry Mintzberg, when studying managers, showed that managers did not generally get their information from reading reports, but by talking to other people (Mintzberg, 1975). Likewise, the conclusion of the (all in all, scarce) research on how politicians use performance information, appears to be that performance reports are neither read nor valued (Pollitt, 2006b; ter Bogt, 2004).

Such an approach to "use" would be very narrow. Policy makers cannot possibly mean that performance information has no effect whatsoever on their decisions, or on their way of looking at organizations. The use of performance information is probably less formalized than the existence of performance reports or league tables suggests. Decision makers engage in a "problemistic search" and seek out supplementing sources of information, rather than just relying on one predefined set of information (Cyert and March, 1963).

Carol Weiss's research on how program evaluation outcomes influence policy provides us with alternative ways of looking at use (see, e.g., Weiss, 1979; Webber, 1991). One alternative way is the symbolic use of performance information, where the information is used for persuasive or legitimation purposes. Another – more difficult to study – use of information is conceptual use, whereby information supports general enlightenment. Rather than being used in a straightforward and direct way, performance information permeates or "creeps" into the organization's mindset (Weiss, 1980). Such an approach does more justice to the incomplete and ambiguous character of much performance information.

A performance information community

We have seen the development of a performance information community in the public sector and even a performance indicator industry (Hood, 1991: 9). This community consists of officials and other actors who are experienced users of performance information. They know how to interpret performance information, they know the strengths and weaknesses of performance information, they know how to data-mine the information and how to present it in an accessible and/or convincing format. They are the performance information wizards who know the magic words for talking about organizational performance and improvement. Talking about organizational performance using indicators signals competence. Yet, there is a possibility of parts of this performance information community becoming isolated from the organizational reality that is being measured. As a result, performance information becomes a production stream in the organization in its own right.

A measurement culture is not necessarily a performance culture. Yet, it is undeniable that the performance information mindset has changed the way of working in the public sector. Performance information has permeated the public sector, and organizations have developed routines to deal with this information. There are of course instances where performance information is used in a conspicuous way in decision making. Performance information is then used for its legitimating or communicative value. Even more attention goes to the abuse and misuse of performance information. But we cannot reduce study of the use of performance information to a study of dysfunctions. Performance information has been around for too long to make this credible, and we have seen too many well-intentioned innovations to simply discard performance information.

Research implications

The study of the use of public performance information, to which this book seeks to contribute, needs to move beyond the study of decision-making processes. Rare are the cases where a single discrete decision can be traced back to a well-defined set of performance indicators. Both the decision-making process and performance information are much too incoherent for this (March, 1987). Performance information is more than the generally agreed-upon colorful graphs and tables in annual reports, and organizational decisions are generally not made by a unitary decision maker at a precise point of time (Majone, 1989: 15).

The aim of this book is to demonstrate how to move beyond the technicalities of performance measurement and performance information. Studying performance information use is in essence a sociological study. It combines a focus on organizational structures for collecting, disseminating, evaluating, and using performance information, with an analysis of the cultural changes related to the increased use of performance information. The use of performance information reflects more than a mere change in the technicalities of public sector decision making. It is indicative of the continuing emergence of a performance information mindset that has influenced officials, politicians, and citizens alike.

Overview of the book

This book grew out of a series of meetings of the *Study Group on Performance in the Public Sector* (formerly Study Group on Productivity and Quality in the Public Sector – www.publicsectorperformance.eu) of the European Group of Public Administration (EGPA). The Study Group had meetings during the annual EGPA conferences in Ljubljana (2004),

Bern (2005), Milan (2006), and Madrid (2007) with calls for papers on "performance measurement and public management reform," "the contingencies of performance measurement systems," "utilization and non-utilization of public sector performance information," and "measuring and comparing the performance of public sectors and public institutions." In addition, a joint ASPA-EGPA Transatlantic Dialogue was held in Leuven in June 2006, attracting over 100 international academics discussing how to improve the performance of the public sector, and how to know that we are improving. All this resulted in series of high-quality papers.

This book is not just a collection of conference papers. During the past couple of years, the Study Group has also created an informal network of academics studying "performance in the public sector." The chapters in this volume each take a different approach to the phenomenon of performance information use. The book is divided into two main parts. The chapters in Part I look at the use of performance information within public sector organizations and by public managers. The chapters in Part II look at the use of performance information at the intersection of these organizations with politics and society. As such, the book presents a progressive set of chapters introducing readers to a widening set of issues and approaches to the use of performance information in the public sector.

The book starts with a chapter by Wouter Van Dooren, who looks at continuity and change in twentieth-century performance movements. He shows that the concepts used by eight distinct performance movements have been remarkably stable, and that there has been a political dimension to each of these movements. The major evolution, he argues, has been the intensification of use in all corners of the public sector. That is the reason why recent movements seem to have had a more profound impact on public administration than ever before.

Performance information, says Donald Moynihan in Chapter 2, is not comprehensive or objective, but always incomplete and ambiguous. The use and interpretation of performance information therefore emerges from an interactive dialogue between actors in public organizations. Drawing from the literature of organizational learning, he investigates the potential for performance information to foster goal-based learning in the public sector.

Performance steering is often presented as a tightly integrated system, whereby performance information triggers decisions. In Chapter 3, Per Lægreid, Paul Roness and Kristin Rubecksen use the Norwegian Management-By-Objectives-and-Results performance management system to show how performance information and performance steering interact in practice. They find a fragmented system where organizational objectives, performance indicators, performance reporting, and performance steering are, in fact, loosely coupled.

The reason why some would argue that performance information does not matter to decisions is that they insist on a very narrow definition of information use. Patria de Lancer Julnes explains in Chapter 4 why, when studying the use of performance information, we should move beyond traditional conceptions of use as an instrumental process and refocus our attention on how information informs a dialogue.

In Chapter 5, Geert Bouckaert and John Halligan take a macro-level approach and compare the implementation of performance management frameworks in the United Kingdom, the United States, Australia, and Canada. Using four ideal types of managing performance, their comparison reveals that practice often falls short of aspirations, and that countries have followed different pathways and implementation styles.

Dysfunctions of performance information systems are often the result of undue attention to performance measurement and reporting, rather than to performance management. Zoe Radnor, Chapter 6, synthesizes the debate about organizational gaming in the public sector and presents us with a gaming typology. Knowledge about the types of gaming behavior may help us to improve performance management systems, and may be a first step towards a more normative discussion.

Kathryn Denhardt and Maria Aristigueta in Chapter 7 discuss the problem of accountability when using performance information in a collaborative public management context. Partnerships and collaboration between agencies and programs blur clear lines of accountability, and therefore change the nature and purpose of performance measurement. With its focus on social indicators and the pressures created by the publication of such indicators, this chapter immediately provides the link to the second part of the book – the use of performance information by politicians and citizens who are outside the administrative system.

Jostein Askim analyses the role of performance information in political decision making. Pessimists in the debate have argued that politicians do not actually use traditional performance information. Just as some of the other authors in this volume, Askim demonstrates in Chapter 8 that we need to broaden our scope of research and also look at other types of information use, and at the different factors influencing politicians' use of information.

In Chapter 9, Carole Johnson and Colin Talbot look at the political use of performance information, with a focus on Parliamentary scrutiny committees involved in scrutinizing government activity in the United Kingdom. They find wide variety across the committees, combined with a strong undercurrent of a lack of change in traditional forms of scrutiny.

Åge Johnsen in Chapter 10 analyses the use of performance information in making public policy, and presents a case of education policy in Norway. Using a life cycle of performance management practices, he stresses that we need to look at the politics and interests behind the use or non-use of information. Political considerations explain why avoiding low performance may be a more powerful incentive than achieving a high level of service.

In Chapter 11, Dennis de Kool uses policy monitors in Dutch urban policy to explain why we need to take political and cultural factors into account when explaining the dynamics of such monitors. Performance information is used for different purposes. Knowledge about and recognition of the interests of all actors may greatly improve the effectiveness and legitimacy of monitoring instruments.

The last two chapters extend the analysis to citizens and society. Alfred Ho, in Chapter 12, highlights the importance of involving citizens in designing and using performance information. Approaching performance measurement systems as technical issues and implementing them top-down ignores the fact that performance is not a neutral concept. Involving citizens improves accountability because it gives them the right and opportunity to define what counts as performance and what doesn't.

Through a focus on rating and ranking systems, Steven Van de Walle and Alasdair Roberts demonstrate in Chapter 13 how performance information may create an illusion of rationality, order and control. The move towards ranking services' performance is based on a number of behavioral assumptions. Rather than viewing this change as a technical innovation, we should see it as indicative of wider changes in society and as an attempt to deal with uncertainty.

In an epilogue, Harry Hatry reflects on the future of performance information in the public sector, and the central role of "use" in the changing performance measurement landscape. Using the material presented in this book, he develops a taxonomy of use and suggests how the findings may be used to further public management research and public management practice.

Part I
Bureaucracy

1
Nothing New Under the Sun? Change and Continuity in the Twentieth-Century Performance Movements

Wouter Van Dooren

In a critical analysis, Radin (2006) argued that the concern for performance in the United States has become so ubiquitous that it has taken the form of a movement – the performance movement. It is characterized by a mindset of long-term and mid-term goal setting, indicators, and quantitative measurement. In this chapter, I argue that we have witnessed not one, but several performance movements that have attempted to measure government outputs or outcomes in the twentieth century.

Others have studied the history of performance measurement before. Williams (2003) for instance analyzed management practices in early twentieth-century New York, and found many of the features of contemporary performance measurement. These analyses paint a somewhat sobering picture. They seem to suggest that a whole century of public administration study and practice mainly led to stagnation. This observation is also somewhat puzzling. If this is true, why then is there such a vigorous debate about the dysfunctional aspects of performance management? If it really is old wine in new bottles, why, then, does Radin argue that the challenge of performance management to the foundations of traditional public administration is unprecedented? How did the face of performance management change for it to make an impact that it did not have before?

In order to answer these questions, we need to analyze *in what respect* performance measurement and management has changed or has not changed. We will argue that it is mainly changes in use that account for the impact of the contemporary performance movements. First, however, we briefly discuss the most important performance movements in the twentieth century.

Performance movements in the twentieth century

A number of performance movements developed between the end of the nineteeth century and the end of the twentieth century. Early movements emanated from different milieus, respectively social reformers, engineers and specialist administrators, and large corporations. All movements were a response to the social context of industrialization, poverty and social unrest, and governments plagued by corruption. The performance movements of the day sought the answers to these societal issues through the rationalization and quantification of policy and administration.

First, there was the social survey movement that comprised social reformers who needed facts about social problems (Bulmer, Bales and Sklar, 1991). The best-known work of the social survey movement is Charles Booth's study on the "Life and Labour of the People of London" (1886–1903) (Linsley and Linsley, 1993). Booth believed that the poverty debate was underdeveloped because three questions were unanswered; how many people were poor, why were they poor, and what should be done to alleviate poverty? The work shows that the social survey movement sought to quantify the (lack of) results of government. Social science was an i nstrument to influence a policy agenda.

While the social survey movement mainly targeted the social inequalities resulting from industrialization, the second movement, scientific management and the science of administration, was mainly an answer to industrialization itself. New industries and urbanization required more regulation of society, and government institutions therefore needed a professional workforce. Administration was now seen as a profession and a science in its own right. Measurement of government was part of this profession. The principles of both scientific management and the science of administration were according to Mosher (1968: 72–3): (1) Rationality: the applicability of the rule of reason; (2) Planning: the forward projection of needs and objectives; (3) Specialization: of materials, tools and machines, products, workers and organizations; (4) Quantitative measurement: applied as far as possible to all elements of operations; (5) "One best way": there is one single best method, tool, material and type of worker; (6) Standards and standardization: the "one best way," once discovered, must be made the standard.

A third evolution in the early twentieth century was the development of cost accounting. The development of cost accounting was a joint venture of the public and the private sector. Claims of control and openness echoed in both the public and private sector (Previts and Merino, 1979). Stronger information systems were also needed in order to manage increasingly large and complex organizations and corporations. Cost accounting is in essence the process of tracking, recording and analyzing costs associated with the activity of an organization. Through cost accounting, output indicators are integrated into the financial system. Cost accounting has become institutionalized in the private sector. In the public sector, it is still considered innovative in most OECD countries (Pollitt and Bouckaert, 2004).

The New York Bureau of Municipal Research (NYBMR) (Schachter, 1989; Williams, 2003) was a synthesis of scientific management, cost accounting and the social survey. The NYBMR developed many of the performance measurement concepts that are in use today. Data collection was embedded in accounting practices. Record keeping in the form of time sheets and work plans, as well as output and outcome indicators was developed. These indicators were supplemented by social indicators. The information was used for several purposes. A first purpose was the reporting of efficiency and effectiveness. Unit costs and gains and losses were perceived to be an important device for making the operations of the city transparent for citizens. Second, the information was integrated into a functional budget developed to compare similar work units. Third, the information was used for productivity improvements (Williams, 2003).

The mission statement of the fourth performance movement, performance budgeting, resounded in the fifth finding of the first Hoover Commission (1947) stating that "the budgetary processes of the Government need improvement, in order to express the objectives of the Government in terms of the work to be done rather than in mere classification of expenditure" (The Hoover Commission report in Shafritz and Hyde (2004: 162)). Performance budgeting became well established in the 1960s with the introduction of the Planning Programming Budgeting Systems (PPBS). New program expenditures had to be weighed against the marginal benefits of each program in a systemic way. PPBS was a child of its time. The search for big systems that describe the organization and its relation with the environment left its mark on the management tools of the day. PPBS overcommitted itself to this systemic dimension which eventually led to its collapse (Hood, 1998). Nonetheless, performance budgeting inspired subsequent initiatives such as Management By Objectives (MBO), Zero Based Budgeting (ZBB) and the Government Performance and Results Act (GPRA) (Kelly and Rivenbark 2003).

In the 1960s and early 1970s, the fifth performance movement emerged in parallel with performance budgeting. It was called the social indicator movement. After almost two decades of economic growth and prosperity, the limits of economic growth were felt, and the development of the welfare state triggered the demand for social data (De Neufville, 1975; Dowrick and Quiggin, 1998). The social indicator movement sought to construct standard measures of the state of health, crime, well-being, education and many other social characteristics of a population. However, the economic crises of the second half of the 1970s and the cutback management of the 1980s explain why the movement ran out of steam during that era (Bulmer, 2001). Nevertheless, the social indicator movement did have an impact. The statistical apparatus of governments was expanded to cover more phenomena, and new time series were developed. Moreover, the extended statistics on the social condition of the population allowed performance measurement systems to cover the outcomes of government action better. We still see the impact of this movement in contemporary social indicators such as quality of life, happiness or sustainable development.

While the social indicator movement aspired to substantiate the outcome side of performance measurement, the sixth performance movement, called "the quality movement," was aiming at the management side, that is, input, processes and output. The mention of quality in "quality management" seems to suggest that this movement is not about measurement. This is not the case since the quality models do prescribe performance measurement. Rather, quality means that measurement is focused on all relevant aspects of organizational management models. The quality models were developed in the 1950s and the 1960s. In the 1970s and 1980s, they were implemented in Japanese industry on a large scale (Bouckaert and Thijs, 2003). The success of the Japanese economy lent the quality movement its credibility. In the 1980s, the models were imported to the United States and Europe; first, in the private sector and, later, in the public sector.

In the 1980s, a number of countries, notably New Zealand, Australia and the United Kingdom, experimented with managerial approaches in the public sector (Zifcak, 1994). This resulted in a diffuse set of management reforms that spread globally in the 1990s and became known as the New Public Management (NPM). NPM, the seventh performance movement, prescribes that public agencies should be subdivided into small policy oversight boards and larger performance-based managed organizations for service delivery. The latter organizations were to compete with private sector organizations. Performance was to be the criterion to evaluate agencies, and this required measurement in an all-inclusive way. Under the colors of NPM resides a broad array of management tools, with contested compatibility (Hood, 1991; Williams, 2000). The use of performance information is not restricted to policy advice or budget and planning documents. It is integrated in almost all management functions.

The eight and most recent performance movement is Evidence-Based Policy (EBP). EBP has a predominantly British origin (Solesbury, 2001) and was initially pursued in the medical and public health sector (Davies, Nutley, S. M. and Smith, 2000). By the end of the 1990s, EBP had spread to virtually all policy sectors. Solesbury (2001) identifies three conditions that furthered the EBP movement in the United Kingdom. First, there has been a utilitarian turn in research funding policy and practice: Research should not only lead to understanding of society, it should also offer guidance on how to make things better. Second, he observes a decline in confidence in the professions. He speaks of a "retreat from priesthood" (p. 6). Third, New Labour propagated the replacement of ideology by pragmatism. Policy was said to be founded on evidence about what works rather than ideological predispositions.

Change and continuity in the performance movements

There have been at least eight performance movements from the end of the nineteenth century to the end of the twentieth century; social surveys, scientific management and the science of administration, cost accounting, performance budgeting, social indicators, quality management, NPM, and evidence-based policy. Notwithstanding the withering away of some of these performance movements, quantification of government activity has been a recurring tendency. Next, we discuss some change and continuity in the history of performance movements.

Continuity

The eight performance movements resemble each other in some remarkable ways. Probably the most striking similarity is the conceptual stability. The performance mindset did not change dramatically throughout time. Other elements of constancy are the coexistence of policy and management movements, the political nature of the movements, the presence of a stable set of carriers of ideas, and the existence of a deliberate strategy to diffuse practices to other administrations and countries.

Conceptual stability

Concepts are the intellectual artifacts we use to get a grip on reality. Williams (2003) demonstrated that most of the concepts we use to make sense of the very broad area of performance were already used by the NYBMR. He argues that by 1912, performance measurement exhibited many of the features associated with contemporary practice: measuring of input, output, and results; attempting to make government more productive; making reports comparable among communities; and focusing on allocation and accountability issues (2003: 643). The conceptual framework that sees government intervention as a process of turning inputs into outputs that subsequently should have effects in society is a recurring feature of all performance movements. Performance of government is the result of a transformation process of inputs to outputs and then outcomes.

Management and policy movements: coexistence, not a pendulum

Each performance movement has either a policy or a management orientation. Some performance movements were mainly concerned with output and efficiency, while others focused on outcomes and effectiveness. The social survey, the social indicator and the EBP movements were mainly policy-based movements. Scientific management, cost accounting, PPBS, and the New Public Management were predominantly management-based movements.

What is the trend? How do policy and management movements relate to each other? Is there a pendulum that swings from management to policy and back, or do policy and management movements coexist? The pendulum hypothesis seems attractive, since the deficiencies of a too-strong focus on management might be remedied by a stronger focus on policy, and vice versa. Yet, this does not seem to have been the case. Movements coexist. Social surveying and scientific management ran parallel in the early twentieth century. The NYBMR integrated elements from both movements (Stivers, 2000). Measurement for policy and measurement for management were not opposed to each other. A similar pattern of coexistence is found in the 1970s with the performance budgeting and social indicator movements running parallel. In the 1990s, the evidence-based policy movement and NPM overlapped as well.

This is a notable observation. In the twentieth century, policy and management turned to quantification every 30 years or so. The coexistence of performance movements in policy and management may point to a *Zeitgeist* that values quantification as indication of both rational policy making and rational management. This line of reasoning follows the argument made by Feldman and March (1981) that the use of information symbolizes a commitment to rationality. Displaying measurement as the symbol of rationality reaffirms the importance of this social value. The activity of measurement thus becomes the definition of managerial performance.

All performance movements are political

All performance movements are political in the sense that they all have a power dimension. Performance movements have been the subject of tactical maneuvers between legislatures, and executives, between politics and administration, between horizontal and vertical departments, and between political parties. The early twentieth-century attempts to separate politics from administration purposed a power shift from political appointees to administrators. The politico-administrative agenda of performance budgeting reforms in the United States and Australia in the 1990s was to reinforce executive control over departments and agencies (Van Dooren and Sterck, 2006). In Australia, the performance budget reduced the power of Parliament. The Parliamentary appropriation of budget items was set at such a general outcome level – "a safer Australia" – that Members of Parliament had trouble assessing what was lying underneath. Similarly, PPBS was an attempt by the executive to get a grip on a fragmented public sector. During the Great Depression, many new programs had been set up in response to new problems. This led to a disintegration of the executive branch of government. PPBS was expected to re-establish executive control through a clear line of executive authority (Kelly and Rivenbark, 2003). Finally, the rise of the EBP movement under the Blair government in Britain can also be seen as a political strategy. Burnham (2001) typifies the political strategy of New Labour as "the politics of depoliticization." It can be argued that the pragmatism of evidence-based policy making ("what matters is what works") is also a convenient strategy to retreat from strong ideological standpoints that inhibit the making of compromises.

Performance movements have a similar set of carriers

Movements are informally organized. In order to be recognized as a movement, some ingredients are needed. These are the carriers of a movement. First, all movements have had some main proponents that symbolized the movement. Names such as Frederick Taylor (scientific management), Gulick and Urwin (science of administration), or the quality gurus such as Juran or Deming are emblematic of their respective movements. These figures make movements identifiable throughout place and time. Second, associations usually promote the ideas of the movement. The International City/County Management Association, for instance, had a long history in disseminating performance measurement in the local public sector. A more recent example is the Public Management Section (PUMA) of the OECD, which promoted NPM concepts in its member countries. Third, all movements have their biblical texts. (Semi-) academic texts, usually written by the main figures of a movement, are used to disseminate the ideas of the movement. These key texts are used for research, training and advocacy. One of the key texts of the NPM movement, for instance, has been Osborne and Gaebler's Reinventing Government (1992). It is well written and persuasive. Although the book is practice oriented, it is larded with scientific argumentation. Other movements have had similar key texts. The social indicator movement, for instance, is often traced back to Bauer's (1966) assessment of the side-effects of the space program. Fourth, a successful movement will succeed in influencing the curricula of universities. Almost all twentieth-century movements set up courses, academic conferences and even their own journals.

The export of practices has been a deliberate policy

In the twentieth century, the export of performance practices has become a deliberate policy of actors in performance movements. The NYBMR intentionally exported its work to other communities through the provision of services and through contacts with agencies and officials. The PPBS system too was intentionally promoted in other countries. The same applies to NPM. In the late 1990s, many international delegations visited the NPM champions such as New Zealand and the United Kingdom. German local government officials traveled to Tilburg – a medium-sized Dutch city that was an acknowledged NPM champion. It led a Dutch academic to conclude that everyone seemed to be applying the Tilburg model, apart from Tilburg. While the city was hiring an external consultant to organize the reception of delegations, the city itself was already moving away from the model (Kickert, 2003).

Change

Despite the continuities, there are some remarkable changes too. First, in the last few decades there has been a technological revolution that enabled the reinvention of old concepts. Second, analysis techniques have become more sophisticated but also more decoupled from users. Third, and most importantly, use has changed.

Technological evolution enables the reinvention of old concepts

The technological infrastructure for measuring performance has improved tremendously. The most relevant evolutions have been the unparalleled increase in the processing power of computers and the development of networks. Information technology has enabled better generation, display and analysis of performance information. Performance data can be generated more easily thanks to the automation of administrative record keeping. Even field workers, using palmtops, can now more efficiently record performance data. This is, in particular, helpful for collecting output data. Outcome data usually are not embedded in administrative information systems and therefore remain notoriously difficult to collect. The display and diffusion of performance information is strongly enhanced by online applications. The increased computational power of computers permits more sophisticated analysis techniques.

These technological evolutions are particularly relevant because they enable the reinvention of old concepts. Geographic Information Systems (GIS) are a good example (Goodchild and Janelle, 2004). In essence, they are information systems providing knowledge about what is where, and when. The modern concept of building a spatial data infrastructure is not fundamentally different from Charles Booth's attempts to build a social map of London where social characteristics were attributed to spatial data (the location of the houses). Modern techniques have expanded the amount of data linked to the reference file, but the basic concept of mapping social phenomena has remained the same.

Analysis techniques have become more sophisticated, but decoupled from utilization "outside the box"

Major progress has been made with regard to techniques for analyzing performance information. Analysis techniques bridge the gap between data and information. Data are the plain numbers. Information is interpreted data upon which decisions can be based. The interpretation of data is often implicit and *ad lib*. In such an approach, a drop in unemployment is explained as a result of successful policy without taking external factors into account. Alternatively, data can be interpreted in an explicit way, using tools for analysis. In this case, unemployment figures in one constituency are, for instance, compared to those in other constituencies and external factors are filtered out by running regressions.

The sophistication of techniques for analysis has increased substantially. A corollary of this technical sophistication has been the increasingly technocratic nature of the analyses. This evolution goes hand in hand with specialization in Western societies in general and the professionalization of measurement in particular (see below). The increasing econometric and statistical complexity seems to have become a problem for actors that are not part of a profession or dealing with measures on a more or less daily basis. Typically, these actors are citizens and politicians. These users "outside the box" no longer understand the technology behind the results. Statistical sophistication sometimes puts up a smoke screen for inadequate conceptualizations, poor quality data or hidden agendas. Other contributions in this volume show that special efforts are required to reach these groups (see, e.g., Chapter 8 by Askim and Chapter 12 by Ho).

Institutionalization, professionalization and specialization of use

Probably the most important change in the subsequent performance movements is the use of performance information. Performance measurement and management has become: (1) more institutionalized; and (2) more professional; and as a result, there is (3) an increased tension between a specialist supply of performance information and a generalist demand.

(a)   The use of performance information (outputs and outcomes) has gradually become more institutionalized. Early twentieth-century movements such as the social survey and the NYBMR consisted of peripheral actors that wanted to influence government policy and management. Although these movements were innovative and their work influenced many, the impact on the government of the day should not be overrated. Davidson concludes that although senior researchers of the Social Survey Movement were appointed to positions in the British government, there is little evidence of impact (1991: 360). Similarly, it took scientific management and the science of administration several decades to penetrate the core of government. Arguably, this happened when the PPBS system was implemented (Schick, 1966). By that time, the science of administration was included in the curricula of the most important schools (Williams, 2003). Cost accounting, on the contrary, has never been institutionalized in government. Nowadays, measurement is done on a more regular basis – often laid down in management scorecards and management information systems. Increasingly, measurement is seen as an integral part of good management. Of course, this view is open to debate. We argued before that a commitment to measurement can also be of a symbolic nature; a commitment to rationality. Yet, since contemporary performance movements such as the quality movement and NPM are furthering this discourse, it becomes real in its consequences.

(b)   Another trend in use has been the increasing professionalization of measurement. This trend has two dimensions. On the supply side of information, professionalization implies that measurement has become a profession, with a mounting number of measurement professionals; management accountants, management consultants, policy advisors in think tanks, analysts in statistical offices, and so on whose job it is to draw conclusions from measurement. This management profession may run counter to traditional professions that see measurement as an intrusion on their autonomy (see also Chapters 10 by Johnsen and 13 by Van de Walle and Roberts).

On the demand side, there is a more professional way of dealing with information. The way in which information is used has become increasingly complicated. The most important trend seems to be that performance information has gradually become embedded in systems of accountability between the executive and top managers of departments, between tiers of government, between institutions (schools, hospitals) and central departments, and between employees and their bosses. These systems of accountability may run counter to the use of performance information for learning or advocacy (see also Moynihan in Chapter 2), or in Hood's (2007a) words, systems that envisage intelligence. Systems for accountability have the tendency to become beauty contests, while systems for intelligence necessarily need to be critical.

(c)   The third trend is an increasing tension between specialized supply and generalist demand. The supply of performance information has become increasingly specialized. The growing specialization of policy sectors has led to a supply of information that most of the time remains within the policy sectors. Policy movements, such as the social indicators and EBP movements were concerned that this rich sectoral knowledge base would be insufficiently opened up for decision makers (Bauer, 1966; Davies, Nutley and Smith, 2000). The social indicator movement failed to solve this problem. One of the many explanations was its overly technocratic and somewhat naive approach. It assumed that numbers would be used once they were provided. The gap between the increasingly specializing supply and the generalist demand of political decision makers is an enduring issue in performance measurement. It is probably too early to assess whether the EBP movement will be more successful than the social indicator movement in bridging this gap.

Discussion

Let us now briefly return to the central question of this chapter. Notwithstanding the long tradition of performance measurement and management – we identified eight in the history of performance measurement – no movement seems to have had the same influence on public administration as the current ones. What is so particular about the contemporary performance movements (mainly NPM and to some extent EBP) that they have had such a profound impact?

The answer is simple. Performance information needs to be used to have an impact. No other performance movement promoted the use of performance information in such a wide array of management functions. No other movement succeeded in integrating performance information in public management reform packages that focused on the whole of government. No other movement exported its ideas on a similar global scale (Pollitt and Bouckaert, 2004). No other movement coupled performance measurement as closely to accountability structures, in particular in the Anglo-Saxon version.

The change in the nature and extent of utilization contrasts sharply with the conceptual stability of the performance mindset. The conceptual stability may create an impression of absence of change. This is only true for certain aspects. We argue that the history of performance measurement and management in the twentieth century has been a history of use. This is an obvious, but important insight. If we want to study the successes and failures of performance movements, we have to study the use of performance information. We can not confine ourselves to the concepts and techniques.

Conclusion

It is often suggested that most change is superficial spin while the bottom line remains untouched. Mintzberg (1993), for instance, argued that it is always our own age that is turbulent and that therefore turbulence is normalcy. Does this apply to measurement in and of the public sector too? Are recent measurement efforts normalcy rather than change? We don't think so. Although there are tides of reform, every performance movement leaves some sediment which is acquired for future movements. The mapping of poverty was something novel in the late nineteenth and early twentieth century. Nowadays, poverty indicators are an institutionalized means of assessing government performance in the provision and redistribution of prosperity.

One of the most notable evolutions in the twentieth century performance movements has been the ever-increasing integration of measurement in the core of the public sector. The quantification of government started outside government. It was the third sector that began to measure results of the public sector as a tool for advocacy. The twentieth century has witnessed a growing integration of measurement within and by the public sector itself. Quantitative approaches to policy and management – in this order –have become an inclusive part of government. The elaboration of statistical systems led to the government-wide existence of policy indicators.

NPM was the first movement that included quantitative information in public management on a government-wide scale, on an international scale and in all management functions. However, NPM did not come out of the blue. It was conceptually conceived by the NYBMR. Only after an incubation period of nearly a century, does the performance mindset seem to have permeated the fibers of government, for better and worse.

2
Advocacy and Learning: An Interactive-Dialogue Approach to Performance Information Use

Donald Moynihan

This chapter examines how agencies use performance information, and in particular the potential for performance information to foster goal-based learning in the public sector. The most crucial indicator for whether measuring performance is worth the effort is whether public managers are using performance information (Hatry, 2006). It is also the most difficult aspect of performance management, requiring individuals and organizations to change deeply entrenched decision behaviors by widening the scope of the information considered.

This chapter portrays performance information use as emerging from an interactive dialogue between interested actors. As the dialogue contains a greater variety of conflicting interests, performance information will be exploited for subjective ends, reducing the prospects of consensus. This is because performance information itself is not comprehensive or objective, but incomplete and ambiguous. It is subject to selective measurement, presentation and interpretation based on the interests of the actors involved. The full implications of the interactive-dialogue model are explored in Moynihan (2008). In this chapter, I focus on two main implications of the model for information from the perspective of generic agency-level actors.

The first use of performance information by agency staff is for advocacy purposes. Performance information provides a means by which agencies can present their perspective in the policy arena. The second use of performance information is for goal-based learning, that is, where formal performance targets foster an investigation and improved understanding of how to achieve those targets. The interactive-dialogue model suggests such learning is most likely to occur within agencies

24

because there are fewer competing interests, and less disagreement between interests, than elsewhere in the policy arena. In the wider policy arena, stakeholders, central agencies, competing agencies, the media and elected officials are likely to disagree on the meaning of performance information because of ideological or institutional perspectives. For example, the budget process finds line agencies, central agencies and elected officials often disagreeing on what information should be collected, and what performance data reveals about funding decisions.

While public organizations have become quite adept at developing routines of performance information creation and dissemination, they have little experience in creating routines of use, or learning forums. Drawing from the literature of organizational learning, I identify the factors that facilitate goal-based learning. The latter part of the chapter explores the management issues associated with developing learning forums, which include the balance between accountability and defensiveness, the policy-making   potential of learning forums, and the importance of organizational culture for learning to succeed.

The interactive-dialogue model of performance information use

One belief, repeatedly expressed by the public managers that I have interviewed and observed in three different State governments at the agency and central agency level, and of central agency officials at the Federal level, is that performance information can be used to represent them, as a way to communicate their job and the challenges they face (Moynihan, 2008). Performance information can help them to advocate for particular management or policy issues, to defend or expand their budget. One state manager said: "I think it provides a hell of a defense when people come to rob you of resources of any kind."

But only some measures represent the viewpoint that agencies wish to present, and they therefore tend to favor certain data. The motivation for doing this was best summarized by the rhetorical question of one budget official: "what agency in their right mind is going to include measures that are going to reduce the chance of success in getting their damn money?" Some become skilled at using data to tell a compelling narrative about the agency. Measures are selected, presented and interpreted to fit with that narrative. One manager talked explicitly about his role in using numbers to develop a coherent story about the agency: "Understand that measuring policy is not a science. It is an art. It is words, and pictures and numbers. And you create impressions, beliefs, understandings and persuasions." Three state corrections departments agencies I studied, in Vermont, Virginia and Alabama, selectively measured, presented and interpreted information in such a way as to present their perspectives: some used data to portray efficiency and effectiveness in management practices, others used data to make the case for the success of new policy programs, and others used data to emphasize budget needs by pointing to input measures or workload indicators, or output/outcome goals that required more funding (Moynihan, 2008).

Performance management doctrine has tended to assume that performance information is objective, standardized, indicative of actual performance, consistently understood, and prompts a consensus about how a program is performing and how it should be funded. But the actual use of performance information exposes the limits of these assumptions. A theory that recognizes the use of performance information should recognize its interactive element, as actors try to persuade others to look at the performance information they consider important, and see it in the way that they do. The interactive-dialogue model presented here seeks to fill this gap, and is based on a number of assumptions (for more detail, see ch. 6 in Moynihan, 2008):

- Performance information is not comprehensive
- Performance information is ambiguous
- Performance information is subjective
- Production of performance information does not guarantee use
- Institutional affiliation and individual beliefs will affect selection, perception and presentation of performance information
- The context of dialogue will affect the ability to use performance information to develop solutions

Information is ambiguous (March and Olsen, 1976). Performance data do not tell us why performance did or did not occur, the context of performance, how implementation occurred, how outside factors influenced performance, how to choose which program measure is a priority, and tradeoffs with other programs. Performance information does not necessarily provide a definitive account of performance. You and I might look at program data and disagree about whether it is performing well or not. Assuming that we can agree that the program performed poorly, we might disagree on the cause of performance. You might argue that the problem is a management issue, while I might see it as a resource allocation issue. Even if we agree that performance information should influence resource allocation, performance data does not tell us how.

Should funding be cut and the program abandoned as a failure, or should more resources be provided to help make the program a success? The ability to answer this question depends a great deal on our understanding of why performance failed to occur and whether the program can be remedied, issues that are subject to disagreement. Values play a role. We are less likely to abandon programs that we feel have an important purpose.

There is likely to be no single definitive approach therefore to: (a) interpreting what performance information means, and (b) how performance information directs decisions. The meaning of performance information is constructed, and therefore the same performance information can support different arguments. The use of information will never meet some objective ideal because information will always be selected by people who bring with them their own personal and institutional biases (Majone, 1989; Stone, 1997).

Performance information use as advocacy

The interactive-dialogue model suggests that whether performance information is used, and how it is used, depends on the motivations of potential users, and the utility of performance information to their goals. In short, the use of performance information is a subjective exercise that often amplifies rather than reduces the ambiguity of data. Actors will selectively present performance data that supports their point of view, discount conflicting information, and put the best possible spin on the data (Hood, 2006). Brunsson (1989) has argued that organizations have strong incentives to use information to communicate the importance of their services and the values they represent. Organizations will strive to present external values consistent with the demands of the environment, values which may not have a strong relationship with activities. Performance information is a helpful tool here, allowing the organization to "claim to possess a variety of positive qualities: they are efficient, they are service-minded, or they exist for the benefit of the public. Goals are even more useful in this context. If an organization cannot quite fulfil some particular norm, it may at least be a good idea to emphasize a firm intention to do so" (Brunsson, 1989: 5). As long as the external values secure the legitimacy of the organization, and its funding, such an "organization of hypocrisy" is a natural and useful strategy.

We should put aside notions that performance data is neutral, scientific or definitive, but assume instead that it represents the interests of an advocate seeking to persuade. A major use of performance information for agencies is for advocacy purposes. Such a realization prompts us to ask probing questions rather than accept performance information at face value: Who collected the information? How was it measured? What alternative measures exist? What is the context of performance?

Principal-agent problems have not disappeared with the introduction of performance data, they have simply taken new forms. Agency theory proposed performance data as an alternative to the price mechanism and a means to reduce information asymmetry between political principals and bureaucratic agents. But given the breadth of possible information any moderately complex program could legitimately produce, and the range of interpretations associated with this information, it becomes clear that the substantive expertise of the public manager remains important. It is nearly impossible for decision makers to make informed judgments on what mounds of performance information indicate for a particular function. There will never be enough information to substitute for the expertise and knowledge of those who run the programs, and there will be too much information for human cognitive processes to deal with.

Even if a government accepts the transaction costs involved in auditing performance data, and requires detailed records of how data were created, agents have an advantage in terms of being the most credible actors to determine what information should be selected, measured and diffused. For this reason, governments frequently delegate the process of information creation to agencies. Even if governments accept the additional transaction costs (and agency resentment) involved in having a central agency or other third party take over all or some of the process of information creation, the information advantage of agency actors puts them in the best position to offer plausible explanations as to the meaning of the performance data and what it tells us about future action, for example, "performance was lower than expected because we lacked staff at critical points – more resources will remedy this problem." Where governments ignore the interpretation of agencies, they run the risk of being accused of neglecting expertise.

For agencies, the purpose of advocacy is to meet the demands of an external audience. In the policy arena there will be multiple competing perspectives about the worth of the agency's goals, how successful it is at achieving these goals, and how it should be managed and funded in the future. The agency is just one actor among many trying to assert hegemony of understanding over these issues (Kingdon, 1984). Stakeholders, elected officials, central agency officials and constituents may also press their views, sometimes in opposition to the agency. These actors are representatives of ideologies, parties, programs, groups of citizens, organizations and political institutions. How an individual interprets and understands information will be shaped by their political role. Conditions of ambiguity and disagreement will therefore be exacerbated across political institutions that are designed to check one another and represent opposing viewpoints.

These conditions give rise to the following proposition, which I explain in greater detail below: All else being equal, dialogue routines which are institutionally more diverse (in terms of the mix of political/administrative actors involved) are less likely to use performance information to solve problems, and more likely to use performance information for advocacy. The more diverse the institutional actors involved, the greater the number of interpretations of performance data. This is the central reason that performance budgeting, despite its perennial popularity, struggles to actually work. Traditional budget routines have a limited ability to create dialogue which generates solutions. Agency staff or stakeholders presenting information to the central budget office or the legislature have good reason to act defensively. In such situations, information will be used strategically by advocates who are fully aware that they argue in a decision environment that does not closely resemble a strict performance budgeting model.

The political nature of decision making will interact with, rather than be replaced by, performance information. Of course, advocates are biased in their assessments, but all parties of aware of this, and it does not mean that they are wrong. In fact, the greater the degree to which they can use performance data to support their position, the less biased and more rational they appear. A summary of the key hypotheses of the interactive-dialogue model would be as follows:

- Different actors can examine the same programs and come up with competing, though reasonable, arguments for the performance of a program based on different data.
- Different actors can examine the same performance information and come up with competing, though reasonable, arguments for what the information means.
- Different actors can agree on the meaning of performance information/program performance and come up with competing solutions for what actions to take in terms of management and resources.
- Actors will select and interpret performance information consistent with institutional values and purposes.

- Forums where performance information is considered across institutional affiliations will see greater contesting of performance data.

What do the above hypotheses suggest for decision making? Performance information, when used, will not necessarily engender consensus and agreement. This depends greatly on the homogeneity of the actors involved, their interpretation of the data, their ability to persuade others and their power in the decision process. In some cases, what one group of decision makers concludes is a reasonable interpretation and an appropriate response may be completely at odds with another group looking at similar information. The nature of the performance information is therefore not predictive of decisions. Different actors might take the same set of performance data and offer plausible and logical arguments for either option. In settings that limit a diversity of institutional views, many of the problems that arise from performance information ambiguity and subjectivity are reduced, because there is a reduced incentive and potential for advocacy.

Goal-based learning

The first part of this chapter detailed the reasons why performance information is used for advocacy purposes. It is tempting, then, to suggest that performance measurement has largely failed as a management tool and only works as a political tool. But this would represent a flawed and narrow understanding of performance information use. Actors use performance information in different ways, depending on their purpose, their audience, the context, and the decision under consideration. The same agency may use performance information for advocacy purposes to secure external legitimacy, while at the same time use it for internal management purposes (Brunsson, 1989). The second part of this chapter argues agency actors can use performance information to foster learning.

Interactions with central agencies, elected officials or the public offer agencies an opportunity to use performance data to advocate. If they are successful in asserting their version of events, the agency can win legitimacy and funding. But advocacy within an agency is unlikely to win such prizes and is therefore a less fruitful strategy. Advocacy within agencies is also less necessary because of the relative homogeneity of the actors involved. While subject to the tensions of political struggles, they can manage these tensions for a number of reasons. Agency staff is less diverse than the body politic, share a common culture, fall under a single hierarchy that has authority to direct employees, and are more likely to agree on shared goals. Such actors are more concerned with issues of implementation than other actors in the governance process, and therefore more likely to seek uses of performance data that improve management. Together, these factors help reduce the potential for different perspectives between actors within the same organization, reducing the potential for rival and irreconcilable interpretations of performance information to emerge. With relative agreement on the meaning of performance, agency actors have greater potential to identify and implement management actions based on goals.

Looking to learning

Hopes that performance measures are used ultimately rest on a theory of learning. Decision makers are expected to learn from performance information, leading to better informed decisions and improved government performance. However, performance management reforms have largely failed to draw from a well-established literature on organizational learning to better understand how to facilitate performance information use. This literature is helpful in understanding how interactive dialogue fosters performance management in three ways:

1. identifying the types of learning that organizations can engage in;
2. identifying different routes towards learning; and
3. identifying the characteristics of forums where dialogue can foster learning.

Types of learning

The work of Chris Argyris and Donald Schön has been instrumental in developing the concept of organizational learning and in identifying different types of learning. Single-loop learning is "instrumental learning that leads to improvement in the performance of organizational tasks" that "changes strategies of actions or assumptions underlying strategies in ways that leave the values of a theory unchanged" (Argyris and Schön, 1996: 20). In the context of governance, single-loop learning is appropriate for routine, repetitive operations, when public sector goals are clear and widely accepted. In terms of performance management, it implies specifying goals to the point where they are measurable; tracking achievement of goals; and judging these results in the context of a point of comparison, whether it is pre-set targets, previous performance, the performance of other organizations or other parts of the same organization. Such comparison prompts a dialogue that analyzes the factors and processes that underpin performance, and how they might be changed. In short, single-loop learning allows organizations to do the same things better.

Double-loop learning is "learning that results in a change in the values of theory-in-use, as well as in its strategies and assumptions [...] Strategies and assumptions may change concurrently with, or as a consequence of, change in values" (Argyris and Schön, 1996: 21). Double-loop learning occurs when public actors test and change the basic assumptions that underpin their mission and key policies. It is more relevant for complex, non-programmable issues important to the survival of the organization, rather than short-term efficiency gains. Double-loop learning means questioning the goals of a program, asking whether the program is worth pursuing, or worth pursuing in the public sector. In the context of performance management, it implies a willingness to revisit the basic organizational mission, goals and strategies. While performance management reforms have tended to emphasize single-loop learning, there is evidence that performance management can help to facilitate both single- and double-loop learning (Moynihan, 2005a).

Structural and cultural routes to learning

The organizational learning literature identifies two different routes to learning, one cultural and the other structural. The cultural approach is the better-established and more widely pursued, reflecting the influence of the human relations school on the organizational learning literature. In the cultural approach, learning is based on shared experiences, norms and understandings (Senge, 1990). Characteristics of a learning culture include high employee empowerment, participation and discretion (Fiol and Lyles, 1985).

Lipshitz and colleagues (1996) criticize the abstract nature of the cultural approach. They argue that learning can be better studied and promoted through a structural approach, what they call organizational learning mechanisms (OLM): "institutionalized structural and procedural arrangements that allow organizations to systematically collect, analyze, store, disseminate, and use information that is relevant to the effectiveness of the organization" (Lipshitz, Popper and Oz, 1996: 293). While a cultural approach emphasizes creating shared and functional norms among workers, the structural approach denotes a reliance on formal rules and procedures to enable learning.

Reformers favor structural approaches, since structure and procedure are amenable to change via formal mandates. In performance management, this preference for structure is reflected in statutory or administrative mandates that lead to formal rules and procedures to generate, collect and disseminate performance information. These mandates are clear and specific reforms that elected officials can adopt to demonstrate that they care about results-based government. In contrast, cultural reform is slow, difficult, hard to observe and largely shaped at the agency level.

Performance management reforms have done well in establishing OLMs that create and diffuse information, but have largely overlooked OLMs as routines where data is examined and interpreted – learning forums. Learning forums are dialogue routines specifically focused on solution seeking, where actors collectively examine information, consider its significance and decide how it will affect future action. Such routines are unlikely to occur as an organic reaction to the simple provision of quantitative information. Managers prefer to spend their time interacting with people and collecting oral data, not contemplating quantitative data (Mintzberg, 1975). Learning forums therefore require a commitment of time by staff. The interaction between knowledgeable staff can generate innovations and solutions that would not occur if such staff were acting by themselves.

Building learning forums

Designers of performance management systems need to take the routines to consider and discuss data as seriously as they take the routines to collect and disseminate data. Without learning forums, performance management is an incomplete structural approach to learning. The organizational learning literature and case studies of goal-based learning offer insights into the factors that convert interactive dialogue to learning. These insights are summarized in Table 2.1.

Learning forums are more likely to succeed if they are an organizational routine rather than an extraordinary event (Levitt and March, 1988). The key characteristic of such forums will be to exchange dialogue as a precursor to learning. Performance data highlights the relative success or failure of a unit or process, but only a dialogue can help identify and disseminate the reasons why success occurs. Managers often live in "psychic prisons," limited by norms and habits that lead them to view their organization and its problems from a single frame (Bolman and Deal, 1991). Dialogue allows participants to examine their own thinking, look at old problems in new ways by experimenting with multiple frames, and to create common meaning. Dialogue gives managers an opportunity to "practice," experimenting with decisions styles in a way not feasible in real-life.

Table 2.1   Elements of learning forums

- Routine event
- Facilitation and ground-rules to structure dialogue
- Non-confrontational approach to avoid defensive reactions
- Collegiality among participants
- Diverse set of organizational actors responsible for producing the outcomes under review
- Dialogue-centered, with dialogue focused on organizational goals
- Identify, examine and suspend basic assumptions (especially for double-loop learning)
- Employs quantitative knowledge that identifies success and failure, including goals, targets, outcomes, and points of comparison
- Employs experiential knowledge of process and work conditions that explain success, failure and the possibility of innovation

Senge (1990) suggests that the necessary aspects of a successful dialogue include the suspension of assumptions, facilitation that explains and enforces the ground rules for dialogue, active involvement of members, collegiality among participants, and willingness for members to raise the most pressing organizational issues. These standards are similar to the advice given by argumentation theorists on standards for structuring conversations. In facilitating a critical discussion, all participants must be willing to clearly discuss their viewpoints, willing to accept, on a provisional basis, the presumptions of others, and cooperate with one another in evaluating the relative plausibility of inferences drawn from such presumptions (Walton, 1992).

Mintzberg (1994) argues that forum participants should be the decision makers expected to use performance information, and not planners who are removed from managerial realities. For single-loop learning, this implies including lower-level employees who oversee organizational processes; for double-loop learning, it implies more senior-level employees who have an understanding of the entire organization and its environment. Kaplan and Norton (1996) argue that diversity of expertise improves the potential for team learning, and advocate teams that are both cross-functional and that mix senior and operational managers. This makes sense because it overcomes a classic bureaucratic malady – "those who have the necessary information do not have the power to decide, and those who have the power to decide cannot get the necessary information" (Crozier, 1964: 51). Bringing together lower-level managers with senior officials joins operational knowledge with the authority to change processes.

Kaplan and Norton (1996: 252) also emphasize linking dialogue to critical organizational goals. Learning is enabled by "a team problem-solving process that analyzes and learns from the performance data and then adapts the strategy to emerging conditions and issues." Such analyses should be open to both quantitative and qualitative evidence, including correlations between process changes and intended outcomes, in-depth management gaming/scenario analysis, anecdotal evidence, interim review of the progress of process changes, and peer review of performance.

A sense of professional pride is a strong motivator for using performance information (Moynihan, 2005a). Commitments given in front of peers are taken seriously and usually prove binding. Learning forums therefore not only prioritize performance information and identify solutions, but also can change the attitude employees hold toward their tasks. DeHaven-Smith and Jenne (2006) point to Habermas's theory of communicative action to suggest that structured discourse can shape values and motivations, noting the "tendency for people to feel bound by their promises, to give reasons for their beliefs and actions, and to accede to the better arguments and more justifiable claims of others" (2006: 67). Dialogue forms a basis of social cooperation, and people feel committed to the agreements researched in such a context. Interactive dialogue therefore acts as a social process that helps to create shared mental models, has a unifying effect, and helps to develop credible commitment for the execution phase. An important caveat is that the willingness to pursue learning forums is strengthened when agencies have some autonomy in selecting goals. Externally imposed goals, especially those that are at odds with professional values, are more likely to engender compliance rather than the type of collective goal-based learning described here.

Two recent quantitative studies provide additional empirical support for the learning forum concept in very different settings – Norwegian municipalities (Askim, Johnsen and Christophersen, 2008) and Texas state employees (Moynihan and Landuyt, 2008). Askim and colleagues use senior management participation in benchmarking exercises as their primary measure of learning forums, while Moynihan and Landuyt (2008) track the impact of work groups with learning forum characteristics (they incorporate the views of many actors, receive adequate feedback, involve those who are actually involved in decision processes, and are willing to challenge the status quo). Both find that learning forums are positively associated with organizational learning. In the Texas study, such learning forums had a greater positive impact on learning than any other significant variables, including the quality of information systems, the mission orientation of individual employees, and the discretion provided to employees.

Managing learning forums

This section of the chapter considers some of the prominent management issues that arise from learning forums. The first is the danger that a desire for accountability may crowd-out the potential for learning. The second is the importance of culture to learning, even for structural approaches to learning. The third is the potential for double-loop learning to lead to policy change.

The balance between accountability and defensiveness

The literature of organizational learning suggests that confrontational uses of data leads to defensive reactions rather than learning, so an open and collegial approach is preferable to a top-down analysis of failure. Collegiality defuses defensive reactions and encourages information sharing. Heinrich (2003) cites an example of such learning in North Carolina, where city government officials share financial and performance information on a range of services. They come together to talk about why high- and low-performing services, and the simple process of discussing performance, is motivational and provides information. The cities involved have no authority over one another, so the process is motivated by solution seeking, and characterized by equality among participants.

In the absence of equality among participants, a top-down political pressure for accountability may encourage learning (Andrews and Moynihan, 2002). A top-down pressure to perform characterizes the use of performance data to improve organizational performance in the growing "Stat" approach to performance management. The original CompStat policing program for New York police operations has spawned many followers, including the CitiStat program in Baltimore, and the PowerTrac policing model in Broward County, Florida (Behn, 2006; deHaven-Smith and Jenne, 2006; Henderson, 2005).

The Stat model emphasizes the use of near real-time information on the performance of a variety of public programs. Performance is illustrated using geospatial mapping, making problem areas obvious. Senior managers are required to present and defend the performance of their agencies in a learning forum with executive branch officials – in the case of CitiStat, this included the Mayor of Baltimore. At the meeting there is discussion of performance, why problems are occurring, and what resources and strategies are needed to improve performance.

Many of the characteristics of learning forums exist in the Stat model. There are frequent meetings to discuss performance, a variety of different actors involved, a reliance on quantitative measures and experience, and a discussion of the variables that affect performance. But a key difference from the learning forums described above is the unequal footing of participants and the sometimes confrontational nature of the interactions in the Stat approach. The meetings create a pressure to perform, tying responsibility to perform on agency heads rather than discovering improvement as a collective experience. In the search for accountability, the tone of the dialogue becomes "why are you failing?" rather than the "how can we improve?" tone that characterizes more collegial approaches to learning. Agency officials are expected to answer tough questions from political officials, implying the need for learning to occur within the agency before or after the meetings, rather than at the meeting itself (Behn, 2006; Chetkovich, 2000).

At some point top-down pressure in the name of accountability will foster defensive reactions, which ultimately weaken a shared focus on problem solving and encourage agency staff to circumvent, game or discredit performance information systems. To be successful, therefore, the dialogue must retain a basic level of legitimacy. If agency staff see learning forums as exercises in political blame assignment rather than solution seeking, they become disillusioned. As the officials involved seek strategic advantage, the forums devolve into advocacy sessions where different sides present conflicting accounts of the meaning of performance information. An example comes from the PowerTrac system in Florida (deHaven-Smith and Jenne, 2006). Senior officials focused on uncovering performance problems, preparing pre-scripted questions and evidence that embarrassed agency staff. In response, agency managers viewed it as acceptable to collude in evading performance management controls, leading deHaven-Smith and Jenne to conclude: "To the extent that administrative discourse is seen as a game of 'gotcha', it will reinforce rather than expose and dissolve defensive thinking" (2006: 71).

Aligning culture with goal-based learning

Performance management reforms reflect a structural approach to learning, characterized by OLMs for performance creation and diffusion.

The definition of OLMs presented earlier also makes clear that they incorporate routines to use information. Learning forums might therefore be considered another aspect of a structural approach, albeit one given less attention thus far. However, any examination of learning forums reveals the difficulty in separating organizational culture from the structural bases of learning.

Organizational culture frames whether learning forums are welcomed and supported. Most organizations struggle to create such routines of information use because the concept is foreign. The idea of setting aside time to collectively consider performance data appears odd, or brings to mind images of pointless office retreats that distract employees from their real work. The characteristics of learning forums are also unfamiliar. Few organizations, except those that are new or in crisis, have much incentive to question the norms and values that ushered them into existence and have accompanied their survival. Setting aside these ways of thinking is remarkably difficult. Whether and how organizational actors decide to create and participate in routines depends on norms of appropriate behavior for their organization (March and Olsen, 1989). This returns us to the issue of culture. Actors will learn if they have the information to learn, but also if the organizational culture portrays routines of data consideration as appropriate organizational behavior.

The risk of pursuing accountability at the expense of problem solving discussed in the last section further illustrates the importance of culture. Hierarchical structures make some actors more powerful than others, and foster a presumption among higher-level officials that they hold superior knowledge to lower-level actors, who must be monitored to avoid shirking. If the organization features a culture of antagonism and conflict between operators and managers, or between managers and political officials, it becomes more difficult for these actors to set aside their assumptions about one another.

The discussion of the Stat experiences also illustrates the importance of leadership to any effort to build a culture conducive to learning. Leadership matters because employees attempt to discern how seriously senior managers and elected officials take performance management. If employees see real support, they are more likely to devote attention to implement performance management and to actually use performance information (Moynihan, 2005b; Moynihan and Ingraham, 2004). If it is regarded only as a symbolic reform or a burden that must be complied with, employees invest the minimum effort necessary.

The most direct indicator of leadership support is actual participation in learning forums, as exemplified in successful applications of the Stat approach. Askim and colleagues (2008) find that political participation in benchmarking exercises was positively related to learning. They also found that resources were positively related to learning, pointing to another way in which leadership matters. To actually use performance information requires the investment of resources, including specialized staff to develop learning forums, and the willingness to take staff from other tasks to participate in such forums (Moynihan, 2005b). Both Askim and colleagues (2008), and Moynihan and Landuyt (2008) find that resource adequacy is positively associated with learning outcomes. In tight budget constraints, the willingness of leaders to provide human and financial assets for learning forums recognizes learning as an organizational priority.

There are other ways in which culture and structure interact. The organizational learning literature sees high employee empowerment, participation and discretion as conducive to learning, and Moynihan and Landuyt (2008) provide empirical support for these claims. In contrast, punishment-oriented control systems tend to discourage learning and lead to defensive reactions (Argyris and Schön, 1996). Centralized structures reinforce past behaviors and make new learning more difficult. The public sector has traditionally relied on centralized rules to govern the use of human and financial resources. Even with the introduction of new rules and procedures designed to facilitate learning, the failure to remove the old rules will thwart change. Individuals need to "unlearn" past behaviors before new learning can take place (Hedberg, 1981). The ability to unlearn is most at risk when old cognitive frameworks are in contradiction with new ways of thinking.

Performance management provides agencies a tool with which to engage in policy change

Performance management has largely neglected the possibility of double-loop learning. Nathan comments that, "the preponderance of attention and literature on managerial oversight in government has focused on rigid numeric goal setting" (2005: 210). Single-loop learning appears to be the only type of learning recommended to practitioners and realized in mandates: bureaucrats are expected to figure out ways to achieve organizational goals more efficiently, not challenge these goals (Barnow, 1999).

What explains this oversight? To a large degree it reflects the normative assumptions about decision making in the public sector, that is, the hoary politics/administration dichotomy. As a reform, performance management harkens to the concept of the neutral administrator seeking to most efficiently implement the goals they are given by elected officials. While the dichotomy has suffered many a battering, no reform has ever enhanced its potential for adoption by explicitly rejecting its existence. Performance management reforms certainly did not advertise themselves as a means to empower bureaucrats with policy-making authority, or to question the nature of the goals they pursue. The widespread success of performance management reformers is due in part to the willingness to reaffirm the dichotomy and overlook how performance management practice can violate it. Reforms are promoted as a way in which elected officials can reassert control over administrators, by virtue of setting goals in the strategic planning stage, and closely overseeing outputs. If double-loop learning is to occur at all, it is the presumed province of elected officials, not bureaucrats.

It is, therefore, an uncomfortable truth that performance management gives agencies a tool to engage in policy innovation. A seemingly neutral administrative tool has the potential to empower agency actors to make, in effect, major policy decisions. For example, Moynihan (2005a) detailed how the State of Vermont Department of Corrections used strategic planning and performance measurement as a vehicle to develop a new corrections philosophy, goals and programs. There are reasons to welcome such learning. First, legislators are less likely to use performance information than agency staff, and so the best hope for coherent and evidence-based policy development within government rests with agency actors. The restorative justice philosophy developed in Vermont was a response to a failed rehabilitative approach and a nascent punitive approach, neither of which had strong evidentiary backing. However, the punitive approach had political support and would have dominated criminal justice policy without the influence of the agency. Second, concerns about the loss of democratic control are overstated. Agencies depend on governments for funding tied to specific programs, and cannot choose to ignore the legislature's instructions. To comprehensively change programs and implement new goals, they need legislative support. In Vermont, agency staff had to develop basic elements of their new philosophy and some evidence of superior performance before they could convince the legislature to support restorative justice programs. In addition, agency actors engaged in double-loop learning are led by (in the USA at least) political appointees who reflect the goals of elected officials. Third, the policy arena saw greater legislative and public debate about justice than would have been the case if the agency simply embarked on a more punitive course. While performance management fostered double-loop learning, and gave the Vermont Department of Corrections the material to advocate its case, it did not usurp decision-making authority from elected officials. Instead, it offered an example of agency advocacy promoting well-considered and effective policy options.

Conclusion

This chapter has used the interactive-dialogue model to make the case that agencies use performance information for advocacy, but that they can also engage in goal-based learning. For organizations to foster such learning, they need to develop routines of performance information use in the same way that they have developed routines of performance information creation and diffusion. Agencies must take care in building learning forums, because they will fail to foster learning if governments use them for accountability rather than problem-solving purposes. The ability to build effective forums is greatly helped by a supportive organizational culture and leaders willing to build such a culture.

3
Performance Information and Performance Steering: Integrated System or Loose Coupling?

Per Lægreid, Paul G. Roness and Kristin Rubecksen

Over the past two decades there has been a significant increase in the use of performance management systems in the public sector internationally. These systems are widely used, but also criticized (Bouckaert and Peters, 2002; de Bruijn, 2002; Holzer and Yang, 2004; Johnsen, 2005; Radin, 2006). Over time, performance measurement has become more systematic, specialized, professionalized and institutionalized (Van Dooren, 2006). Performance information related to goals and objectives, measured through performance indicators and reported through ICT-based systems has increased (Bouckaert and Halligan, 2006). Yet, performance-based strategic steering is limited (Pollitt, 2006c).

One of the main doctrines of New Public Management is managerial discretion combined with transparent targets and *ex-post* control by result or performance (Hood and Bevan, 2004). Setting targets, evaluating output information and applying rewards and sanctions represents a specific type of regulatory system. Thus, according to NPM doctrines, performance management is an integrated system where performance information is closely linked to performance steering through incentives. Performance management allows organizations a lot of autonomy and flexibility in the use of allocated resources and in choosing the means and methods. However, the price public bodies have to pay for their increased freedom is to accept a more rigid performance management system, which includes performance indicators and performance monitoring and assessment. The system is thus a mixed one that prescribes both centralization and decentralization, and it is an empirical question in which direction it will tip in practice.

The topic of this chapter is how performance information and performance steering are related in the Norwegian central government. The Norwegian performance management system, Management-By-Objectives-and-Results (MBOR), is based on NPM doctrines. We will distinguish between four phases of the MBOR process: (1) the formulation of goals and objectives; (2) the performance indicators; (3) the reporting of performance; and (4) performance steering. The first three are seen as different aspects of performance information. We will present some main aspects of the MBOR system and examine how it works in practice by analyzing data from a comprehensive survey of state agencies carried out in 2004. The main research questions are, first, to what extent is MBOR an integrated system with tight coupling between performance information and performance steering, and second, to what extent can we explain variations in performance steering across agencies using variations in performance information and in agency characteristics like structure, culture and environment?

Performance management: the Norwegian way

We will analyze how performance information and performance steering are related in practice by focusing on the case of Norway, where the MBOR system is now widely used in the public sector (Lægreid, Roness and Rubecksen, 2006b). The chief features of Norwegian-style NPM have been the pragmatic introduction of a formalized performance assessment regime. The performance management system is the main tool for regulating relations between ministries and agencies. An essential part of this system is the establishment of a quasi-contractual steering model, whereby the parent ministry allocates resources and specifies targets and goals for the various agencies by means of an annual steering document. The agencies, in turn, are expected to report on performance through formal reports and a formalized steering dialogue. The idea is to make the managers manage by use of performance management techniques.

When the Management-By-Objectives technique was introduced in the Norwegian central government at the end of the 1980s, there was considerable emphasis on the formulation of objectives. Later modifications have focused more strongly on the performance aspect. This shift was expressed in the relabeling of the concept Management-By-Objectives to become Management-By-Objectives-And-Results.

The Management-By-Objectives concept was put into practice through three reform measures. The first, budget reforms, was introduced in 1986 and was intended to make the state budget system more performance oriented. The agencies were given greater freedom in the use of allocated financial resources, but the price for increased autonomy was that the agencies were required to provide more systematic reporting of performance. MBOR was made mandatory in 1990 with the introduction of an annual activity plan for each public sector unit. This reform aimed to make goals and means less ambiguous, focusing on results, introducing a monitoring system and making greater use of incentives. A central feature of this arrangement was the development of a hierarchy of primary and secondary objectives. The third set of reforms was salary reforms. In the early 1990s a new salary system was introduced for administrative leaders in ministries and state agencies. These officials now received salaries based on individual contracts, pay-for-performance elements and an annual assessment of managerial executives. This system was implemented more reluctantly than anticipated (Lægreid, 2000).

MBOR has been further developed in recent years and more broadly applied. It is now more closely connected to the state budget system, less rigid, and more adapted to the special features and tasks of different state organizations. After experiencing problems with measuring outcomes, a more relaxed result concept has been introduced that also accepts performance information based on activity and output performance indicators. Increased flexibility of MBOR may, however, weaken it as an overall control device. Different, shifting and unstable performance indicators can reduce their control potential across time, administrative levels and organizational bodies. A comprehensive model for performance management was introduced through the new Government Financial Regulations in 1996. This includes a Letter of Allocation, which is a contract-like arrangement between the parent ministry and subordinate agencies concerning resources, objectives and performance indicators. Thus, performance budgeting and performance management are central features of MBOR.

MBOR entails more flexibility, leeway, autonomy and discretionary power for subordinate agencies. Yet, it also gives rise to a more formal and rigid control regime because of the extensive use of performance management and contract-like arrangements. Political executives are supposed to specify targets and objectives more clearly, and performance is supposed to be controlled by the use of quantitative indicators for monitoring results and for measuring efficiency.

Database

The database is a survey addressed to all organizations in the Norwegian civil service outside the ministries in 2004. It excludes ministries, local government, state-owned companies and governmental foundations. The civil service organizations are divided into sub-forms of affiliation: directorates/central agencies, other ordinary public administration bodies, agencies with extended authority, and government administrative enterprises. Compared to ordinary public administrative bodies, agencies with extended authority and government administrative enterprises are given some degrees of formal autonomy within or beyond the general governmental regulatory frameworks. The population of organizations also consists of three different agency types, based on whether and to what extent they include a territorial dimension. The first one consists of single national civil service organizations without subordinate bodies (e.g., the Norwegian Competition Authority). The second is that of integrated civil service organizations consisting of a national unit as well as subordinated regional or local branches (e.g., the Norwegian Tax Administration). Finally, there are single units in groups of similar civil service organizations in different geographical areas, reporting directly to one or more ministries (e.g., the County Governors).

Given these criteria, the population adds up to 215 civil service organizations. One questionnaire was sent to each agency, and a central manager was asked to answer on behalf of the whole organization. A total of 150 organizations answered the survey, which constitutes a response rate of 70 percent. There were only small variations in the response rate according to sub-form of affiliation and type of agency and between different ministerial areas. For half of the ministerial areas the response rate was over 80 percent and none was below 50 percent.

Performance information and performance steering: different dimensions

As noted above, we distinguish between four phases of the MBOR process. The first three (the formulation of goals and objectives, the performance indicators, and the reporting of performance) are seen as different aspects of performance information, while the last one concerns performance steering. We will present an overall description of how the Norwegian state agencies score on these dimensions, based on our empirical database. For each of the dimensions we have constructed additive indexes, based on relevant aspects. These indexes will be used in our examinations on whether MBOR is an integrated system or characterized by loose couplings.

Formulation of goals and objectives

According to the instrumental-rational ideas underlying MBOR, performance information takes the goals and objectives of the agencies as the point of departure. Goals and objectives should be formulated by political executives and the parent ministry through a top-down process and in quantitative terms. In the Norwegian context, the annual Letter of Allocation should both present concrete and testable criteria for goal achievement and specify efficiency targets.

In practice, however, many agencies do not live up to such an ideal. One-fifth of the agencies report that they set their goals alone; one-fourth of the agencies have only qualitatively formulated goals; concrete and testable criteria for goal achievement are reported by half of the agencies; and estimates of efficiency or productivity are rather uncommon in the Letter of Allocation.

We have constructed an additive index for the formulation of goals and objectives, ranging from zero to four. The index is constructed by counting occurrences of agencies reporting that the goals and objectives are formulated by the ministry alone or together with the agency, that some goals are quantitatively formulated, that the Letter of Allocation presents concrete and testable criteria for goal achievement, and that the Letter of Allocation specifies efficiency targets. Few agencies (10 percent) report that all criteria for formulation of goals and objectives are fulfilled or that none of them are (12 percent). The majority (57 percent) report that they fulfill two or three of the preconditions for formulation of goals and objectives specified by the MBOR model.

Performance indicators

The MBOR model is not only supposed to measure output, activities and resources used, but also outcome and effects on users and clients. In practice, however, the performance indicators, first of all, give some quantitative information about use of resources and activities and task achievements. There is much less information on quality of services, and outcome (societal effects) is measured to a rather limited extent. Four out of ten agencies report that their performance indicators give little or no information about outcome. A well-functioning MBOR model should have performance indicators that cover all important aspects of the activities of subordinate organizations. However, only one-third of the agencies report that the performance indicators to a large extent embrace the central aspects of their operations and work. Stability in the performance indicators over time is also necessary in order to obtain comparable data about the development of performance and provide meaningful benchmarks in the long term (Lonti and Gregory, 2007). Four out of ten agencies report that performance indicators have remained stable over the past five years, while the normal situation is that there have been some changes in the indicators over time.

The additive index for performance indicators also ranges from zero to four. The index is constructed by counting occurrences of agencies reporting that the indicators cover societal effects to some or a large extent, that the indicators cover quality of services to some or a large extent, that the performance indicators to a large extent cover important aspects of the agency's work, and that the performance indicators remain stable during the budget year. Few agencies (7 percent) report that all four criteria for performance indicators are fulfilled or that none of them are (11 percent). The majority (60 percent) report that they fulfill two or three of the preconditions for performance indicators specified by the MBOR model.

Performance reporting

A third main component in MBOR is performance reporting. The introduction of ICT-based reporting systems has made systematic reporting of performance information easier, and two-thirds of the agencies mention that they use ICT-based systems to document results and performance. Performance indicators are normally integrated into such systems. Four out of ten agencies mention that the performance indicators are used to a large extent in the steering relations between the agency and the parent ministry. There are a variety of channels for reporting performance information from the agency to the parent ministry. Almost all agencies report to the parent ministry through annual reports, and quarterly reports are also common. In addition to the formal reports, there are also formal meetings as part of a steering dialogue between the parent ministry and state agencies. The steering meetings focus primarily on the reporting of performance and achievement of results, but financial and administrative matters are also discussed.

For performance reporting, we use an additive index ranging from zero to three. The index is constructed by counting occurrences of agencies reporting that the performance indicators are used to a large extent in the steering relations between the parent ministry and the agency, that they use ICT-based systems in performance reporting, and that the steering meetings are used for reporting on results and performance. In 27 percent of the agencies, all three criteria of performance reporting are fulfilled, while in 14 percent none of them are. The majority (59 percent) report that they fulfill two or three of the preconditions for performance reporting specified by the MBOR model.

Performance steering

MBOR prescribes that performance indicators should be used to reward good performance and to punish bad. Performance management or steering is thus about acting upon performance information by formulating and using performance incentives (Bouckaert and Van Dooren, 2003). However, when those agencies that use performance indicators in steering relations with the parent ministry are asked about different ways that the information is used, only 49 percent say that it is used as a basis for future resource allocation. Likewise, 46 percent of these agencies report that it is used as an informational basis for organizational learning. In cases where it is used for future resource allocation, normally more than 10 percent of the total budget of the organization is linked to this type of allocation. Overall, as many as 63 percent of the agencies report that the agency is rewarded to a small extent or not at all for good results (i.e., for reaching targets), while 26 percent report that they are rewarded to some extent and 11 percent to a large extent. In most instances of rewarding good performance, this is done through increased resource allocation. Increased autonomy with regard to superior units or regulations, increased discretion for individual employees, or wage increases and bonuses are only used in rare exceptions. About 90 percent of the agencies do not use pay for performance or bonus pay as a way of rewarding performance, and when such measures are used, it is more common for managers than for other employees. When it comes to using sanctions in case of bad performance, this happens to a small extent or not at all for 66 percent of the agencies, 24 percent report that this happens to some extent and 9 percent to a large extent. Punishing bad performance is thus less common than rewarding good performance, but the normal method of applying sanctions is to reduce future resource allocation.

For performance steering through the use of rewards and sanctions, we have used an additive index, ranging from zero to three. The index is constructed by counting occurrences of agencies reporting that performance information based on indicators is used in the steering relations between the agency and the parent ministry as the basis for future resource allocation, that the agencies are rewarded for good results, and that they are sanctioned for poor results. For 36 percent of the agencies there are no rewards or sanctions in use that can be connected to performance measurements or reporting, 18 percent report that they fulfill all three preconditions, 17 percent fulfill two and 29 percent fulfill one feature.

MBOR as a partly integrated system

In an ideal MBOR model there should be high positive correlations between the different phases of goal formulation, development of performance indicators, performance reporting and performance steering. If the correlations are not significant or negative, the MBOR model is not a coherent tool. What we see in Table 3.1 is that there are some tight ties and some loose ties. There are strong positive correlations between performance reporting on the one hand, and rewards and sanctions on the other. Performance indicators are tightly coupled to performance reporting, but not to the formulation of goals or to the issuing of rewards and the imposition of sanctions. Thus, the weak coupling seems to be between formulation of goals and performance indicators, and also between performance indicators and performance steering. Overall, the goals of state agencies seem to be outcome-related societal goals, while performance indicators tend to be activity- or output-based. One reason for this is the problem of measuring societal goals. Weak coupling between performance indicators and performance steering can be related to the fact that performance indicators often do not cover the whole range of the organization's mission, activities or tasks, but are biased towards what is measurable in quantitative terms. Performance steering often has to take a broader scope into consideration.

Often the officially formulated agency goals are outcome-based and focus on effects on citizens, users and clients, while the derived performance

Table 3.1 Intercorrelations between goals, performance indicators, performance reporting and performance steering

	Formulation of goals	Performance indicators	Performance reporting	Performance steering
Formulation of goals	–	0.05	0 .32**	0.22*
Performance indicators		–	0.28**	0.06
Performance reporting			–	0.51**

(Pearson's R. **: Significant at the 0.01 level; *: Significant at the 0.05 level (2-tailed).)

indicators tend to be more output- and activity-based, with rather loose links to the superior general goals, focusing more on societal implications. Even if there is goal agreement, it is often difficult to find measures adequate to the determination of social conditions (Frederickson and Frederickson, 2006). When it comes to performance steering, the agencies incline to pay more heed to the formulated goals than to the performance indicators. This tends to leave the performance indicators in a political-managerial vacuum. If one wants to live up to the ideal performance management model, the challenges are to develop performance indicators that are more clearly derived from the goals and objectives, and to strengthen the link between performance indicators and rewards and sanctions. But it is not obvious that the answer to decoupling is more integration towards the ideal model. It could also be the case that loosely coupled performance management models are easier to implement and use in practice.

Thus, the Norwegian type of managing performance seems to fit best with Bouckaert and Halligan's "management of performances" model (see Chapter 5 by Bouckaert and Halligan in this volume). Management and performance are linked, but the system is rather disconnected and not very consistent and coherent.

The importance of performance information and agency characteristics

As noted above, there is some variation among Norwegian state agencies with regard to the extent they live up to the MBOR ideal. A previous study based on the same survey also shows that agency characteristics such as structural, cultural and environmental features make a difference for how performance management is practiced (Lægreid, Roness and Rubecksen, 2006b). Moreover, comparisons across countries and sectors show that differences in polity features, cultural features and tasks produce considerable variation in the use of performance management (Pollitt, 2006c).

We will here examine whether and to what extent various types of agency characteristics affect performance steering, contributing to loose couplings between performance information and performance steering. These characteristics have previously turned out to be of relevance for explaining aspects of the autonomy and steering of Norwegian state agencies (Lægreid, Roness and Rubecksen, 2006a; 2006b; 2007; 2008). Why they are important is related to different types of theoretical ideas.

Table 3.2 presents the results of a multivariate analysis where different types of independent variables are included, and where (the index of)

Table 3.2 Summary of regressions for performance steering

	Performance information model	Structural model	Cultural model	Environmental model	Combined model
Performance information:	0.06				0.02
– Formulation of goals	−0.08				0.01
– Performance indicators	0.52**				0.30**
– Performance reporting					
Structural features:		0.02			−0.07
– Form of affiliation		0.22**			0.01
– Type of agencies		0.16*			0.06
– Executive board		0.18*			0.00
– Primary task					
Cultural features:			0.21**		0.18**
– Agency age			0.36**		0.20**
– Agency size			−0.14*		−0.12*
– Quality of services					
Environmental features:					
– Market competition				0.45**	0.29**
– External criticism				−0.02	−0.07
Adjusted R^2	0.26	0.10	0.22	0.19	0.40
F Statistics	18.110	4.943	14.394	18.379	8.927
Significance of F	0.000	0.001	0.000	0.000	0.000

(Linear regression. Standardized beta coefficients. **: Significant at the 0.01 level; *: Significant at the 0.05 level (2-tailed).)

Notes: **Form of affiliation**: (0) ordinary civil service organizations, (1) civil service organizations with some form of formal autonomy; **Type of agencies**: (0) agencies without a territorial component, (1) agencies with a territorial component; **Executive board**: (0) no executive board, (1) have an executive board; **Primary task**: (0) agencies with other primary tasks, (1) agencies with service provision or production tasks; **Agency age**: (0) agencies established before 1990, (1) agencies established in 1990 or later; **Agency size**: (1) small (fewer than 50 employees), (2) mid-sized (50–199 employees), (3) large (200 employees and more); **Quality of services culture**: (0) medium or less, (1) very good or good (the agencies were asked to assess 16 aspects of their organizational culture, including quality of service culture, along a scale: (1) very bad, (2) bad, (3) medium, (4) good, and (5) very good); **Market competition**: (0) no, (1) yes (the agencies were asked to assess whether or not they were in a market or a quasi-market characterized by competition); **External criticism**: (0) to a very little or no extent, (1) to some or a very large extent (the agencies were asked to assess to what extent, during the past five years, they had been subject to criticism from other public units, political actors or mass media due to lack of conformity/correspondence with political objectives and preferences, along a scale: (1) has not occurred, (2) to a very little extent, (3) to some extent, (4) to a very large extent).

performance steering is the dependent variable. The importance of performance information is revealed partly by focusing on (the indices of) formulation of goals, performance indicators and performance reporting separately, and partly through the combined model where all independent variables are included. Likewise, the importance of structural features, cultural features and environmental features is revealed by looking at their effect separately, and by including them in the combined model.

Performance information: performance reporting matters

As noted above, there is a strong positive bivariate correlation between performance reporting and performance steering; there is also a significant bivariate correlation between formulation of goals and performance steering; yet performance indicators are not related to performance steering. When controlling for other independent variables, the strong linkages between performance reporting and performance steering is upheld, while the linkages between formulation of goals and performance steering disappear. This is in line with a Nordic perspective on performance measurement decoupling performance indicators, both from the objectives and from the rewards (Johnsen and Vakkuri, 2006). The stronghold of the performance management system is the tight coupling between performance reporting and performance steering, while the critical links are between objectives and steering as well as between indicators and steering. Overall, performance information explains 26 percent of the variance of performance steering, mainly due to the importance of performance reporting.

Structural features: small effect on performance steering

We have examined the importance of four structural features. The first one is the type of affiliation, where we distinguish between ordinary civil service organizations and organizations with various forms and degrees of formal authority. From earlier studies, we know that MBOR seems to work better the further away the organization is from the political executive (Christensen and Lægreid, 2006). Here, however, we find no such effects on performance steering.

The second structural variable is type of agency. We assume that agencies with a territorial component will be more embedded in regional and local networks, which in turn will tend to increase their autonomy and reduce the extent of control by their parent ministry and other superior bodies. This way of reasoning implies that it will be easier to exercise performance steering in agencies without a territorial component than in agencies having this. We find, however, that performance steering is used more often in agencies with a territorial component than in others, and that this relationship disappears when we control for other main types of independent variables.

The third structural variable is the existence of an executive board. From earlier studies, we know that having a board between the agency and the ministry will blur political signals on their way down the hierarchy, providing more autonomy for the agency (Christensen, 2001; Egeberg, 1994). Here, we find that performance steering is used to a lesser extent in agencies without a board than in agencies with a board, but that the relationship is quite weak when we control for other main types of independent variables.

Recent studies of state agencies reveal that there are significant variations in their behavior according to what their primary tasks are (Pollitt et al., 2004). We have made a distinction between different types of tasks or activities as the point of departure: regulatory tasks; other ways of exercising public authority; policy formulation; and service-providing and -producing tasks. The basis of categorization is the agencies' own perception of their tasks. Service-providing and -producing agencies have tasks more similar to private sector organizations, and performance measurement is regarded as being most feasible in product-oriented organizations (De Bruijn, 2002). This way of reasoning implies that it is easier to exercise performance steering in agencies with service provision or production as their primary task than it is in agencies with other primary tasks. We also find that performance steering tends to be used to a larger extent in service-providing and -producing agencies than in agencies with other primary tasks, but that the relationship is quite weak when we control for other main types of independent variables.

Overall, structural features do not explain much of the variance in performance steering, and the significant correlations disappear when controlling for other types of independent variables. Thus, agency form as specified here does not have a strong effect on the degree of autonomy and control in Norwegian central agencies (Lægreid, Roness and Rubecksen, 2006a).

Cultural features: size and age are important

We have examined the importance of three indicators of culture. The first one is agency age. Normally, the development of a distinct culture and tradition takes some time. Older organizations will tend to have developed a stronger identity than younger ones, and the potential for socialization of their members into a common culture is higher. Generally, we will assume that the traditional rule-oriented culture is stronger in older agencies and that modern results-oriented managerial techniques will be easier to adopt in agencies without a long and well-established organizational culture. This would imply that it is easier to exercise performance steering in younger agencies than in older agencies. We find that agency age has a significant effect on performance steering, meaning that rewards and sanctions are easier to use in younger agencies than in older ones.

Agency size is normally regarded as an indicator of structural capacity (Egeberg, 2003), but we may also use it as an indicator of cultural homogeneity. Small agencies may generally have a more homogeneous culture and a more distinct identity than large agencies, and may be more able to live up to the assumptions of the MBOR model. This might not be the case for all organizations. A large organization full of economists may have a more homogeneous culture than a small organization where several disciplines, professions and ideologies are represented. At the same time, small agencies may have less administrative capability to exploit and utilize the MBOR model. We find that agency size has a significant effect, where performance steering is used to a greater extent in large agencies than in small agencies. This result supports earlier findings (Van Dooren, 2006). It also suggests that size as an indicator of structural capacity is more important than size as an indicator of homogeneity and culture.

Finally, internal agency culture may affect how performance steering is practiced. We assume that agencies with a service-quality culture will have a normative correspondence with the MBOR model. This would imply that it is easier to exercise performance steering in agencies with a strong service-quality culture than in other agencies. We find, however, that performance steering is used to a lesser extent in agencies with a strong service-quality culture than in other agencies. This might indicate that tools such as service management and total quality management belong to another family of managerial tools than the performance management tools (Lægreid, Roness and Rubecksen, 2007). Overall, our cultural indicators explain 22 percent of the variance in political steering, and the effects are upheld when controlling for other types of independent variables.

Environmental pressure: market competition matters

A third set of factors describes the autonomy and control of agencies primarily as a response to external pressure (Olsen, 1992). While there may also be an adaptation to internationally based norms and beliefs about how an agency should be run and steered simply because these have become the prevailing doctrine in the institutional environment (Christensen et al., 2007; Roness, 2007), we here examine the importance of the technical environments. Thus, performance-management models may be adopted to solve widespread problems created by economic competition and market pressure in a global economy. Even if some of its origins come from the military (Offerdal and Jacobsen, 1995), MBOR is mainly a management technique developed for private-sector firms (Drucker, 1954). This would imply that it is easier to exercise performance steering in agencies that are subject to competition and operating in some kind of market than in other agencies. Agencies that face market competition usually have tasks that are easier to measure and thus are more prone to performance steering. We also find that this is the case. The strong linkage between market competition and performance steering is upheld when controlling for other types of independent variables.

In addition to the pressure of the market, agencies also encounter pressure from their political environment. Studies have shown that the political salience of their tasks plays a major role for how agencies are steered and managed (Lægreid, Opedal and Stigen, 2005; Pollitt et al., 2004). Agencies in policy areas involving cases and tasks with a high level of political conflict and cleavages will normally have problems in adopting an MBOR model. This way of reasoning implies that it is easier to exercise performance steering in agencies that have not been criticized than it is in agencies that to a large extent have been subject to criticism from other public organizations, political actors or the mass media for lack of conformity or correspondence with political objectives or preferences. We find, however, no such differences. Overall, environmental pressure explains 19 percent of the variance of performance steering, mainly due to the importance of market competition.

Summing up, the performance information model has the strongest explanatory power. Agency characteristics such as cultural and environmental features, and to some lesser extent structural features, must, however, also be taken into consideration to understand the constraining and enabling factors for performance steering.

Discussion

In this chapter we have shown, first, that the Norwegian MBOR model contains some tight as well as some loose couplings. Even if there are strong linkages between performance reporting and the other components, the overall impression is that this model is not a fully integrated system. The way the different components of the model are mixed varies considerably. One size does not fit all and there is not a standardized solution. Performance management systems are fairly well developed, but they are neither tightly integrated nor systemic. One could also raise the question of whether it should be an integrated system or not. A less integrated system may make the implementation easier but may also make it less suitable as a control tool.

Second, as reported by the agencies, performance information is quite extensive: there is a lot of goal formulation going on, the agencies make a strong effort to formulate performance indicators, and there is a lot of performance reporting and increased formalization of the information system. But the Achilles' heel seems to be performance steering. The great challenge is to use the information obtained to make decisions and formulate policy, but "steering by indicators" is rather unusual in the Norwegian case, as has also been revealed in other countries (Ingraham, Joyce and Donahue, 2003; Pollitt, 2006a). There is a strong link between performance steering and performance reporting, but a weak link between performance steering and performance indicators and formulated objectives. One implication of this is that what is reported is not necessary based on performance indicators or related to specified objectives. Despite this, performance reporting is extensively used in performance steering. The agencies invest a lot in systems of performance measurement, but they subsequently make limited use of them (De Bruijn, 2002). Overall, the majority of agencies are not rewarded to any great extent for good results or punished for poor results. Pay-for-performance systems are only introduced in a small minority of the agencies. The system has great potential for increased centralized control and steering. The loose coupling, however, provides opportunities for flexibility and adaptation to local conditions.

Third, several types of factors affect the non-use of performance information for performance steering, and in total we have been able to explain a fair amount of the variance in performance steering. Performance information explains a relatively large part, mainly due to the importance of performance reporting. Structural features do not seem to make a difference, except for agency size (as an indicator of structural capacity). Thus, large agencies are subject to more performance steering than small agencies. Performance steering is also easiest to apply in young agencies. External pressure through market competition also has some explanatory power. Thus, agencies that operate in some kind of market competition tend to be subject to performance steering to a larger extent than other agencies.

Conclusion

From its introduction in 1990 and its implementation up to the mid-1990s, the MBOR performance management system in Norway has become less rigid and more flexible, which makes it easier to implement but more difficult to use as a control tool. We have described a rather fragmented system with loose coupling between objectives, performance indicators, performance reporting and performance steering. Overall, performance steering is most widespread in agencies that have a well-developed performance reporting practice, that were established in the 1990s or later, that have more than 200 employees, and that are subject to some kind of market competition. For old and small agencies that have weak performance reporting and no competition, the conditions for the use of rewards and sanctions are rather poor.

Performance information can be used for different purposes and not only for control (Bouckaert and Van Dooren, 2003). One of those is to use it in the policy cycle to evaluate, learn and improve policy. This is done to some extent in the Norwegian case, but there is a long way to go before there is an evidence-based policy cycle, and one probably often has to go beyond performance measurement to get the necessary information. Results-based reporting will not disappear, but expectations must be revised and become more realistic.

Performance information can also be used to increase accountability. We have primarily focused on the accountability of decentralized or devolved agencies to parent ministries. Performance information is essential in the steering of autonomous agencies, and MBOR is primarily a tool for steering between governmental bodies at different administrative levels. The important component for performance steering is performance reporting and not the development of performance indicators or the formulation of objectives.

4
Performance Measurement Beyond Instrumental Use

Patria de Lancer Julnes

Performance measurement has been expected to produce information that can be used to make better and more rational decisions. In the United States, this belief is directly related to performance measurement's lineage – scientific management and its perceived contribution to better government (see also Van Dooren in Chapter 1). In the early 1900s, organizations focused on developing procedures and measurement techniques to improve efficiency and increase the productivity of workers. For public organizations, the interest in efficiency, which is built into the traditional approaches to accountability (Brunsson, 1989: 5; Radin, 2002) was a reaction to the pervasiveness of patronage and corruption in the way government conducted its business. Thus began a series of efforts to replace rather subjective assessments of government performance with systematic and more precise measurement. There was an optimistic view that performance measurement would automatically lead to rational decision making and, thus, to good government (see also Chapter 13 by Van de Walle and Roberts). Performance measurement in this chapter refers to measures or indicators of inputs, outputs, efficiency, effectiveness and outcomes.

This optimistic view of rational decision making presumes what Weiss (1998) calls instrumental use, wherein the information gathered directly leads to changes in the program or unit being assessed. The expected changes can range from allocating resources to modifying program processes and activities, to expanding or terminating a program. However, empirical research in various fields has shown flaws in this line of thinking. First, the use of information in decision making, and the use of performance measurement information in particular, has been shown to be a complex and challenging process. Second, the term "use" itself is now understood to be a multi-dimensional concept instead of a catch-all word (Burke and Costello, 2005; de Lancer Julnes and Holzer, 2001; Solberg, Mosser and McDonald, 1997; Weiss, 1998). As a result, although public organizations seem to be increasingly committed to performance measurement, the actual use of the information, at least in its instrumental form, is not as prevalent (Behn, 2002; de Lancer Julnes and Holzer, 2001). And even the use that is reported might actually be overstated (see Burke and Costello, 2005, for a discussion of this phenomenon).

I argue here that our failure to find more evidence of the use of performance measurement may be due not only to the complex nature of the organizational environment in which measurement occurs, but also to our insistence on a narrow definition of knowledge/information use and not differentiating use from purpose: what are we measuring for and how are we actually using the measures? Moreover, we often limit ourselves to some purposes and forget others. By doing so, we miss the more subtle manifestations of use. Specifically, while performance measures do not drive decisions in some automatic, mechanical way, it often forms the basis for discussions that lead fairly directly to decisions. Using performance measurement information to inform dialogue among decision makers, therefore, should be considered a positive contribution of performance measurement rather than a failure.

I assume that organizational context influences the mode of use. Therefore, the next section briefly discusses the organizational conditions that facilitate or obstruct the use of performance measurement. This is done to provide a backdrop for the framework of purpose and use that is discussed in the second section, which goes well beyond the narrow perception of performance information for rational decision making. As I suggested above, two defining features of the framework are the distinction between use and purpose on the one hand, and the inclusion of less visible, latent uses and purposes on the other hand.

The context of performance measurement utilization

In their 2001 article, de Lancer Julnes and Holzer demonstrated empirically that the utilization of performance measurement is composed of at least two stages, adoption (developing a performance measurement system – a capacity to act) and implementation (actually using the information – knowledge converted into action). These two stages help to explain why organizations usually report that they have some form of performance measurement system in place. That is, they have or are developing a capacity to act. The question is to what extent this capacity to act is also put to work.

According to de Lancer Julnes and Holzer (2001), adoption does not necessarily lead to implementation. That is, the capacity to act does not necessarily lead to the conversion of that knowledge into action. Furthermore, each of these two stages is differentially affected by organizational factors. For adoption, the most important factors hinge around a rational/technocratic capacity and include: internal requirements; support from internal interest groups (management and employees); availability of adequate resources; technical knowledge about performance measurement; and a goal orientation. On the other hand, factors that affect implementation are primarily political support and involvement of external interest groups – citizens and elected officials (de Lancer Julnes and Holzer, 2001). I discuss further some of these organizational factors.

A first, rather evident, factor is leadership. Studies on managing for results have consistently shown that executive branch leadership positively influences strategic planning and performance measurement (Berry, 1994; King, Zeckhauser and Kim, 2004; Moynihan and Ingraham, 2003). Conversely, a lack of leadership and employee motivation have been found to relate to a perceived lack of usefulness of managing for results (Burke and Costello, 2005). In the field of program evaluation, researchers like Patton (1997) and Cronbach and colleagues (1980) have pointed out that without these identifiable individuals or groups, evaluation would largely go unused. According to Newcomer (2007), support from our congressional leaders for these efforts is lacking. She reports that although some members of Congress support using performance data to inform decision making, others have rejected the idea, while still others have chosen to ignore it.

The primacy of politics in performance measurement is another contextual factor (see Askim in Chapter 8). Some authors argue that by nature, performance measurement is a political activity (see Johnsen in Chapter 10) because what gets measured gets attention. Furthermore, different actors are likely to have different and often conflicting perceptions of what constitutes performance (Kelly, 2002; Stewart and Walsh, 1994). Thus the different meanings assigned to the concept of performance are usually rooted in different values and priorities. As a result, no set of performance measures is found satisfactory by all actors and the assessment of performance becomes a value judgment.

Two other political factors can have negative effects on performance measurement efforts: political ideology and partisanship. For example, in their study comparing the performance measurement efforts in two states in two different countries, de Lancer Julnes and Mixcoatl (2006) found that in Champeche, Mexico, legislators tended to support governors' initiatives and remained at the margin of the implementation process when the governor was of the same party. For them, partisanship was more important than ideology. This was not the case in Utah in the United States, where party identification of both governors and the great majority of legislators is such a given that political ideology takes precedence. Specifically, the Utah Legislature is considered to be one of the most conservative in the United States. According to de Lancer Julnes and Mixcoatl (2006), the legislators were not as complacent as their Mexican counterparts in supporting the performance measurement initiative, which, although coming out of the Legislature, was fully embraced by the Governor. Similar to the response of US Congressional Members to efforts at the national level (Newcomer, 2007), some Utah Legislators rejected the initiative while others simply ignored it in the hope it would go away.

These different observations lead to the conclusion that both rational and political factors are necessary, but insufficient conditions for performance measurement to function. Thus, technical capacity matters little without political support. On the other hand, personal support will only be successful when the essential technical infrastructure, including training in performance measurement, is present. As concluded by Ho (2007), without the appropriate technical capacity performance measurement risks to become a paper-pushing exercise. However, political factors seem to outweigh technical ones. The most important difficulty is to overcome political power struggles resulting from disagreement on the performance that the measurement system is supposed to reflect.

Another important factor affecting the utilization of performance measurement is timing. For example, the political environment might be perceived as too volatile for program changes when there is a change in leadership. In other instances, a change in leadership will precisely entail a window of opportunity that brings fresh air in the governance structure. Another example is a change in the client characteristics or needs which may, in turn, result in a need to make changes to the measurement system. However, if the program is not perceived to be in a state of crisis, the decision might be to maintain the status quo (Weiss, 1998). Each of these situations would lead to a misfit between measurement systems and the needs of the organization, which in all probability will lead to future changes – when the time is right.

To conclude, there are many factors that can have an impact on the utilization of performance measurement and discussing them all goes beyond the scope of this chapter. However, these factors can be categorized as the internal and external organizational context, which according to Van de Walle and Bovaird (2007) also includes some elements related to power and accountability. Getting to the utilization of performance measurement requires entrepreneurs who see Kingdon's windows of opportunity (1984) and thus bring together actors and agendas at the right time.

Exploring a framework for uses and purposes of performance information

Given the context of performance measurement, what expectations, if any, should we have for use? I argue that just as the process of performance measurement is not monolithic, the use and purposes of performance measurement information have many facets too. These facets can be found beyond the instrumental use and traditional purposes of performance measurement information. To see accountability as the sole purpose of performance measurement is a waste of its potential.

Behn (2003) has identified eight managerial purposes of performance measurement systems. Although he concedes that the ultimate purpose of performance measurement is to manage, he nonetheless describes the purpose of performance measurement as falling into one or more of eight categories. Thus, the purposes, he argues, are not necessarily distinct from one another, and in fact overlap. They include: evaluating; controlling; budgeting; motivating; promoting; celebrating; learning; and improving. While these different purposes do not necessarily contradict each other, Behn argues that they require different measures. Thus, for example, measures for the purpose of controlling may not be as useful when the purpose is celebrating successes.

In a seminal address to the American Evaluation Association, Carol Weiss (1998) emphatically pointed out not only that there are many factors that can interfere with the use of evaluation results, but also that there is more than one type of evaluation knowledge use. Weiss (1998) identified four distinctive types of use: (1) Instrumental, when the evaluation findings influence the decision of what to do next about the program or policy in question; (2) Conceptual, when findings change the understanding of what the program is and does; (3) Persuasion, when the information is used to mobilize support for an already held position; and (4) Enlightenment, influence on other institutions and events, when evaluation findings add to the knowledge accumulated and contributes to shifts in thinking and actions. For the most part, proponents of performance measurement define success of use of performance measurement information in terms of instrumental behavior. That is, we look to see if the information has been used to hold someone accountable, to make decisions about program budgets or personnel, or to make significant changes such as expanding, cutting back, or terminating a program. The lack of such decisions often leads to the conclusion that performance measurement has failed.

Weiss's differentiation of knowledge demonstrates the complexity of knowledge use which fully applies to those promoting the utilization of performance measurement in public organizations. These actors are in the business of producing knowledge, and mostly they do it with the expectation that it will be used. Besides pointing to the complexity, Weiss also gives us hope; not all is lost because the organization appears to have failed to launch into action based on performance measurement information.

Weiss's typology also highlights the fact that at different points in time different stakeholders will implement the same information about programs for different purposes. Moreover, these purposes are not necessarily incompatible. And although the purposes may not be incompatible, as suggested by Behn (2003), some types of performance measures will be more useful than others for different purposes.

The framework presented in the two-by-two table (Table 4.1) incorporates Weiss's categorization of knowledge use by categorizing the use of performance measurement information as instrumental or non-instrumental. The framework also takes into account the intended audience of the performance measurement information. Inside the two-by two table are purposes of performance measurement information. Again "purposes" is a different concept than "use." Purposes represent knowledge converted into action or implementation of performance measures. Use, on the other hand, is an underlying concept that provides meaning to purposes. The concept of use provides a helpful structure for better understanding the different purposes of performance measurement information.

As shown in the first quadrant (upper left hand corner) of Table 4.1, for internal audiences an instrumental purpose of performance measurement information is program improvement. These stakeholders are interested in performance indicators that will allow them to answer the question of what changes, including re-allocation of resources, need to

Table 4.1   Purposes of performance measurement

	Primary audience	
Nature of knowledge use	Internal	External
Instrumental	Improvement	Accountability
Non-instrumental	Understanding	Mobilization

be made in order to improve the program in question. Most likely, when these audiences focus on improvement, they will want information on program outcomes, processes and efficiency. The program process indicators may help explain why the outcomes are what they are. However, these indicators do not provide a complete picture. Program evaluators will be reluctant to reach conclusions about causation based on performance information. Nonetheless, as I have argued elsewhere (de Lancer Julnes, 2006), there are certain situations when one can have confidence in the performance measurement information and make changes based on that information. Those situations include:

1. The program theory is not flawed; that is, the program and its expectations are based on a sound theory of cause and effect.
2. The program is not very complex. This would be the case for what Perrin (1998) calls mundane programs such as street cleaning or a vaccination program where the results (e.g., not getting the disease) are clearly attributable to the program.
3. The nature of the program and problem allows for the use of a simple follow up procedure to complement and verify performance information. For example, in some cases doing an implementation evaluation can be all that is needed to understand why results are not as expected.
4. The performance measures were developed based on program evaluation findings that remain relevant. In such cases there can be confidence in the meaning of the indicators of results.

Practice, however, does not provide much evidence of use for improvement purposes. Newcomer (2007) found that only 23.5 percent of US government agencies actually made funding and other resource allocation decisions based on performance measurement information. Comparing these six separate surveys conducted by the different organizations between 1997 and 2003, she does, however, find a slightly positive trend. At the municipal and county levels of government similar findings exist. For example, Melkers and Willoughby (2005) reported that in their study, between two-thirds and three-quarters of respondents stated that performance measurement information was not important or only mildly important in the budget process.

The second purpose is accountability which is categorized as representing an instrumental use with an external audience. For this audience, inputs and outcomes, and to some extent efficiency, would be the preferred performance measurement information. When it comes to citizens, though, the bottom line is outcome or results. Koppell's (2005) typology of accountability provides good insights into how performance measurement information may be used for this purpose. The typology identifies five dimensions of accountability of which three can be directly addressed using performance measurement information (2005: 96). The first dimension is transparency, which asks the question whether the organization reveals the facts of its performance. This kind of accountability requires a conspicuous reporting of performance information to a broad audience. The second dimension, controllability, is about conformity with the principal's concerns (e.g., Congress, President). The third dimension is responsiveness. Did the organization fulfill the substantive expectation (demand/need)? Control and responsiveness can be satisfied by reporting on the accomplishments of the agency or program. These last two dimensions also require a linkage between objectives and indicators of performance.

Accountability, mostly observed in the form of reporting to external audiences, is one of the most often mentioned purposes of performance measurement by survey respondents. For example, 35 percent of the respondents in a study at the local level conducted by Poister and Streib (2005) stated that performance measurement information was reported to the public on a regular basis. In another study, at the state and local level, de Lancer Julnes (2006) reported that 50 percent of informants stated using performance measurement to report to elected officials, and 50 percent explicitly spoke of accountability as the reason for having a performance measurement system. In the 2003 GAO's survey on the use of performance data at the federal level (discussed in Newcomer, 2007), a large majority, 63 percent of respondents, stated that they have performance data that could demonstrate to external audiences whether they are addressing their intended result – an accountability purpose. At the same time, 57 percent felt that performance measurement information was being used for the purpose of holding managers accountable for the accomplishment of agency strategic goals as measured.

In the third quadrant the claim is made that a non-instrumental purpose for performance measurement information intended for external audiences is mobilization. As suggested by Weiss (1998), in discussing program evaluation, it is not unusual for managers to have a preconception of what needs to get done to improve or change a program. In this case, the evaluation information is not necessarily used to effect change, but rather to mobilize support for the manager's position. It may also be used to garner support for the program or agency by promoting the findings of performance measurement, as suggested by Behn's fifth goal of performance measurement, which is that of promoting (Behn, 2003). In this case, outcomes, which call attention to results achieved, can be particularly useful.

The fourth quadrant contains a non-instrumental purpose for internal audiences: understanding of the program. Performance information provides ideas about possible future changes and directions managers may want to pursue, without coupling these insights to formal allocation decisions. Newcomer (2007) reports that approximately 54 percent of federal managers use performance data to understand and improve. But because these two different purposes were part of the same question, it not possible for us to ascertain what proportion of this percentage refers to the understanding purpose and what proportion refers to the improvement purpose. Understanding how a program works and what it does may benefit from outcome and process measures.

It should be noted that understanding is a perfectly legitimate reason for conducting performance measurement; however, in most instances the likelihood is that the stated purpose is program improvement. Complex environments often complicate straightforward use. As a result, performance measurement does not get used in an instrumental manner; it is used by the internal audience to understand how their program works and what it does. With this shift in use, the purpose of measurement moves from instrumental improvement to non-instrumental understanding.

Building on the purposes shown in Table 4.1, the concept of purpose is further differentiated from the concept of knowledge use. Figure 4.1 depicts the four purposes above as well as five additional elements. These elements represent distinct categories of knowledge use that are, in turn, associated with the different purposes of performance measurement. Thus, each type of knowledge use can contribute to one or more purposes of performance measurement. Conversely, each purpose can be fulfilled by one or two types of knowledge use.

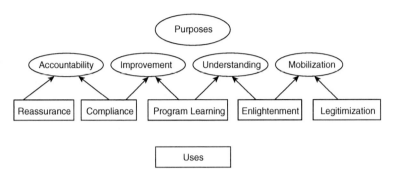

Figure 4.1   Types of knowledge use and purpose

The use for reassurance is to make sure that everything is going well and is under control; government is doing what it is supposed to be doing with taxpayers' money. The performance measurement information, when intended for external purposes, can be used to reassure citizens. This use would highlight indicators that, for example, would lead citizens to feel secure in their neighborhoods. This is also the kind of information that would point out that the city has a reason to be proud because of the cleanliness of the streets and the accomplishments of local schools. The measures would attempt to demonstrate that citizens do not need to be concerned about this year's drought because their city is prepared. And, they can be confident that costs are being kept down even though the quality of services is high.

The next use is compliance. Because of laws and administrative regulations that call for performance measurement, government agencies will feel compelled to use performance measurement to comply with these requirements. For example, in order to receive funds under the US "No Child Left Behind" legislation, schools are required to report test results. It is quite possible that unless they are required to do so, schools or other agencies would not measure the performance of programs, or would measure performance but would not report findings. The non-profit sector provides another example of the need for performance information for compliance. For many years, the utilization of performance measurement in nonprofit organizations was the exception rather than the rule. However, funding agencies have started to ask more questions about the effectiveness of the programs and require performance information to demonstrate effectiveness (Newcomer, 2008). Consequently, nonprofit agencies are now collecting performance information in order to comply with their funders' requirements.

Both reassurance and compliance uses can contribute to accountability (Figure 4.1). But accountability, even in the case of reassurance, can be a double-edged sword. For some, the information poses a threat, while for others it may be an opportunity. There is an opportunity to benchmark, to praise, to reflect. But since the information inevitably leads to judgment, it can lead to fear and defensiveness (de Lancer Julnes, 2006; Solberg, Mosser and McDonald, 1997). Practitioners fear that there is no telling who is going to get a hold of the information and what they are going to do with it. Thus, they feel the need to be careful about how the information is reported. Because of these fears, stated Ammons (2001), some public officials prefer to maintain the status quo rather than allow the performance of their organization to be compared with others. However, since it is not possible for everyone to be above average, Ammons (2001) suggests that knowing where one stands in the performance scale should be about a desire to improve, not a desire for publicity and praise.

In order to discuss program learning (Figure 4.1), we need to reconsider the political nature and the capacity requirements for performance measurement. Given the political nature, some have argued that the information should be used as a means to the end of helping to understand accomplishments of programs, how they work, and what might be done to improve them (Stewart and Walsh, 1994). Thus, the expectation should not be that the information will automatically lead to changes in a program. Further, as has been argued by Weiss (1998), discussions of evaluation impacts tend to refer to users as individuals. However, programs and projects are part of organizations, and it is the organizations and their interaction with the environment that provide the context for knowledge use. These ideas have led to the theory that it is the organization that "learns." Yet, "learning organizations" have some special characteristics. To some extent the theory, grounded in studies of private firms, is about the survival of the fittest, where organizations that do not change (learn) in response to changes in their environment are expected to disappear. The following are some definitions that have been put forth to describe a learning organization:

- A learning organization is a place where people continually expand their capacity to create the results they truly desire, where new and expansive patterns of thinking are nurtured, where collective aspiration is set free, and where people are continually learning how to learn together (Senge, 1990: 1).

- A learning organization is an organization skilled at creating, acquiring and transferring knowledge, and at modifying its behavior to reflect new knowledge and insights (Garvin, 1993: 80).
- A learning organization is an organization that facilitates the learning of all its members and continually transforms itself (Pedler, Burgoyne and 1991: 1).
- Learning organizations are characterized by total employee involvement in a process of collaboratively conducted, collectively accountable change directed towards shared values or principles (Watkins and Marsick, 1992: 118).

In the larger scheme of things, these definitions are useful. However, they are not entirely applicable. A key assumption in these definitions is that learning always leads to transformation or change. In reality, as suggested by Weiss (1998), in order for changes to occur, organizational conditions may have to be changed. But organizations and the programs that operate within them "function within rigid limits imposed by law, tradition, procedures, regulations, accustomed habits of doing things, and restraints from other organizations in the inter-organizational field" (Weiss, 1998: 28). Therefore, even if the organization has learned from performance measurement information, program learning may or may not lead to improvement. Instead it may contribute to a better understanding about the program, which may in turn lead to a more informed dialogue. That, too, is a useful contribution of performance measurement (see also Moynihan in Chapter 2).

The previous discussion leads us to enlightenment. Although most research on knowledge use has tended to focus on finding evidence of instrumental uses, enlightenment may be the most prevalent use of performance measurement in the public sector. Certainly, public officials tend to agree that performance measurement information adds value to budget decisions, informs debate, and somehow influences action. But they also agree that it does not replace traditional considerations when it comes to resource allocation (de Lancer Julnes, 2006; Melkers and Willoughby, 2005). Internally, enlightenment could lead to more informed decisions; because stakeholders are more educated about the program in question, the content of discussions is enhanced with new insights. Also, previously held perceptions can be challenged and in time can lead to organizational transformation. As stated by

Niven: "Simply understanding the firm's strategies can unlock many hidden organizational capacities, as employees, perhaps for the first time, know where the organization is headed and how they can contribute during the journey" (2003: 22).

Externally, a broader form of enlightenment can lead to mobilization of support for a particular course of action. Performance information can be used to put an issue on the political agenda. For instance, waiting lines in service provision may add up to a general sentiment that "something has to change." Conversely, by educating the public about how the program is doing and the benefits that the program brings to the community, program leaders can get support. Beyond program changes, Weiss (1998) suggests that over time the accumulation of evaluation knowledge can influence "large-scale shifts in thinking" – and sometimes, ultimately, to shifts in action.

The last category of knowledge use is legitimization. In this case performance measurement information is used to rationalize, justify or validate current, past and future course of actions or decisions (Ansari and Euske, 1987). For example, performance measurement information plays a supporting role in the budget process of public organizations (de Lancer Julnes, 2006). The information is used to justify budget requests, not to drive decisions. Similarly, Modell and Wiesel (2007) conclude from a comparative study of three state agencies in Sweden that there was a tendency for agencies to use performance measurement to legitimize current practices. In some instances legitimization was a response to external pressure, as was the case of Statistics Sweden. The agency used customer satisfaction indexes to defend itself from criticisms raised by the National Audit Office. When agencies use performance measurement to legitimize the position, the information can contribute to the purpose of mobilization of support.

Conclusion

In this chapter, I have attempted to provide more depth to our understanding of the use of performance measurement information by taking into account the complexities of the context of performance measurement as well as the multiple dimensions of knowledge use. To that end, I have articulated a framework that goes beyond traditional conceptions of use of performance measurement information, differentiating use from purpose and making distinctions between the needs of different audiences. I argue that such a framework is a better tool for assessing the failure or success of performance measurement. Not all use is instrumental, and performance measurement serves more purposes than just accountability.

One implication stands out. Different audiences, different purposes and different uses require different kinds of performance measurement information. This will present new challenges to those developing and implementing performance measurement systems. Decisions have to be made as to which measures would best serve which uses and purposes. Moreover, the uses and purposes may not always be clear and, more often than not, will change along the way. Consequently, the system has to be flexible enough to adjust to different requirements for information. In essence, the system has to learn.

5
Comparing Performance across Public Sectors

Geert Bouckaert and John Halligan

This chapter compares the models for managing performance of four countries and the extent to which they have been implemented. The approach is, first, to examine the countries in terms of their official models and how these compare to an ideal type of Performance Management. The second part addresses how the country models work in practice, focusing on the main dimensions of performance. The countries have well-developed performance management systems, but practice falls short of aspirations, and questions remain about the quality and use of performance information in the budget process, internal decision making and external reporting. Details of the country material and references are in Bouckaert and Halligan (2008).

Framework for comparative performance: ideal types and country models

This chapter presents a framework developed to analyze managing performance and seeks to make comparisons across several countries with well-developed performance management systems. In contrast to the standard approach of focusing on specific management functions, a cross-cutting issues approach is favored here. This involves analyzing components of managing performance, their relationships in four ideal types, and applications to six different countries (Australia, Canada, The Netherlands, Sweden, United Kingdom and United States) in terms of their country models.

The analysis of managing performance involves specifying three components and their relationships. Performance is seen in terms of the pursuit of defined objectives of measuring, incorporating and using performance. In order to extract meaning from the diverse applications and combinations of the three, a framework has been developed. A logical sequence is envisaged of, first, collecting and *processing* performance data into information; second, *integrating* it into documents, procedures and stakeholder discourses; and third, *using* it in a strategy of improving decision making, results and accountability. Four ideal types of managing performance are identified, each with an increasing span and depth of performance, and improved levels of coherence, substance and consolidation (Table 5.1).

The four types are: Performance Administration, Managements of Performances, Performance Management, and Performance Governance (discussed in Bouckaert and Halligan, 2008). Each represents an ideal type, and the four can be applied to the historical development of, and to trace the evolution of, managing performance over time and as a basis for analyzing and comparing country orientations to performance and as a means for thinking analytically about performance management and its components. The focus in this chapter is on one type, Performance Management.

Material from country files (see Bouckaert and Halligan, 2008 and the methodological appendix) provides the rationale for the assignment of countries to ideal types in Table 5.2. Of the countries that did not fit the Performance Management category, those in Performance

Table 5.1 Four ideal types of managing performance

	Performance administration	Managements of performances	Performance management	Performance governance
1. Measuring	Administrative data registration, objective, mostly input and process	Specialized performance measurement systems	Hierarchical performance measurement systems	Consolidated performance measurement system
2. Incorporating	Some	Within different systems for specific management functions	Systemic internal integration	Systemic internal and external integration
3. Using	Limited: reporting, internal, single loop	Disconnected	Coherent, comprehensive, consistent	Societal use
4. Limitations	Ad hoc, selective, rule based	Incoherence	Complex, perhaps not sustainable as a stable system	How controllable and manageable?

Table 5.2   Management ideal types and country models

Ideal type	Country
Performance Administration	France, Germany
Managements of Performances	Netherlands, Sweden
Performance Management	Australia, Canada, UK, USA

Administration are readily explained. Performance Administration is distinguished in measurement by limits to the span and depth and by design that is ad hoc; incorporation is disconnected and variable; and there is limited use of performance information.

A more developed case is the Managements of Performances category. This ideal type encompasses several of the features of Performance Management – for example, depth of measurement, management emphasis – yet there are several key differences such as disconnected policy and management. Countries that fit this type are the Netherlands and Sweden. Why do the Netherlands and Sweden not qualify for Performance Management when they both have long commitments to a performance approach? Have they opted to be out rather than in because they see the limits of performance management or because they are unable to apply that level of discipline in their systems?

Comparing country models within the Performance Management type

Turning to the Performance Management type, the focus here is on the country models or frameworks that encapsulate official aspirations and rhetoric. There are several means by which Performance Management can be realized in official frameworks, but the basic features must be present. In terms of span, it ranges across inputs, outputs and outcomes. With regard to depth, the type needs to encompass several management systems and their interconnections. There must be an overriding integrated performance focus with strong policy and political dimensions.

Four countries from our case studies fit the Performance Management type. While other candidates have not been systematically investigated, it is expected that few countries approximate this type. The available information for the early 2000s suggested that Canada and the United

States fitted Managements of Performances, but as their respective reform agendas progressed towards the mid-2000s their official models moved sufficiently to qualify for inclusion in the Performance Management type.

Australia has a fully fledged model that fits within the Performance Management ideal type. This agenda has been pursued since the mid-1980s with increasing elaboration and refinements to a comprehensive approach. The official model is a developed system based on an outcomes and outputs framework that covers individual and organizational dimensions and their management interrelationships. This model reflects the situation at the federal level, but in some sectors the model is being increasingly applied to the state government.

The United Kingdom model of public service reform is based on top-down performance management, plus competition and contestability in service provision, citizen choice and voice and strengthening officials' capability; all of which have performance elements. This has supported a comprehensive model of performance management based on Cabinet Office and Treasury agendas, but with the centerpiece being the latter's regular spending reviews and the Public Service Agreement Framework. This framework is a multifunctional system that generates performance information that can be used for different purposes, including coordinating, steering and integrating government under a system-wide performance regime that supports the Treasury's role in priority setting. The result has been a national system that is unlikely to be achieved in federal systems.

Canada now has a developed performance management framework at the federal level. Its unifying structure is centered on the Management Resources and Results Structure (MRRS), which is designed to establish the link between results of programs and departmental management and structure, and to link program activities to strategic outcomes, resource information and performance measures and departmental governance. Strategic outcomes and program activities are aligned with Government of Canada outcomes. The Whole of Government planning and reporting framework, which is based on MRRS, provides a comprehensive overview of resources and results. Finally, the Management Accountability Framework provides building blocks for anchoring the performance focus.

The United States model is centered on PART and follows on from the congressional GPRA initiative. During the Bush era, the focus has been on making GPRA more effective, using PART as a complementary and major tool for performance improvement. The philosophy is one of managing for performance. The mechanism is to evaluate, to assess and to publicly judge the performance by offering information on performing and not-performing agencies. The purpose is to integrate, use and improve performance information. The GPRA/PART infrastructure links strategic objectives to outputs and resources with periodic assessments using performance measures for different purposes. The ultimate purpose is to guarantee performance for the public.

The four systems can be observed moving through stages that correspond to the ideal types. The United States led early in the use of measurement, and with more complex experiments with PPBS, budget savings and productivity. Canada and the United Kingdom also contributed to the advocacy of improved measurement and management. In the actual shift from an inputs and process focus to managing for results, the United Kingdom and Australia were able to install programs, outputs and outcomes in the 1980s and 1990s, and new approaches to managing resources. In the last decade, the focus has been on how to make something of outcomes and register impacts on society. At the same time, performance management systems have been developed in North America and been refined and improved in all systems. In the 2000s, all four countries have been working through variations on a performance management approach.

The country models exhibit common features that determine their grouping under the Performance Management type, but there are also significant variations in how they approach the key aspects of a performance management framework. These variations partly reflect different approaches but also institutional contexts (see Bouckaert and Halligan, 2008).

Measuring and incorporating performance information

Measuring performance information

Four dimensions are important. First, the set of criteria for a good performance indicator and performance measurement system. Second, the process of measuring and managing performance measurement, including the prescribed stages in an operating procedure for measuring performance. Third, the context of what is being measured and what models are used, including what is being measured and the extent to which there is a range of indicators on resources, activities, outputs, effects/outcomes, environment; linkages between indicators; and policy on developing standards for performance levels. Finally, there is the question of the handling of audit and quality control of measurement and management.

In terms of span of measurement, there may be a pronounced architecture as in Australia and Canada. In Australia a distinction is made between indicators for outcomes, outputs, and administered items (which include transfers and subsidies) and detailed specifications exist for outputs and outcomes. On the other hand, the United States leaves such details open.

With regard to criteria, the degree of detail is most operational in the United Kingdom (with FABRIC and SMART). The United States has a mechanistic checklist defined under PART. The United Kingdom lists criteria for good indicators such as relevance, attribution, timeliness, reliability and verifiable; and a good performance measurement system should be focused, appropriate, balanced, robust, integrated and cost effective (FABRIC). Australia has applied the criteria of alignment, credibility and integration, and placed emphasis on an accrual based Outcomes and Output Framework.

Quality control is sometimes linked to audit and is sometimes part of the executive. All four countries have a strong audit tradition. External audit has been stronger than internal audit, and internal audit has been inclined to lag behind. Some systems, such as Australia, have routinely emphasized both for many years. For the United Kingdom, the external auditor is the Comptroller and Auditor General, who is supported by the National Audit Office, and all departments have an internal audit unit that operates within the Audit Policy and Advice Unit of HM Treasury. Canada took steps to develop a departmental internal audit function decades ago, but reviews indicated shortcomings, and attention to internal audit increased after the sponsorship scandal of 2003 and the re-establishment of the Office of the Comptroller General. The United States is strong on performance audits, and has Offices of the Inspector General as independent units for conducting and supervising audits and investigations on agency programs and operations.

Incorporating performance information

The analysis of the incorporation of performance information focuses on tools, methods and techniques for anchoring measurement and management practices in documents and processes. These might be framework documents, budget formats and links between planning, budgeting and reporting. Overall, all countries used the budget cycle for incorporation of performance information. All emphasized budgeting and reporting, but different types of documents were used.

The Australian Outcomes and Outputs Framework was legally anchored by the Financial Management and Accountability Act. For human resource management the Public Service Act provides a legal framework and responsibilities of heads of agencies. In linking a planning and reporting cycle to a yearly budget cycle, performance management is tangible. The responsible minister, after consultation with the relevant agencies, decides on outcomes. The Outcomes and Outputs Framework is connected to the budget process through the outcome statements in the budget bills, portfolio budget statements and annual reports. The framework requires financial management and reporting to budgeting on a full accrual basis and outputs and outcomes reporting. Agencies identify explicit outcomes, outputs and performance measures. Agency heads are assigned clear responsibility and accountability for performance. Reporting occurs through budget plans (Portfolio Budget Statements) and financial year results (annual reports). Outcome statements are linked to Portfolio Budget Statements, which are linked to the Annual Reports. Outcomes are crucial since this is the appropriation level. The Department of Finance provides minimum requirements for the Portfolio Budget Statement and, together with agencies, provides more detailed information to the Appropriation Bills. Portfolio Budget Statements should follow general principles containing sufficient information, explanation and clarification for Parliament to understand objectives and agency performance. Criteria for annual reports are determined by the Department of the Prime Minister and Cabinet and approved by a Parliamentary committee.

The design of an architecture of information for documents guarantees a standardized approach to incorporating performance information in management and policy cycles. Canada uses the Management Resources and Results Structure (MRRS), which establishes the link between results and the results of programs that connect with departmental management and structure. MRRS contains performance information at a more detailed level and is linked to cost data. MRRS consists of strategic outcomes; Program Activity Architecture (including an inventory of all program activities of departments in relation to strategic outcomes, resource information and performance measures); and governance structure (processes and structures for exercising departmental decision making). Departments have been asked to align strategic outcomes and the relevant program activities with Government of Canada outcomes. The requirements for departments are codified and integrated through Reports on Plans and Priorities and Departmental Performance reports. Finally, the Management Accountability Framework anchors the performance focus by providing deputy ministers with tools to assess and improve management practices.

The United Kingdom has a complex set of documents to report on in the planning, control and reporting cycle. Departments conclude a Public Service Agreement, a two-yearly agreement with HM Treasury on prior policy objectives and targets for the next three years (see also Chapter 9 by Johnson and Talbot which deals with PSAs). PSAs are translated into targets for agencies. Departments plan an implementation trajectory to reach the PSA Targets, and report to Cabinet Office and HM Treasury on the implementation of their Targets and Delivery Plan. Other reporting covers the Annual Report and Accounts in which departments and agencies submit to parliament their yearly report and accounts; the Framework Document established by the responsible minister and the agencies to define tasks and objectives; and key ministerial targets determined by the responsible minister and the agencies. In spring, there is a departmental report to Parliament on progress and plans; in autumn, a departmental annual report and accounts (outputs, performance, accounts) (Scheers, Sterck and Bouckaert, 2005).

United States agencies have been required by the GPRA to submit a three-year strategic plan and both an annual performance plan and performance report. Steps have been taken to transform the performance plan into a performance budget. At the agency level, the GPRA requires departments and agencies to produce a three-year strategic plan, which contains a description of the relationship between annual performance goals in the performance budget and the long-term goals in the strategic plan. Agencies now have to submit a performance budget organized as a hierarchy of goals linked to performance and cost information: strategic, long-term performance and annual performance goals. Agencies also have to report the results of the PART assessment and the performance goals used in the assessment of program performance under the PART process in their performance budget. The annual performance report provides information about departments' and agencies' performance and progress in achieving the goals in the strategic plan and the performance budget. Cabinet departments and nine independent agencies have to integrate the annual report required by the GPRA with the accountability report. The annual report contains a comparison of actual performance with the projected levels of performance as set out in the performance goals in the annual performance budget; explanations for unachieved performance goals; and evaluation of the performance budget for the current year. Information on every PART program is assessed as part of the budget formulation for the fiscal year.

These countries – Australia, Canada, the United Kingdom and the United States – have developed generally accepted performance principles for measuring and incorporating performance information. First, a logical and connected chain of inputs-activities-outputs-effects/outcomes-trust is developed, refined and operationalized. Second, incorporation is connected to stages in the policy cycle (design, decision, implementation, reporting) on the one hand, and service delivery on the other hand. There is an increasing coherence within and between the policy cycle and service delivery cycle. Third, this is institutionalized using new roles for existing actors, and creating new actors such as internal auditors, or autonomous statistical services.

Using performance information

There are three main dimensions to using performance information: internal use by agencies and individuals, budget decisions and process, and reporting.

Using performance information internally

The Australian outcome and output structure of the performance measurement system has the potential for several management functions. Documents in the budget cycle, such as portfolio budget statements and departmental annual reports, are used by the administration and government to communicate to Parliament on an *ex-ante* and *ex-post* basis. Performance information that is collected and used internally results in awareness of its use and an extra motivation for external reporting. Performance information runs through the management and policy cycle in the different stages of design, decision, implementation and evaluation, and the related financial stages of budgeting, accounting and auditing.

The Canadian main estimates are structured as a traditional program budget, but departments and agencies report on their plans and priorities in the main estimates to inform Parliament about the outputs and outcomes they want to achieve with the authorized resources. Including output and outcome information in the budget, however, does not necessarily mean that this information is used in the budget process. The reporting cycle in 2006 shows how reports providing performance information relate to the financial calendar and the estimates.

In the United Kingdom, there is a cascade of Public Service Agreement (PSA) related documents which support internal use such as delivery plans and reports, annual reports, framework documents, corporate plans, departmental reports and charters with an increasing challenge to make them coherent.

In the United States, the potential to use performance information internally is significant. The largest potential for real payoffs from using performance information may be in agency management of resources once they have been provided in the budget process. Even if the performance information has not played a significant role in the budgetary approval process, it can still influence the execution of the budget in the agency. Agencies have a significant discretion in allocating resources between programs and between regional units. Also, performance information is connected to internal managerial issues such as adopting new program approaches, setting individual job expectations, rewarding staff, and developing and managing contracts.

Reporting of performance

Understanding reporting requirements and practices is only possible within the context of the measurement focus and the framework of a performance system. It also should be put in a sequence of documents that should have a cyclical coherence.

In the Australian case, outcome appropriations are linked to portfolio budget statements, which are linked to the annual reports. Outcomes are the intended and expected impact of the public sector on a particular policy field. Outcomes are at the same strategic level as the mission of an organization, but are supposed to be more external and less value laden. There is a list of requirements for a good outcome description. Portfolio Budget Statements (PBSs) are part of the budget papers and provide explanatory memoranda on the provisions of budget bills. Detailed information is provided on the outputs and the administered items at portfolio level. The official criteria for agency annual reports include: review of the preceding year; overview of the department's functions and outcome and output structure; report on performance; review of performance in terms of efficiency of outputs and effectiveness in achieving planned outcomes; actual results against PBS performance standards for outcomes and outputs; and management and accountability.

The Canadian guide for Reports on Plans and Priorities (RPPs) and Departmental Performance (DPRs) has been integrated for the reporting cycle to reinforce their complementary roles. The RPP presents planned spending information on strategic outcomes and program activity, and covers priorities, expected results and resourcing for a three-year period. The DPR records results achieved against performance expectations in the RPP, with explanations of progress made towards strategic outcomes. The report may be structured in a way suitable for telling the department's performance story, but consistency is maintained through mandatory sections for both RPP and DPR (departmental overview, including program activity architecture; and analysis of program activities by strategic outcome). Annual guidelines are set for plans and priorities and departmental performance reports based on reporting principles and integrating principles that reflect their complementary features. The combined documents are designed to indicate the links between plans, performance and achievements, and with the Whole of Government planning and reporting framework, which provides a comprehensive overview of resources and results.

The United Kingdom has a complex set of reporting documents based on different institutional linkages and the related documentary requirements in the planning, control and reporting cycle. Ministerial departments have the two-year Public Service Agreement (PSA) with HM Treasury on prior policy objectives and targets for three years. PSAs consist of an aim, objectives, performance targets, value-for-money targets, and a responsibility statement, plus a technical note to explain measurement itself. The operationalization of the PSA is through Delivery Plans for departments to plan an implementation trajectory to reach PSA targets, and Delivery Reports for departments to report to Cabinet Office and HM Treasury on implementation. They are presented to the Cabinet Committee on Public Services and Expenditure, and are neither communicated to Parliament nor made available to the public. Departments submit an autumn report to Parliament on the performance of the previous year (outputs, performance and accounts), including an annual report and accounts; and a spring report on progress and plans. For policy and management control, the annual report, the statement on internal control, and the Statement on Resources by Aims and Objectives are crucial.

United States agencies are required by the GPRA to submit a three-year strategic plan, an annual performance plan and an annual performance report. Steps have been taken to transform the performance plan into a performance budget. The performance budget is organized as a hierarchy of goals linked to performance and cost information: strategic goals (aim and purpose of the agency, spanning several programs and several agency organizational units); long-term performance goals (outcome goals at program level); outcome targets and resources (full cost); annual performance goals (output goals at program level); and output targets and resources (full cost). The annual performance report provides information about departments and agencies performance and progress in achieving the goals as set in the strategic plan and the performance budget. Cabinet departments and nine independent agencies have to integrate the annual report required by the GPRA with the accountability report and submit this combined performance and accountability report.

Using in practice

Performance information

The quality of Australian financial information is regarded as having improved as a result of the outcomes/output framework and explicitly identifying performance indicators (Department of Finance and Administration, 2006a). However, performance measurement of outcomes has provided difficulties, despite its centrality to the resource management framework (Wanna and Bartos, 2003). Australian output performance measures are generally more appropriate and measurement more reliable. In a review of performance reporting in departmental annual reports, the Australian National Audit Office (ANAO) has indicated the need for improving information with respect to specification of the performance framework and the quality of measures and the reporting of results. The Auditor-General reports that performance information is being used by decision makers for policy development and allocating resources but the actual "influence of outcomes and outputs information on decision making was mixed" (McPhee, 2005: 3–4).

In the United States, there is in general a positive evolution in the percentage of agencies measuring performance. This can be explained by the fact that in 1997 the GPRA was implemented only in pilot projects whereas it was implemented fully in 2000. In 2003, 54 percent of the federal managers reported having output measures to a great or very great extent (General Accounting Office, 2004: 36).

The UK National Audit Office looked at indicators used in *Public Service Agreements 2001–2004*. Evidence demonstrates that the majority of the indicators used (43 percent) are collected by departments, 19 percent have Non-Departmental Public Bodies, and 14 percent National

Statistics origins (National Audit Office, 2001b). The remaining indicators are from local government, the Health Service and international organizations. The same survey showed that the initial distribution of indicators changed. The proportion of indicators changed from 7 to 5 percent for input, from 51 to 14 percent for process, from 27 to 13 percent for outputs, and from 15 to 68 percent for outcomes.

In Canada, for each strategic outcome and program, resource allocations and performance indicators have to be defined. However, reporting on outcomes has been difficult. An assessment of departmental performance reports of 2001 showed that only 31 of the 84 examined reports were focused on outcomes, but many of these could be classified as outputs produced by the department and focused on activities under its control. The assessment of the departmental performance reports of 2002, showed a stronger focus on outcomes, although many reports were still largely focused on activities, outputs and immediate or intermediate outcomes.

According to Curristine (2005) almost 75 percent of countries reporting in the 2005 OECD survey mentioned extending coverage, a strong focus on outputs, and about 52 percent are moving to outcomes. In general the United Kingdom, United States, Canada, and Australia are significantly above the average practice.

Performance and budgeting

Performance information is meant to inform the budget process. For Australia, budget information is now "more comprehensive, based on external reporting standards, and provides better alignment between appropriation Acts, PB Statements and agency annual reports" (Department of Finance and Administration, 2006b: 11). The Australian outcomes policy provides for agencies to use performance information in budget decision making, but the potential has not been achieved because of the variable influence of this information on decisions and resource allocation. The Finance Department is exploring means for improving the use of performance information by revising the information required for new policy proposals and making greater use of reviews, regarded as an instrument through which performance information can be fed into budget decision making.

In Canada, main estimates are structured as a traditional program budget, but since 1995 departments and agencies report on their plans and priorities in the main estimates to inform parliament about the outputs and outcomes they want to achieve with the authorized resources. Including output and outcome information in the budget, however, does not necessarily mean that this information is used in the budget process.

According to the OECD 2005 survey the majority of finance ministries use performance measures in budget processes, but measures or evaluations are rarely used for eliminating programs and cutting expenditure (Curristine, 2005). The practice is that performance information is there to inform but not to determine budget allocations.

Individual and organizational performance

The alignment between agency goals and organizational priorities and their performance management systems is variable. Many Australian agencies lacked systems for supporting performance management, and were not assessing the internal impact of performance management systems. As a result, performance management was not contributing to effective business outcomes (Australian National Audit Office, 2004). The credibility of performance management systems as they affect individual public servants has been raised by inquiries, with performance pay systems being problematic. The ANAO concluded that the significant investment in performance-linked remuneration delivered patchy results and uncertain benefits. Performance management in Australia was depicted as a "work in progress" with major challenges on the issues of credibility and staff engagement (Halligan, 2007).

In the United Kingdom, at central and local government levels there is an "instrumental-managerial" focus on performance measurement (Sanderson, 2001). In combination with the top-down conditioning of performance, the individual and organizational performance may be in tension. In the Annual Report there is a brief description of how the various elements of remuneration were determined for the members of the management board and, if the latter was done following a standard process, a reference to the appropriate report of the Senior Salaries Review Body suffices. Details of remuneration or a reference to where such information is given is provided in the notes to the accounts.

Agency variation

There is considerable variation among agencies in how they engage and implement performance management. This reflects in part the nature of agencies, with some types more able to demonstrate effective use of performance information. Significant variation exists in the quality of and information used in annual reports. Variability also exists in the alignment between the goals and organizational priorities of many

Australian agencies and their performance management systems. In the United States, the PART scores demonstrate the variance. In Canada, the Treasury Board Secretariat (TBS) and the Office of the Auditor General (OAG) have developed scoring systems to measure the quality of performance reporting. All these scores show a significant variance between organizations. Crucial issues are whether there is a policy for a bottom line of measuring, incorporating or using performance information, whether there is a culture of champions (with publicized scores, or red/orange/green labels), and whether there is a maximum tolerated variance.

Reporting of performance

The reporting of outputs and outcomes in Australia is generally appropriately specified in annual reports and the quality of performance reporting has improved since the introduction of accrual-based budgeting. Nevertheless, improvements in annual reporting frameworks have been urged to enhance accountability and transparency to stakeholders, particularly parliamentarians, because of shortcomings in the presentation and analysis of performance information in annual reports. In Canada, the success of performance reporting seems to be positively correlated with evidence that the information is used for decision making or program improvements. The Treasury Board Secretariat reports that departments with satisfactory to very good departmental performance reports scored high on the use of performance information for learning and for decision making. In most cases the performance information has a strategic element with an outcomes focus and a clear logic between departmental activity and how this contributes to outcomes (Treasury Board Secretariat, 2003).

System assessment

Administrating, managing or governing performance

To what extent are the countries actively cultivating and managing performance? The approach in the United Kingdom has been a combination of strategies of the two primary central agencies, the Cabinet Office and Treasury over ten or more years.

The Australian approach has been to combine framework reform at intervals with regular strategic adjustments and fine-tuning. The steering is centered on the Department of Finance with occasional oversight reports on issues from the Management Advisory Committee (MAC – a collective of departmental secretaries), and annual reporting on the state of the service by the Public Service Commission. This is under the guidance of the public service head, the Secretary of the Department of Prime Minister and Cabinet, who makes regular statements about reform and whose department monitors delivery and manages Whole of Government initiatives. The Management Advisory Committee has reviewed performance management with the application of a strategic framework. More recently there have been the Australian National Audit Office analysis (Australian National Audit Office, 2004) and the Australian Public Service Commission's annual surveys, which rely substantially on the MAC report.

Canada was one of the first countries to explore management reform, but was slow to incorporate and institutionalize it. Despite having never fully embraced managerialism through a sustained reform program at the national level, the Canadian public service exhibits many standard management features and has experienced the tensions and conflicts produced by attempts to change the administrative culture. The Audit Office often filled the vacuum left by lack of sustained leadership from senior politicians and lead central agencies. The verdict of observers was critical (Aucoin, 2001) with slow progress in using information on results; weaknesses in the management reform process; divided responsibility for human resource management; and limited Parliamentary review. The Office of the Auditor General continued to raise issues about the quality of information, the lack of focus on outcomes, and the coverage of performance data. By the mid-2000s, these questions had been responded to, although there appears to be a shortage of independent analysis, and skepticism about performance management and the mandatory federal agenda (Clark and Swain, 2005). The new approach is top-down, featuring central agencies, particularly the government's "management board", the Treasury Board Secretariat.

The United States has had a significant historical influence on other Western countries in managing performance in the public sector (e.g., PPBS has been exported to OECD countries). Then there was a break until a new era started with GPRA and the National Performance Review (NPR) in the early 1990s. However, NPR was more ad hoc than institutionalized, and not connected to GPRA. It took some time before GPRA became the standard for practice. However, there was an effort to consolidate and to create a converging strategy of managing performance. Under Bush, the focus has been on making the GPRA more effective, using PART as a complementary and major tool to push for performance. The purpose has been to integrate performance information, to use this information, and to improve performance. According to Posner in a General Accounting Office (GAO) testimony to a congressional committee, "one way of improving the links between PART and GPRA would be to develop a more strategic approach to selecting and prioritizing areas for assessment under the PART process" (General Accounting Office, 2004: 10). The mechanism is to evaluate, to assess, and to judge publicly the performance by offering information on performing and non-performing agencies.

Overall assessment

Australia has a fully operational performance model that incorporates and uses performance information. The early program and results focus laid the foundation for evolving towards a more comprehensive system. Financial information has improved with the Outcomes/Output framework in registering government preferences (intentions and results) and identification of performance indicators (Department of Finance and Administration, 2006a). However, measurement of outcomes has continued to provide difficulties. Output information is considerably better, performance measures are generally more appropriate and measurement more reliable than those for outcomes measures (McPhee, 2005). As for using performance information, there are improvements and continuing shortcomings, including variation among agencies. First, budget information is more comprehensive, and there is better alignment between reporting documents. The outcomes policy provides for the use of performance information in budget decision making, but the potential has not been realized because of the variable influence of this information on decisions and resource allocation. Second, with regards to reporting, outputs and outcomes are appropriately specified in annual reports and the quality of performance reporting has improved. Nevertheless, improvements in annual reporting frameworks have been urged to enhance accountability and transparency to stakeholders, particularly parliamentarians (Halligan, 2007). The official Australian model fits within the Performance Management Type, but implementation has not been fully realized, and work continues on how to achieve more effective performance management.

Canada fitted into Managements of Performances for a long time, but a sustained program has moved it into the Performance Management type. The current model was preceded by a sequence of initiatives that produced an ambitious scheme for departments. Given Canada's earlier reputation for weak implementation, recent initiatives have been promising. Performance indicators have been expanding and are under review. There has been a developmental logic that is cumulative at this stage, but the Canadian system appears to have reached a turning point. The lack of fuller information makes it difficult to form a firmer judgment on practice. Canada appears to be at the stage where the mandatory and centralized approach to management improvement is unsympathetic to variation.

The United Kingdom's PSA regime has been "a novel and ambitious tool for steering and coordinating public activity" that was designed to reduce fragmentation by bringing central government under one performance system and "to promote Treasury influence over the priority setting of bodies beyond central government" (James, 2004: 398–401). Reported limitations include frequent changes to targets, the weak link with systems where relevant activity occurs, and the use of presentation strategies for blame avoidance. Moreover, PSA objectives are not necessarily clear on priorities and PSAs appear to have weak incentive effects on priorities (James, 2004). In theory, measures cascade from PSAs to other frameworks and plans at regional and local levels. In practice further plans, strategies and indicators may need to be taken into account. The Treasury is central to the agreement on a limited number of targets and indicators, but is not formally involved in the cascade process; it is the departments that have discretion over the application of PSA objectives and targets. Research suggests that cascading indicators were multiplying but there was a lack of priority among indicators at the local level, and a disconnection between PSA and Best Value regimes. Measurement systems may not influence behavior to produce the delivery in terms of priorities (Neely and Micheli, 2004). The 2007 Comprehensive Spending Review is designed to go beyond 2004 aspirations for efficiency. The focus on reforming service delivery involves "strengthening accountability, as part of an overall framework for devolved decision making [...] to ensure that public services are responsive to needs and preferences of individuals and communities." It covers clear goals and national standards, front-line flexibility and capability, community and citizen engagement and empowerment of users (HM Treasury, 2006: 140–2).

The official US evaluation of PART is rather positive according to the GAO and the Office of Management and Budget (OMB), the review process stimulating agencies to increase their evaluation capacity and the available information on program results (US Government Accountability Office, 2005a). However, even if the PART process helped OMB's oversight of agencies, stimulated agencies' efforts to improve program management, and created or enhanced an evaluation culture within agencies, most PART recommendations have focused on improving outcome measures and data collection, not on short-term observable performance improvements (US Government Accountability Office, 2005c).

Dissonant voices come from the academic world with Radin (2006) arguing that PART is detrimental to increased performance. Also Gilmour and Lewis observe that PART shows that "if the measurement process is not neutral, political considerations may warp the assessment, as well as their application [...] PART scores influenced budget allocations for programs housed in Democratic departments but not other programs. This last finding underscores the difficulty of using performance information in an impartial way" (2006: 750–1). The greatest accomplishment of PART, has been to produce "useful assessments of 800 programs. OMB is on track to finish assessments of all federal programs in 2007. There is evidence that PART assessments have an impact on allocation decisions in the president's budget. Yet, thus far there is little evidence that PART has caused significant changes in program management" (Gilmour, 2006: 6). The GPRA/PART infrastructure links strategic objectives to outputs and resources. There are periodic assessments in a context of using performance measures for different purposes. The ultimate purpose is to guarantee performance for the public, including trust. This corresponds well with a Performance Management ideal type.

Conclusion

This chapter has focused on the Performance Management ideal type and countries that fit within it in terms of their official models. The second task was to examine practice with the official models in the four countries.

The countries examined have been highly committed to performance management over two decades during which they have refined their measurement and performance framework and increased their capacity to monitor performance. They have followed different pathways within a performance management framework during these two decades. Their early implementation styles differed in terms of conceptions of the relationship between outputs and outcomes, the responsibilities given to chief executives, and the roles of central personnel agencies in handling performance oversight. The exigencies of reform agendas have produced a considerable convergence on public management during the 2000s.

Yet there remain significant differences in approach and with the technical treatment of outcomes and outputs. In terms of their reform cycles, two countries have been implementing the main initiatives that qualify them for the Performance Management type (Canada and the United States). The Netherlands also is implementing a new approach, but like Sweden, which seems to have been the less mobile of the six, falls outside the Performance Management category. The country models continue to evolve and be refined in Australia and the United Kingdom.

More importantly, practice continues to fall short of aspirations, and significant questions remain about the quality and use of performance information in the budget process, internal decision making and external reporting, and the variable engagement of agencies. There continue to be other issues about the level of application by public managers in practice and significant challenges to accomplishing sophisticated performance management and limits to a heavy reliance on this approach (Bouckaert and Halligan, 2008).

Appendix: Note on methodology

The study relies on two major methodological pillars: ideal types and concrete country case studies that result in a description of a country model. The empirical material used is based on comparative research that considers the "official" or dominant performance models of central governments. Official country models are communicated through legislation, circular letters or handbooks and are an expression of the desired information architecture, the emphasis on content, its incorporation, and its use. In many cases this is a program of change and improvement that needs to be implemented.

The structure of this empirical material relies on ideal types as defined by Max Weber. Four ideal types are developed. Ideal types fit into Weber's methodology of "singular causal analysis." From a process point of view, a causal chain consists of, first, *measuring*, then *incorporating* this information, in order to ultimately *use* it. Based on implicit or explicit concepts or even definitions of performance, the practice is to observe levels of performance. To the extent that these are systematic observations, one could label them as the practice of "measurement." The processing of data into information means that this performance data needs to be incorporated into documents, circulated, and generally made available, the "incorporation" stage. Once there has been "measurement" and "incorporation," performance information should be fit for the intended purpose, that is, using it to manage. The final stage is therefore use of performance-related information, which includes all positive and negative, intended and unintended, short-term and long-term effects and types of use.

Six countries (Australia, Canada, The Netherlands, Sweden, the UK and USA) are examined using the scheme for analyzing managing for performance and defining country models.

A distinction is made between three modes in analyzing managing for performance: "ideal types," "country models" and "degrees of implementation" of the "country models" (Figure 5.1). These three dimensions interact with one another. "Ideal types" may influence and inspire the "country models." On the other hand, the starting positions of countries, and their capacity to implement, may influence the choice of "country model." Both existing practices and their official versions can be compared and assessed against the coherence and the logic of an ideal type.

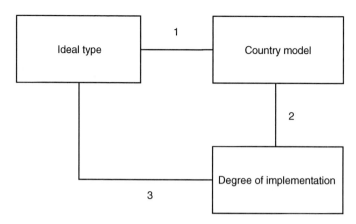

Figure 5.1 Three modes of "realities" for analyzing managing performance

6
Hitting the Target and Missing the Point? Developing an Understanding of Organizational Gaming

Zoe Radnor

Public services are by their nature complex (Moore, 2002), involving a large number of stakeholders. As a result, the number of public sector performance measures can quickly rise in order to reflect this complexity and to be accountable to the various stakeholders. Hood gives an example of the Health Department in England, where ten top-level targets "were translated into some 300 lower-level targets for various public sector health-delivery organizations" (2006: 515). In many countries we have seen a rapid proliferation of policies introducing performance indicators and targets in all areas of the public service sector, from local and central government to education, health and community care.

These performance indicators serve different aims. Some would argue that performance regimes are primarily about accountability and control (de Haas and Kleingeld, 1998; Fisher, 1995), whereas others would argue they are also about improvement and motivation (e.g., Neely, 1998). Performance indicators are used for controlling public expenditure, demonstrating accountability and for improving public services (Wilson, 2004). When targets are put in place to drive activities and behaviors in a particular direction to improve performance, a control element is introduced in the system.

Performance measurement, reporting and management

It is important to differentiate the terms "performance measurement," "performance reporting" and "performance management." Each has its own set of activities and issues. The three activities can be defined as follows (based on Radnor and Barnes, 2007):

- Performance measurement is the valuation of the quantity or quality of the input, output, outcome or level of activity of an event or process.
- Performance reporting is providing an account, and often some analysis, of the level of input, activity, output or outcome of an event or process, usually against some form of target.
- Performance management is action, based on performance measures and reporting, aimed at improvements in behavior, motivation and processes and promotes innovation.

A systems views suggests that a performance management system should provide information on the matters of importance, promote appropriate behavior, provide a mechanism for accountability and control, and create a mechanism for intervention and learning (de Haas and Kleingeld, 1998; Fisher, 1995; Neely, 1998). Yet, evidence (e.g., Hood, 2006; Pollitt, 2005) suggests that within the public sector much of the attention has gone to performance measuring and reporting, focusing on target achievement and positioning in league tables, rather than to the use of the performance metrics to directly improve services. This chapter has the underlining premise that too much focus on measurement and reporting means that performance measures and indicators are not so much used as a tool to improve the performance of an organization but become ends in themselves.

Dysfunctions of performance information systems and gaming behavior have received considerable attention in the literature (Bouckaert and Balk, 1991; Hood, 2007a; Smith, 1995; van Thiel and Leeuw, 2002). Unintended consequences of measurement and reporting are often related to targets and league tables. Hood describes "gaming", as "[the] deliberate massaging or outright fabrication of numbers collected with the intention of improving the position of an individual or organization" (Hood, 2007a: 100). He summarized the three major types of gaming (related to targets and rankings) as *ratchet effects*, where targets are set as an incremental advance and where managers as a result restrict performance to below their possible level; *threshold effects* where uniform output targets provide no incentive to excel and do not encourage top performers; and finally *output distortion* or *manipulation* of reported results (Hood, 2006).

In this chapter I will address the consequences of a disproportionate focus on performance measurement and performance reporting, rather

than on performance management. The chapter will use UK government-
or department-based documents and academic journal articles and
summarizes the main issues related to organizational gaming. It will
concentrate on the degree of gaming and the impact of such gaming on
organizational performance and improvement, that is, the consequences of gaming. This review will then be used to suggest a possible
typology of gaming within organizations that will help to understand
the effects of gaming.

Dysfunctions related to performance measurement

Some organizations use performance information systems that give
undue attention to performance measurement. A "measurement culture" is different from a "performance culture" (Public Administration
Select Committee, 2003). An organizational measurement culture is
one of tracking quantitative achievement, whereas a performance culture is concerned with building an organization's capacity. The danger
of a measurement culture, according to the Public Administration Select
Committee in the United Kingdom, is that excessive attention is given
to what can be easily measured at the expense of what is difficult to
measure, even though this may be more appropriate to the service. In
some cases, a measurement culture may regard delivering on targets as
more important than delivering on services. The Select Committee
report refers to a by now well-known example from the ambulance
service. Concerned with response times, it used "lay responders" to hit
the target even though these individuals may not be appropriately
trained in meeting the needs of the emergency conditions (Public
Administration Select Committee, 2003).

　　Academics have also analyzed measurement error and measurement
dysfunctions. Hood (2007a) outlines that measurement error arises
from several sources: simple mistakes (e.g., clerical error), sampling error
(e.g., time-period is not representative), categorization error (e.g., cases
are poorly fitted into categories) and gaming (or cheating). He suggests
that simple mistakes, sampling error and categorization error can occur
within most measurement systems, but that the likelihood of gaming
can be expected to be highest where measurement is used for targeting
and ranking purposes, rather than just for intelligence purposes (Hood,
2007a: 100). Some managers are "working the system" and deliberately
misreport performance and distort individual behavior (Pollitt, 1989).
The performance indicator culture is, according to Smith, "likely to

push managers increasingly towards a superficial view of the service, in which indicators are cited when convenient and ignored otherwise" (Smith, 1990: 69).

Several authors have studied types of unintended consequences of performance measurement. Bouckaert and Balk (1991) listed 13 measurement diseases in the public sector, some with quite fancy names: the Pangloss disease, the impossibility disease, hypochondria, hypertrophy, atrophy, the Mandelbrot disease, the pollution disease, the inflation disease, the enlightenment/top-bottom disease, the time-shortening disease, the mirage disease, and the shifting disease. Their 13 diseases reflect that measurement is always a representation of an organizational reality. As such, performance measures create meaning. Smith (1995) wrote an elaborate article defining eight types of potential unintended consequences of performance indicator systems. These consequences are due to divergence between organizational objectives and the measurement, to the inability to measure complex phenomena, to the inability to process performance data correctly, and to the inability of measurement systems to respond to new challenges (Smith, 1995: 283). The unintended consequences are listed as tunnel vision, sub-optimization, myopia, measure fixation, misrepresentation, misinterpretation, gaming and ossification.

The "dangers" of performance measurement have long been recognized (Ridgway, 1956). A constant in these overviews appears to be the observation that unintended consequences of measurement systems will always exist, no matter how well-intentioned the system (van Thiel and Leeuw, 2002: 270). The best we can do, it appears, is to search for optimal measures to minimize dysfunctional effects (Bouckaert and Balk, 1991). Others argue, however, that distortions are primarily a consequence of the way performance indicators are used, rather than of measurement or the quality of measures (Van Dooren, 2006: 191–225). We need a better understanding of why certain performance measurement regimes lead to unintended consequences. This is an area that warrants further study (Pidd, 2005).

Radnor and McGuire (2004) evaluated a framework developed by the Public Services Productivity Panel, to assess whether "performance management in the public sector is fact or fiction." The panel developed a performance management framework for public services which aimed to represent the five building blocks of performance management including: developing a "bold aspiration"; targets that needed to be "SMART" (Specific, Measurable, Accurate, Realistic and Timely); ownership for every target; targets and the delivery of them to be regularly and rigorously reviewed; and finally, success in delivering targeted performance by reinforcement through incentives (Public Services Productivity Panel, 2000). In two case studies – a health authority considering implementing a Balanced Scorecard and a large government agency developing a reward-based system – they found that the role of the managers in performance measurement and management is far more about being administrators than about acting as managers (Radnor and McGuire, 2004). In order to achieve or respond to the various stakeholders, much time was spent on "form filling" and chasing information rather than changing or managing the process. Rather than developing a strong set of measures, evidence was found that organizations were "working the system" with the Hospital Trust Chief Executive asking "which boxes do I need to tick?" The lack of ownership was indicated in both case studies with not one organization in the health authority wanting to pilot the Balanced Scorecard and the government agency having the targets being set by an outside body. It was found that a review was difficult as too much time was spent on collecting the data and information in order to satisfy "government" requirements rather than ensuring that they were the right measures in the first place and using them to meet the needs of the consumer and citizen in delivering outcomes. Finally, the research found that, particularly for the agency, there was little understanding of the baseline target, illustrated through the example of one unit whose target was set based on case clearance expressed as a percentage of the total number of applications received. Therefore, achievement of the target was vulnerable to a significant increase in demand of the service and the number of applications received.

Gaming and performance reporting

In particular in an environment where targets and rankings are used, gaming behavior becomes quite prevalent in the reporting of performance information. The phenomenon of "targetology" (Rouse, 1993) refers to a situation where organizations narrow their focus to specific targets which affects aspects of service delivery. The Public Administration Select Committee report, mentioned in the previous section, clearly outlines the perverse consequences of targets and gives a series of examples. One example showed how Accident and Emergency (A&E) patients were left sitting in ambulances because the clock measuring the four-hour target to see patients did not start ticking until patients enter the building. Another example is schools which were measured by the number of students obtaining good results in their exit exams (GCSEs and A levels in the UK), who then excluded more students and so contributed to more petty local crime.

The report indicates "allegations of cheating, perverse consequences and distortions in pursuit of targets, along with unfair pressure on professionals [...] and league tables often seen as untrustworthy and misleading" (Public Administration Select Committee, 2003). The report concluded that there was a lack of understanding about the objectives of the targets and a feeling that the targets were plucked out of thin air. It was felt that targets had become an end in themselves rather than providing a measure of progress towards the organization's goal and objectives. The targets were seen as imposed by central government and its agencies. Although it was recognized they can be "good servants they are poor masters" (Public Administration Select Committee, 2003).

The report also mentions league tables as "particularly misleading and demotivating," because they tend to make everyone except the *league champions* look and feel like a failure. League tables stress absolute positions rather than improvement, and as a result they may present considerable improvement as failure. Because of the effects this may have on the individuals in the organizations, some targets have been referred to as *P45* targets, after the document you receive from your employer in the United Kingdo when you are made redundant (Pitches et al., 2003).

Pitches and colleagues (2003) wrote a guide in the British Medical Journal for "corrupt managers and incompetent clinicians" on how to optimize data, and refer to practices used by various healthcare organizations. In this article, they suggest that a position in a clinical league table can be achieved by "coding creep" ("excessive or inappropriate coding of risk factors that are required for calculating risk adjusted mortality"), transferring of patients, changing operating class, denying treatment and "cream skimming" of healthier patients.

In July 2001, a report about the UK National Health Service (NHS) waiting lists listed six NHS trusts where the waiting lists had been inappropriately adjusted (National Audit Office, 2001a). Further work discovered that a total of nine NHS trusts had inappropriately adjusted their waiting lists, three of them for more than three years. This had affected nearly 6,000 patient records (National Audit Office, 2001a). The adjustments varied in their seriousness, from staff following established, but incorrect, procedures through to deliberate manipulation or misstatement of the figures. The impact on patients also varied from little or no impact to patients waiting longer for treatment (National Audit Office, 2001a). In response the majority of the nine trusts suspended individuals and launched an enquiry, which led to some actions including policy and procedure reviews, improving lines of accountability and raising the seniority of decision making.

The recommendations of the National Audit Office report was focused on individual responsibility, that is, assurance from chief executives, putting in place disciplinary procedures and enquiries, and tightening up the employment process (National Audit Office, 2001a). However, the report did not address the wider question of why individuals felt the need to adjust the figures. As a result, it mainly dealt with the consequences of the action, but did little to uncover the underlying causes of the action or the deeper issues in the system.

Gaming or cheating?

The evidence suggests that in an environment dominated by targets and league tables, and where there is a measurement culture rather than a performance culture, there is a vicious cycle of target obsession, gaming, cheating, lying and blaming. People within organizations feel that if the target is not achieved, they will be blamed or even sacked. To avoid this they game the process, lie about the results or cheat by misreporting the output.

The previous section, when dealing with waiting lists, already briefly touched on the consequences of gaming. While the behavior is generally referred to as gaming, some gaming behaviors may have more severe consequences on the service than others. Gaming behavior varies widely, and many officials appear to distinguish between gaming and cheating, and between acceptable and unacceptable gaming. One respondent in Hood's research described "outright falsification or making up of numbers as cheating" and thought that "creative classification or interpretation" could be considered gaming (Hood, 2006: 518). In a later paper, Hood raises the point that "we know relatively little about the extent of gaming or cheating in target or ranking systems, or indeed where the culture draws the lines in practice between what is seen as gaming as what as cheating" (2007a: 100). It is furthermore the case that the existence of dysfunctional effects in the performance measurement regime does not necessarily imply "that such a regime fails on balance to improve organizational performance" (Kelman and Friedman, 2007).

Is it possible to ethically distinguish between acceptable and less acceptable gaming? Should the line be drawn differently for different organizations in different contexts? The evidence tends to show not only that gaming exists, but also that there are different types, or levels, of gaming, with some having a greater impact than others. The next section will reflect on this by attempting to develop a categorization of the various types of gaming.

Developing a typology of organizational gaming

This section will attempt to unpack the evidence surrounding gaming at an organizational level in order to suggest a categorization, or typology, of gaming. This typology could help in understanding the degree and impact of the gaming. Often the word "gaming" is mentioned as a catch-all phrase. Developing a classification can help support the design of future performance measurement and performance reporting systems, and thus contribute to genuine performance management.

Within this chapter the differences between performance measurement, performance reporting and performance management have been outlined. It highlighted the effects of a performance measurement and performance reporting culture focused on targets and league tables, and cited evidence and examples of unintentional consequences of the desire to achieve targets. The examples cited in this chapter and in the wider literature (NAO, 2001; PASC, 2003; Hood, 2006) showed the lengths an individual within an organization is willing or is expected to go to in order for the organization to reach its target. In an environment dominated by targets and league tables the focus is on organizational, not individual, achievement of targets and the position in a league table. Therefore, a possible definition of organizational gaming could be the "creation of (both formal and informal) activities which allows a target or regulated deliverable to be met when the result leads to unintended consequences on the internal or external service delivery."

However, developing a definition of organizational gaming still does not allow us to understand the extent, range or impact of this gaming. Hood (2006) attempts to make a distinction between four types of gaming. He looks at the degree by which performance data is creatively interpreted, dropped or invented. He also considers the effect of this gaming on the underlying performance in the provision of services, where some gaming alters the actual service delivery. He identifies one type of gaming as acceptable, another as unacceptable gaming, a third as a "fact of life in bureaucratic politics," and finally a fourth as cheating

(Hood, 2006). Van Dooren (2006) makes a distinction between the manipulation of actual output and the manipulation of measurement, which is a representation of output.

The typology presented in Table 6.1 attempts to build on the ideas by Hood (2006) and others, by presenting possible types of organizational gaming. In Table 6.1, the axes are "impact of gaming" and "level of gaming" within the organization. Reflecting on Hood (2006), the level of gaming can be viewed as "low" if it is just the output data that is changed, that is, creatively interpreted, contrived or spun. The level becomes "high" if the actual activities change in order to hit the target. With "high" levels of gaming, little consideration is given to effect on the service, and the focus is on creating or managing activities in order to achieve the target. In terms of the impact of gaming, the internal impact is within a department or organization, that is, the result of the gaming only really effects the organization. External impact means that the gaming impacts and affects the stakeholder, citizen, consumer, customer, patient or an element of what could be considered as the "authorizing environment" (Moore, 2002). The table suggests four types which move in a hierarchy from Type I to Type IV which will be explained and illustrated through examples.

Type I organizational gaming occurs when performance indicators are creatively interpreted. The impact of this is mainly felt internally. An example would be where a museum counted as "visitors" all the people not directly working for the organization who come into the building, that is, catering suppliers, contractors and so on, in order to raise the visitor count (Jackson, 2002). Type I gaming is facilitated by performance indicators that are poorly defined and provide leeway in their application.

Type II organizational gaming reflects the manipulation of measurement, but with an impact on service users. An example of this would be admission dates on patient records (Pitches, Burls and

Table 6.1   A typology of organizational gaming

		Impact of gaming	
		Internal	External
Level of gaming	Low level – only measurement	Type I	Type II
	High level – also activities	Type III	Type IV

Fry-Smith, 2003), or moving patients from one official waiting list to another so meeting the waiting list targets (which are reported by absolute numbers rather than patient names) or starting the clock at different points in time in order to hit the eight-minute response time for ambulances dealing with life-threatening emergencies (PASC, 2003). In these cases the external receiver of the service, that is, the patient is directly affected by the desire to hit the target, but the activity is not fundamentally changed, only the way the data is reported.

Type III organizational gaming is where, again, the PI or target is clear and understood, but the activities are (creatively) developed or implemented in order to achieve it. Examples including the UK Research Assessment Exercise (RAE), where universities chose to include or change the titles of staff, buy-in new staff and set up "research centers" in order for them to be included in the "count." Also the changing of trolleys to beds in the Accident and Emergency departments of hospitals in order to hit a waiting time target (Pitches, Burls and Fry-Smith, 2003) are examples of maneuvering with the impact really only affecting the internal organization and not the receivers of the service, that is, the patient was still treated.

Finally, Type IV is where the focus on the performance indicator or target is so strong that gaming becomes the purpose and it could be argued that the meaning of the service delivery has been "lost." Here activities are deliberately changed, implemented and even encouraged in order to "hit the target," even if it results in poor service delivery and outcomes for the actual recipients. Being left in an ambulance because the Accident and Emergency department is concerned with meeting their four-hour waiting target, being attended to by a "lay responder" so the ambulance service can hit their response time target, or a central agency call centre hanging up your call as they have not answered enough calls, are all examples of deliberate activities developed and implemented to "hit the target but miss the point" (Pitches, Burls and Fry-Smith, 2003; Radnor and McGuire, 2004).

If performance management is about improving, as the definition and system view presented in this chapter recommends, then the examples and typologies presented here do little to confirm this idea. They instead portray examples of performance measurement and reporting which negatively impact on improving the service delivery. The typology may help to understand different degrees of gaming and contribute to developing strategies, ideas and systems to minimize both the game playing and the impact of the gaming. The discussion below will reflect on the evidence, models and ideas presented in this chapter in order to highlight the value of an organizational gaming typology.

Discussion and conclusion

Using evidence and arguments from writings from various disciplines within academia, as well as practitioner documents, this chapter has attempted to synthesize the various strands of debate and discussions about organizational gaming in the public sector. Differentiating between performance measurement, reporting and management, and using explicit examples and characterizations of gaming behavior, a typology of organizational gaming was developed. Gaming is often used as a catch-all phrase without recognition of its various levels of impact both internally and externally. The typology is presented as a valuable conceptual model by which gaming in the public sector can be analyzed. The organizational gaming typology can act as a useful conceptual tool which could help in "unpacking" gaming, unintended consequences and ineffectual activities. From the examples, it is possible to recognize that as gaming moves from Type I to Type IV, both the impact and level of gaming increases leading to a more "dangerous" outcome for the citizen or recipient of the public service.

The line between gaming and cheating may be difficult to draw. The typology may help us to distinguish between "outright falsification or making up of numbers" (cheating) and "creative classification or interpretation" (gaming) (Hood, 2007a). In our typology, Type I and Type II could be considered as gaming, while Type III and Type IV is cheating. However, for this typology, cheating would, rather than just the falsification of numbers, be the falsification, development and/or implementation of activities designed to hit the target.

Much of the existing research has focused on specific examples and occurrences of gaming, yet little attention has gone to answering the deeper question of why individuals feel the need to game. The answer to this lies within both the behavioral aspects of an organization and within the system design in which the individual is operating. The behavioral aspect is an area which probably needs closer analysis and investigation beyond the scope of this chapter. However, the typology may give some insight into how the performance measurement, reporting and even management systems should be designed to avoid the outcome types presented.

The next step, beyond the conceptual analysis presented here, is to develop more examples of gaming so the typology model can be empirically tested. A limitation could be leveled at the 2 x 2 typology in that it may be difficult to place a gaming phenomenon into one single box, as the activity may consist of elements fitting into more than one box. To a degree this is true. In a sense, however, a typology is a conceptual clarification even though the empirical evidence may be more complex. If the typology is considered as a starting point so that a contingent rather than a normative approach is taken, then at least this opens up the opportunity to analyze performance measurement and reporting. This may then allow some form of learning and improvement to be developed so that it can lead to performance management.

Performance management systems are designed to drive action. If this action drives intended consequences, hopefully leading to improvement, then it could be argued that the system is "successful." However, as the examples have illustrated, all too often the action becomes gaming. These unintentional or even perverse actions can impact on both the internal and external environment. Different types of organizational gaming are probably unavoidable in accountability relations involving performance indicators, targets or league tables. What needs to happen is that the gaming energy is diverted towards improving the service delivery not the targets. This will allow performance regimes to become a useful tool for driving improvement and performance, and to move beyond measurement and reporting for its own sake.

7
Performance Management Systems: Providing Accountability and Challenging Collaboration

Kathryn G. Denhardt and Maria P. Aristigueta

Performance measurement systems are promoted as mechanisms of accountability and, thus, enhancements to democratic control. Choices must be made about whether the unit of accountability will be individuals, programs, agencies or larger systems. Focusing on the performance of the individual program or agency has the benefit of establishing clear lines of accountability, and has emerged as the most common focus of performance measurement systems. At the same time, the importance of partnerships and other forms of collaboration have been emphasized in management theory and practice. Complex social problems are typically addressed by multiple organizations inside and outside government, so (at a minimum) coordination among programs is necessary in order to avoid duplication or gaps, as well as to achieve better outcomes. The question is whether, and how, typical approaches to performance management are impacting partnerships and collaborations. Self-aligning collaborations, performance agreements and social indicators are explored as mechanisms for achieving both accountability and collaboration in pursuit of outcomes oriented performance.

Two key strategies pursued in contemporary public management are (1) the development of performance measurement systems to ensure a focus on results and accountability, and (2) the encouragement of collaborative approaches to public service delivery to draw on the strengths, resources and perspectives of multiple agencies within and outside government. Both performance measurement and collaborations are seen as having the potential to improve the management of public services. A body of research is quickly accumulating around each of these strategies, including findings that the strategies have encountered significant barriers.

The development of performance measurement systems has helped governments "move away from the more traditional focus on activities or services provided, toward quantifiable results, outcomes, and impact" (Popovich, 1998: 175). Nonetheless, performance measures have encountered barriers such as resistance, cost, reliability of data, behavior distortions, and the extent to which analysis of the data is utilized in making decisions (Bouckaert, 1990; Greiner, 1996; Kelman, 2007; Schick, 1990).

"Partnerships, alliances and other forms of inter-organizational collaborative arrangements are now a commonplace part of institutional life" and present many opportunities for "collaborative advantage" observes Huxham and Vangen (2000b: 771). "The topics of organizing collaboration across government agencies ('connect the dots') and between government organizations and private ones ('network government,' 'collaborative governance') are now among the most-discussed questions involving the performance of public institutions and achievement of public purposes" (Kelman, 2007: 24). But these collaborations present a set of management challenges such as accountability (Bardach and Lesser, 1996; Behn, 2001) and the tendency toward "collaborative inertia" (Huxham and Vangen, 2000b). Koontz and Thomas (2006) urge that a high priority be placed on examining the connections between collaboration and performance in order that we might better understand the impact of collaboration efforts.

This leads us to exploring the question: Do our efforts to achieve accountability through agency-level performance measurement hinder our efforts to achieve collaborative efforts with other organizations?

Performance measurement in government

Performance measurement may be described as the gathering of information about the work effectiveness and productivity of individuals, groups, and larger organizational units (Larson and Callahan, 1990). Performance measurement models have two distinct purposes:

- Accountability to stakeholders in order to improve perceptions of government; and
- Managerial improvement that, through the collection of performance information, aims to improve government (Aristigueta, 1999).

The Organization for Economic Cooperation and Development (OECD) reports that the performance measurement movement (which OECD calls "service quality initiatives") had the common characteristics of requiring government organizations to be more responsive and outward-looking, and that these initiatives changed the relationships between citizens, public servants and elected officials (OECD, 1996). For example, the United Kingdom launched the Citizen's Charter initiative in 1991 (Schiavo, 2000) to publicize performance targets for various public services. The US federal government initiated widespread performance measurement and management through the Government Performance and Results Act of 1993 (GPRA); earlier initiatives were found at the State level in the United States.

Along with this focus on performance and accountability has come the increased acceptance of the public as a legitimate stakeholder in most government activities and planning processes. In the healthcare system in New Zealand, for example, it is expected that the views of the general public should be incorporated into the performance measurement process (Van Peursem and Pratt, 2000). In *Results for Canadians: A Management Framework for the Government of Canada*, the Canadian public service expresses commitments to assess results of government programs from the perspective of the citizen, to focus on the achievement and reporting of results, to link government spending with results in order to provide "value" for the taxpayer, and to manage its business according to the highest public service values (Treasury Board of Canada, 2000).

Accountability and collaboration

Performance measurement programs represent progress in communicating information to agency stakeholders, but not necessarily progress in collaborating across programs in order to maximize overall outcomes. "Accountability as performance measurement is deeply jurisdictional (city, county, state, nation) and program specific [...] Accountability, thus understood, is a silo idea, an idea that reinforces the boundaries and barriers between jurisdictions, agencies and programs" (Frederickson, 2007: 11).

In a study of Interagency Coordinating Councils (ICC), which were created to lead integration of services for children with disabilities, Baker (2004) found that creating the ICC collaboration was a consistent challenge because it was a new role requiring a new infrastructure and new management behaviors. When allocating scarce resources, managers were sometimes put in the position of having to choose between performance measurement goals and collaboration goals (e.g., between expanding access to services and expanding coordination among services). Those choices tended to be detrimental to the collaboration.

In a January 2003 report, the US General Accounting Office (2003) indicates that the linkages remain weak between individual performance goals and organizational objectives, and do not do enough to encourage collaboration across organizational boundaries. "In particular, more progress is needed in explicitly linking senior executive performance to results-oriented organizational goals, fostering the necessary collaboration both within and across organizational boundaries to achieve results, and demonstrating a commitment to lead and facilitate change" (US General Accounting Office, 2003: 16).

In *Strategic Alliances – A Review of the State of the Art*, Keil (2000) examined collaborative alliances between businesses, and discussed the various issues associated with judging the alliance a success or a failure. Issues such as whether there was economic advantage in the alliance, equitable division of inputs or outcomes among the partnering organizations, efficiency in their collaborations, and the overall costs of managing the relationship were all viewed as important in determining whether participants were satisfied with the collaboration and willing to continue investing in the collaboration. Public sector agencies face a similar set of issues when determining whether to invest in collaborations with others. The "economic advantage" and "equitable division of inputs and outcomes" for these agencies might very well be judged in light of the impact on the individual agency's performance measurements. If investing in collaborations comes at the expense of meeting performance targets for which the agency is accountable, then withdrawing (literally or figuratively) from the collaboration might be a reasonable managerial choice. Given that performance on agency-specific measures might be compromised if the agency invests itself in inter-organizational collaborations, we must address the question of why (or if) collaborations are of essential value in government.

Frederickson (2007) refers to collaboration in public service as a standard of professional excellence. Yet, accountability and collaborations serve different purposes and therefore present great challenges and incompatibilities. Accountability encourages silos as agencies are held accountable for their work. Collaborations require that managers move beyond boundaries in order to achieve results.

Collaborations in public management

This chapter is concerned with the impact of performance measurement systems on inter-organizational collaborations. Barbara Gray defines collaboration as "a process through which parties who see different aspects of a problem can constructively explore their differences and search for solutions that go beyond their own limited vision of what is possible" (1989: 5). As discussed by Hardin (1999), Himmelman (1996) "employs a 'continuum of change strategies' to pinpoint the definition of collaboration and contrast it with the other major ways organizations might work together: networking, coordination, and cooperation".

> Networking is "exchanging information for mutual benefit" [...] Coordinating is "exchanging information and altering activities" [...] Cooperating requires exchanging information, providing access to turf, and altering activities as well as sharing resources. Finally, in addition to exchanging information, providing access to turf, altering activities and sharing resources, collaborating involves "enhancing the capacity of another."
>
> (Hardin, 1999: 3)

Huxham and Vangen (2000b: 1159) observe that there is a "worldwide movement toward collaborative governance, collaborative public service provision, and collaborative approaches to addressing social problems." Examples of such collaborative efforts include the United Kingdom's policy promoting collaborations between central and local governments, government and nonprofit organizations collaborating to provide public services, and partnerships between the business sector and governments to address community problems. Collaboration is central to many of the strategies currently being utilized, and Huxham and Vangen point out that "public sector management in the 21st century will need to be sophisticated in its understanding of the skills, processes, structures, tools, and technology needed for working across organizational boundaries" (2000b: 1159).

What is really expected of a collaboration? Examining networks as a form of collaboration, Mandell and Keast suggest that "many organizations become part of a collaborating network [...] because the way they are delivering services is not working. Instead, the purpose of the network is to find more innovative solutions" (2007: 576). They observe that "the effectiveness of the network is determined by the ability of all organizations in the network to act as a cohesive whole" rather than being judged by the individual accomplishments of members (2007: 575).

But collaborations are far from the norm, and rarely as successful in practice as hoped for. Eugene Bardach concludes that "substantial public value is being lost to insufficient collaboration in the public sector" (1998: 11). In a 1997 report, the US General Accounting Office (1997) outlined widespread mission fragmentation and program overlap throughout the US federal government, and a failure to coordinate cross-cutting program efforts. Such lack of coordination is seen as one of the reasons US agencies failed to recognize the threats that led up to the 9/11 attacks on US sites including the World Trade Center and the Pentagon, and one of the primary challenges to be addressed in the creation of the new Department of Homeland Security that was established in January 2003 (US General Accounting Office, 2003).

Even when collaborations are attempted, they often fall short of expectations. Examining community development efforts in the United Kingdom, Huxham and Vangen (2000a) observe that there is "ample evidence [...] that inter-organizational arrangements are difficult to manage and often fail to meet expectations [...] Instead of achieving collaborative advantage, they often degenerate into a state of collaborative inertia in which the rate of work output is much slower than might be expected." They describe factors leading to collaborative inertia as:

• Difficulties in negotiating joint purposes because of the diversity of organizational and individual aims which those involved bring to the collaboration
• Difficulties in developing joint modes of operating given that the partner organizations inevitably have quite different internal procedures from each other
• Differences in professional (and sometimes natural) language
• Differences in organizational (and sometimes ethnic) cultures, as well as structures and procedures
• Difficulties in managing the perceived power imbalances among groups, and of assuring accountability to each of the represented groups.

They conclude that "collaborative structures need to be understood as ambiguous, complex and dynamic in order that practitioners convening them, or policy makers promoting them, clearly understand the enormous challenges which collaboration presents" (Vangen and Huxham, 2001: 19).

In *Rethinking Democratic Accountability*, Robert Behn describes the dilemma of accountability when we are talking about collaboratives rather than individuals:

> In a traditional, hierarchical bureaucracy, there is little formal ambiguity about who is in charge. The manager at each level is the accountable individual. But in a collaborative of individuals – or in a collaborative of organizations [...] – identifying an accountable individual or even accountable individuals is not easy. And for what should such individuals be accountable? Are they responsible collectively for producing the overall result? Or is each component of the collaborative responsible only for producing its own, specific component of that overall result?
>
> (Behn, 2001: 73–4)

In public management, performance measurement systems have developed, in general, as a means to enhance the accountability of an individual program or agency. When being held accountable for specific results, there is a natural tendency for an agency to attempt to maintain control over factors that might contribute to success in achieving those results – even if that is detrimental to a collaborative effort being pursued simultaneously.

Government Performance and Results Act (GPRA) and collaborations

In 1993, the US federal government adopted the Government Performance and Results Act (GPRA) which required agencies to identify measures and report performance against those measures in order to enhance accountability. Even though GPRA was designed as a performance measurement system, GAO's 1997 report *Managing for Results: Using the Results Act to Address Mission Fragmentation and Program Overlap* (US General Accounting Office, 1997) suggests expectations that GPRA might enhance collaboration. In 2000, GAO issued a follow-up report *Managing For Results: Barriers to Interagency Coordination* (US General Accounting Office, 2000), in which they found little or no progress on addressing issues of mission fragmentation and program overlap during the 1997–2000 time period. The report emphasizes "how important it is that the federal government develops the capacity to more effectively coordinate crosscutting program efforts and to identify and eliminate those programs where redundancy does not serve public policy" (US General Accounting Office, 2000: 19) and expresses optimism about the efficacy of GPRA to address the problems of coordination among federal agencies.

One can only wonder why the GAO could find so little evidence of improved coordination across agencies seven years into the implementation of GPRA, yet remain optimistic that GPRA could help address the problem of inadequate coordination. As Murphy and Carnevale point out, "measurement of performance for crosscutting programs falls outside of the GPRA provisions" and GPRA's "focus on individual departments as its unit of analysis [...] can be misleading relative to causes and effects" (2001: 7). Coordination (and, more optimistically, collaboration) is needed and desirable, but will a performance measurement system promote that outcome? Poister describes the phenomenon of goal displacement "whereby organizational behavior reacts over time to maximize performance on those dimensions emphasized by the system at the expense of other equally or more important objectives" (1992: 201). By institutionalizing a performance measurement system which holds individual agencies accountable for their unique performance measures, GPRA (and other performance measurement systems) might be encouraging agencies to maximize agency-specific performance measures at the expense of broader objectives that require collaborative efforts.

When individual units are held accountable for performance measures, it is possible that goal displacement and conflict can occur even between subunits of the same organization which presumably share a common mission. What follows is a brief description of one early Internal Revenue Service (IRS) effort to utilize performance measures, and the impact it had on collaboration across units.

Case: Early GPRA implementation in the Internal Revenue Service (IRS)

This case was prepared by IRS manager Charles Dietz in a seminar on ethical leadership, conducted by the Brookings Institution for senior IRS administrators in January 2001. The IRS was divided into regions and districts throughout the United States. Each District had divisions focusing on specific elements of the IRS Mission. The collection division's function is to collect delinquent taxes. The collection process begins in regional service centers where delinquent notices are sent out. Approximately 60 percent of all delinquent accounts are paid when written notices are sent to the taxpayer. The remaining 40 percent, not paid after a final written notice, are sent to the automated collection sites where agents attempt to resolve the cases through telephone contact and additional correspondence with the delinquent taxpayer. Most cases are resolved at that point. Less than 5 percent of cases would eventually be referred to a field revenue officer for resolution, usually because the accounts were deemed the most complicated, the highest dollar, or highest risk.

As the IRS implemented the Government Performance and Results Act (GPRA) in the early 1990s these collection division offices began to feel pressure to increase "total dollars collected" as their measure of performance. At a meeting of regional collection division chiefs, the suggestion was made that district collection divisions "go around" the usual collection process and begin to pull selected large dollar cases out of the written notice stream, assigning those cases to the field revenue officers immediately rather than first making written and telephone contact with the delinquent taxpayer. This would enable the field revenue officer units to claim huge increases in dollars collected with only a minimal investment in additional resources. One district collection division chief argued vehemently that this would increase the performance measure of "total dollars collected" for the field officers, but would do so at the expense of the regional service centers. More importantly, the measure being used (total dollars collected) would no longer be an accurate representation of a district office's collection division performance. That regional division chief chose not to change the collection procedure, while the other nine regional division chiefs did change the procedure. One year later, the measures of performance were assessed for the ten regional collection offices. The regional district chief who did not make changes was given a lower performance rating than all the others, and was counseled to "get your numbers up." His numbers did show a considerable increase over the prior year, but were much lower than the inflated increases in the other nine districts.

The GAO and IRS Internal Audit did a subsequent study of these new collection procedures and decried them as a blatant attempt to manipulate numbers and as potentially harmful to taxpayers. The new collection procedures were abandoned. In the fall of 1997, a series of hearings were held by the Senate Finance Committee to evaluate IRS procedures, and in particular the effect that use of their measurement system was having on individual taxpayers. As a result of these hearings, the Reorganization and Restructuring Act of 1998 was passed. This act mandated an entire reorganization of the IRS from a regional and district designed and managed organization to a market segment based organization. This same act also strictly prohibited the use of any enforcement results (such as dollars collected) in any evaluative format.

This case indicates how performance measurement systems can contribute to decreased coordination and collaboration across programs. But the case also indicates that such unintended consequences can be identified and rectified. The IRS did learn from this experience, but the lesson was a costly one in that it created rifts between units within IRS that will not be healed easily, and this may have a chilling effect on future coordination and collaboration across units. Though an unintended consequence, performance measurement systems might be having similar chilling effects on collaborations across public management systems today.

Reforms to achieve both accountability and collaboration

In *Rethinking Democratic Accountability*, Robert Behn argues that we have "created an accountability system that depends upon the self-interested, competitive behavior of legions of accountability holders" (2001: 216). While Behn is specifically critical of accountability systems that place "too much emphasis on finances and fairness and not enough on performance – too much on rules and not enough on results" (2001: 216–17), even performance measurement accountability systems which effectively capture the desired agency-level performance results probably will not reflect the results that might be accomplished in a collaborative endeavor. Behn suggests that "we need to invest some resources and time in experimenting with some alternative concepts and institutions" – concepts that will foster responsibility and mutual, collective public interest (2001: 217).

A natural tension arises between an emphasis of performance measurement with positive agency-level results expected annually, and an emphasis on collaborations in which positive results can be expected only after trust and cooperation have developed over a longer period of time. Administrators experience accountability (positive and negative) for agency-level performance measures long before they will experience any positive or negative effects due to improved outcomes achieved through more effective integration and coordination of services across agencies.

This tension has been recognized by those who study performance measurement systems. Aristigueta's (1999) research on state-level performance measurement systems showed that the measures tended to be utilized for internal agency purposes, but had little relevance to any potential benefits of inter-organizational collaborations. The GAO reports (1997; 2003) cited earlier, as well as Hatry (2006), observe that using performance measures in a punitive fashion may lead to maximizing short-term performance measures. They recommend, therefore, that performance measures not be linked to short-term, individual rewards. Mandell and Keast (2007) suggest that nontraditional measures related to changed relationships among network members be added to performance measurement systems at the agency level if there is to be any expectation that enhanced coordination, networking or collaboration will receive essential attention from public managers.

The strategic plans and goals that serve as the starting point for the development of agency performance measures could be utilized in a way that enhances coordination and collaboration across agencies. Umbrella management agencies, like the Office of Management and Budget (OMB), could utilize strategic plans to identify shared goals across programs, and could develop performance measures that enhance collaboration and alignment across agencies. The alignment could include shared time frames, consistent criteria utilized across programs, and the collection of consistent and reliable data across programs. More importantly, it could include the use of nontraditional performance measures that evaluate relationships and processes that occur in the development and functioning of networks or collaborations (Mandell and Keast, 2007).

Evidence to date, however, does not indicate success in making those alignments and encouraging collaboration. While GPRA and other performance measurement systems in theory provide the necessary framework for coordination and collaboration, it has become clear that, in practice, more intentional mechanisms will need to be utilized in order to encourage the collaborations thought to achieve better performance outcomes. While recognizing that collaboration is not an end in itself (McGuire, 2006), more collaborations will have to be developed and functioning in order to gather the evidence necessary to determine whether better performance outcomes are achieved through collaboration. What follows are some reform strategies which hold promise for achieving both accountability and collaboration.

Self-aligning collaborations

Borins notes that "in areas where coordination is needed, it is becoming increasingly evident that informal coordination and partnerships are better alternatives than central coordination" (1995: 125). Labovitz and Rosansky (1997) suggest that it is possible to achieve a "self-aligning organization" where the focus is on the main thing the organization is to achieve, performance measures should be carefully crafted to give the organization feedback on how well it is staying focused on its main purpose, and by doing so will give units within the organization sufficient information to self-align rather than being forced into alignment. This is also consistent with recent applications of chaos theory to organizational leadership in which it is suggested that chaos "is necessary to new creative ordering" and that "scientists now describe how order and form are created not by complex controls, but by the presence of a few guiding formulas or principles repeating back on themselves through the exercise of individual freedom" (Wheatley, 1999: 13). With regard to the application of chaos theory to organizations, Wheatley writes:

> In organizations, we are very good at measuring activity. In fact, that is primarily what we do. Fractals suggest the futility of searching for ever finer measures that concentrate on separate parts of the system. There is never a satisfying end to this reductionist search, never an end point where we finally know everything about even that one small part of the system.
>
> (1999: 125)

We might consider, then, the futility of focusing ever-more attention on agency-level performance measures. Instead, we might turn our attention to identifying the "guiding formulas or principles" that, exercised by individual interdependent agencies, might develop into a new creative ordering that achieves better results in impacting complex public problems than have thus far been achieved through efforts to impose complex controls on individual agencies.

Studies of inter-organizational dynamics suggest that alliances depend more on loose, informal controls rather than strict, formal controls. Reviewing the theoretical literature on strategic alliances, Keil notes that "psychological contracts rather than formal contracts increasingly govern relationships" in the alliances (2000: 21) and that the ability of an organization to absorb knowledge from another organization (as is expected in collaborations) is a "relationship specific capability," where organizations "are not equally able to develop effective knowledge assimilation with all partners" because of similarities or dissimilarities in the organizations (2000: 29).

Thus, we might conclude that inter-organizational alignment and collaboration is more likely to be achieved by shifting our focus toward understanding and improving the relationships among partnering organizations, especially in terms of joint planning, so that a more natural self-alignment will occur among these organizations in terms of their goals, activities and outcomes.

Performance agreements

Performance agreements are primarily used to align individual performance expectations with agency goals, but also have the potential to foster collaboration across organizational boundaries. Beginning in 1995, the Veterans Health Administration (VHA) decentralized its management structure from four regions to 22 Veterans Integrated Service Networks (VISN). To accomplish its reform goals, VHA gave each VISN substantial operational autonomy and established performance goals to hold network and medical center directors accountable for achieving performance improvements (US General Accounting Office, 2000). As of 1999, the Department of Transportation (DOT) had implemented a total of 26 annual performance agreements with its modal administrators, all Assistant Secretaries, and Office Directors in the Office of the Secretary. The agreements include organization-specific activities that are collectively intended to achieve DOT's performance goals, as well as "corporate management strategies" that cut across organizational boundaries and set additional expectation for administrators, such as the use customer feedback to improve programs (US General Accounting Office, 2000: 35).

By entering into performance agreements with members of a collaborative structure (both governmental and nongovernmental members), it is possible for agencies to move beyond networking, and on to higher levels of mutuality such as cooperating (exchanging information, providing access to turf, altering activities, sharing resources) and perhaps even true collaboration (cooperation accompanied by efforts to enhance the capacity of another organization) (Himmelman, 1996). For example, the Office of Student Financial Assistance's Chief Operating Officer enters into a performance agreement with the Secretary of Education on an annual basis (US General Accounting Office, 2000: 35). The performance agreements (US General Accounting Office, 2000: 6) fostered collaboration across organizational boundaries, encouraging executives to work across traditional organizational lines (or silos) by focusing on the achievement of the results-oriented goal. The performance agreements also enhanced opportunities to discuss and routinely use performance information to make program improvements.

The strategy of entering into performance agreements with other members of a collaborative structure is considerably less formalized than a central agency mandating coordination objectives, and thus it might be more successful. In addition, it has the advantage of being initiated and maintained by the organization members themselves rather than by an outside planning entity. Vangen and Huxham (2001) found leadership in such collaborative arrangements to be very challenging and certainly not guaranteed to succeed. They found it important to mobilize and empower members of the collaborative, to manage information or knowledge exchange between members, and occasionally to engage in "collaborative thuggery" when making progress on the collaborative agenda demands forceful action by the leader to move things along (Vangen and Huxham, 2001).

Performance agreements address several barriers to collaboration. First, they provide a mechanism for negotiating joint purposes despite the diversity of organizational and individual aims brought to the discussion. Second, the agreements encourage the development of joint modes of operating during the time period of the performance agreement. Finally, they encourage alignment of language, structures and procedures. Experience shows that these collaborative performance agreements often start out as very modest agreements, but as success is experienced and trust develops among the partners, these collaborative agreements become broader and more substantive over time (Huxham and Vangen, 2000b). In essence, performance agreements become concrete mechanisms for achieving alignment among multiple agencies. Collaboration becomes achievable when pursued in the iterative process of performance agreements.

Social indicators

Another strategy that goes beyond measures of individual agency performance is the use of "social indicators," which are general indicators of improved social well-being (e.g., reductions in infant mortality, improved air quality, or increases in literacy among adults). Oregon's Benchmarks and Minnesota Milestones are two examples of statewide social indicator programs. Social indicators measure performance on cross-cutting issues that tend to be influenced by programs across a variety of governmental and nongovernmental agencies. No single agency is responsible for all programs that would affect a social indicator, but because the social indicator measure tends to be so highly publicized, it is expected that agencies would find it in their best interest to attempt to collaborate (or at least coordinate) their activities with related agencies in order to achieve improvements in the social indicators over time.

The tension between collaboration and performance measurement of individual agencies has been felt in the use of social indicators as well. Social indicators have been controversial in some governments, and abandoned in others, in part because it is impossible to hold a single agency accountable for success or failure in improving social indicators. New Zealand's Social Monitoring Group tracked a series of key social indicators of significant life events, and published its findings in *From Birth to Death* (New Zealand Planning Council, 1985) and *From Birth to Death II* (NZPC, 1989). But the New Zealand Planning Council was abolished in 1992 when the "ascendancy of economic rationality and the pervasive belief in market forces militated against anything which smacked of 'planning' and government intervention or direction" (Davey, 2000: 54).

Where social indicators are in use, however, it has been found that multiple agencies do align their strategies in a way that helps achieve improved results on the social indicators. For example, Aristigueta, Cooksy and Nelson describe the alignment found in an evaluation of the Agency-School Collaboration Partnership (ASCP) in Delaware:

> ASCP focuses on two of the statewide goals used to organize the indicators: healthy children and successful learners. ASCP supports those goals by working towards improved communication, cooperation, and collaboration between state personnel and school staff who work on behalf of children. [...] ASCP is aligned with indicators such as the rate of teen deaths by injury, homicide, and suicide, and the percentage of third graders tested scoring at or above basic reading levels. At the agency level, the strategic plan [...] states a goal of reducing children's need to return to agency services. One of the performance measures for that goal is the portion of Child Mental Health Service clients who are admitted to a hospital within 30 days of their release. ASCP is intended to contribute to lower rates of readmission within 30 days by ensuring that children receive appropriate services during the transition form the hospital back to school.
>
> (Aristigueta, Cooksy and Nelson, 2001: 263)

At the state government level in the United States, social indicators are sometimes used as mechanisms for coordinating governors' priorities (e.g., the State of Arizona). When the Governor of the state sets specific priorities, agencies throughout the state align their programs and priorities accordingly, albeit informally. A word of caution is in order here, though. Moynihan and Ingraham's study of performance information use in state governments provides evidence that formal top-down approaches are not successfully influencing agency performance: "The emphasis that *agency management* places on performance information has a significant influence on whether it is used for agency activities, while active *statewide leadership* [gubernatorial or legislative] appears to have a *negative* impact on performance-information use" (Moynihan and Ingraham, 2004: 442; emphasis added).

The impetus for using social indicators usually comes from outside an individual agency, and perhaps even outside the political system. *Kids Count*, for example, was initiated by the Annie E. Casey Foundation and has led to social indicators of children's well-being being implemented at the state level throughout the United States. These social indicators measure how well a specific state is doing with regard to children's well-being, yet are not linked to the evaluation of any particular agency.

Social indicators provide the advantages of annual reporting of specific measures of social well-being – measures that no single agency would choose to take responsibility for in their own set of performance measures because the power to influence the social indicators is shared across many governmental, nongovernmental and community groups. But the visibility of these indicators is a powerful motivator. When a document (funded by the nongovernmental Annie E. Casey Foundation) gives publicity to how well or poorly a particular state is doing on these measures, attention can be expected from the public, elected officials, relevant government agencies and nongovernmental organizations that provide service in the arena. Perhaps this provides an impetus for renewed efforts to collaborate in order to achieve better results next time. Social indicators tend to focus attention on obligations to address broad social problems (requiring collaborative efforts in order to impact), while agency-specific performance measures tend to focus attention on accountability to more narrow and short-term goals.

Conclusion

Through assessing recent findings on the impact of performance measurement systems, evidence indicates that these measures enhance internal management of the agency, but little evidence was found that such systems were being utilized to enhance collaboration across organizations and achieve cross-cutting or government-wide objectives.

While the potential for enhanced collaboration exists, the incentives to maximize agency-specific performance measures seem to be stronger than the incentives to collaborate. Therefore, the hew and cry for collaboration that is being heard across the globe is unlikely to be achieved through (or in concert with) performance measurement systems unless some specific incentives are created for aligning agency-level performance measures with social goals that can only be achieved collaboratively.

Evidence suggests, however, that multiple agencies might self-align into collaborative networks by concentrating more focus toward understanding and improving the relationships among partnering organizations, and less focus on more detailed agency-level performance measures. Use of performance agreements and social indicators are two additional strategies that could help to achieve the levels of inter-agency collaboration thought to be necessary in impacting complex social problems. Performance agreements appear to be successful because they are concrete, iterative mechanisms that address the barriers to collaboration while focusing on achievable individual or agency-level performance from year to year. Social indicators appear to be successful because they provide a rallying point that focuses the attention of citizens, elected officials and organizations on broader social problems and obligations. The visibility of these social indicators pulls attention toward addressing broad social goals because they provide concrete evidence of success or failure. The publicity around the announcement of the new results on the social indicator opens up communication among the multiple organizations that seek to have an impact on the indicator.

The development of performance measurement systems to ensure accountability, and the encouragement of collaborative approaches to public service delivery, are both important strategies in public management. However, performance measurement systems will tend to undermine collaborative efforts unless they are accompanied by other strategies intended to provide the impetus for alignment and collaboration across agencies.

Part II
Politics and Society

8
Determinants of Performance Information Utilization in Political Decision Making

Jostein Askim

Performance management has become a defining feature of public administration, especially in OECD countries (Bouckaert and Halligan, 2006; Radin, 2000). Performance management consists of three routinized activities. The first is measuring the outputs, outcomes and throughputs of organizations, people and programs in government, thereby generating what will hereafter be called performance information. The second is analyzing performance information by comparing current performance levels to past ones, normative standards (like goals), and the performance of other organizations. The third activity is communicating performance information to appointed and elected decision makers in government.

Performance management routines ensure that managers and elected politicians receive large amounts of, presumably, decision-relevant performance information, but its mere presence does not necessarily lead to its effective use in decision making (Melkers and Willoughby, 2005; Pollitt, 2006b; Rich and Cheol, 2000; Siverbo and Johansson, 2006). This chapter contributes to an emerging stream of research that attempts to improve knowledge about who makes use of performance information, when and for what purposes. To this end, the chapter reviews existing public administration literature. Special attention is given to findings from recent case and survey research from the Norwegian local government sector, conducted by the author and colleagues.

The chapter first reviews reasons for optimism and skepticism concerning performance information's usefulness in political decision making. Then the chapter asks: Under what conditions is performance information most used by elected politicians? The chapter explores whether and how utilization of performance information is conditioned by politicians' personal background, role characteristics, and their political ideology. The chapter also explores the effects of polity characteristics, and policy sectors.

Decision makers' utilization of performance information is largely overlooked in the performance management literature (Pollitt, 2007b; Talbot, 2005). Due to this knowledge gap, our understanding of performance management's significance to organizational life is limited (Bouckaert and Halligan, 2006). Improving knowledge about how performance information is used helps in understanding performance management's broader consequences. Today, too many scholars give scant attention to the use of performance information when theorizing about performance management's consequences; instead, they discuss consequences they deduce from an abstract logic they attribute to performance management (see, e.g., Nørreklit, 2003). Researching what consequences performance information utilization may have for such things as organizational performance, relations between actors, and decision-making capacity is no doubt an important task, but statements about consequences are poorly grounded as long as knowledge about utilization of performance information is as patchy as it is today.

Focusing especially on politicians' utilization of performance information is merited because performance management research has provided far less knowledge about politicians' than about managers' utilization. When summing up 20 years of research on performance management practice, Pollitt (2007b) calls it "mildly amazing" that there are only a few analyses of what elected politicians do with performance information.

Optimistic and sceptic prospects for utilization

The case for optimism

Scholars who draw on agency theory tend to be optimistic about performance information's utilization in politics because they say politicians, who normally suffer from information asymmetry, can use such information to evaluate the performance of their agents – bureaucrats and agencies. Many students of governmental decision making say the primary purpose of performance information in government is to help determine whether things were done correctly (Behn, 2003; Talbot, 2005).

In the case of Norwegian municipalities, this reason for optimism has been strengthened by reforms in recent years. Norwegian municipalities were delegated new tasks in the 1980s and 1990s. This meant larger budgets and more complex organizations. The municipalities were also delegated authority over organizational matters in this period, and most used it to delegate authority from councilors to administrative managers and from top-level to lower-level managers. Moreover, most municipalities decoupled political and administrative specializations (Aarsæther and Vabo, 2002; Hovik and Stigen, 2004; Kleven, 2002). In sum, these reforms increased information asymmetry between councilors and administrators. It is therefore not surprising that research from Norwegian local government shows that performance information is used as a control tool by managers and councilors alike. For example, a case study by Askim (2004) describes how top managers used information generated by a Balanced Scorecard system to control the behavior of lower-level managers from across a broad range of services. In a national survey, almost no councilors (only one in ten) said they could monitor municipal service production equally well without performance information (Askim, 2007a).

Organizational learning theory also gives reason for optimism. Scholars emphasize that the communication of performance information to decision makers increases the polity's decision-making capacity. Performance information stimulates the political decision-making process by provoking, informing and improving the quality of decisions (Hartley and Allison, 2002; Moynihan and Ingraham, 2004). Research shows that performance information is used to identify problems and to put them on the decision agenda (Halachmi, 2005; Nicholson-Crotty, Theobald and Nicholson-Crotty, 2006). In a study of budgeting practices in US local government Melkers and Willoughby (2005) found that performance information was most useful to decision makers during budget preparation. Askim and colleagues (2008) found that eight out of ten Norwegian municipalities used information obtained through inter-organizational benchmarking to identify issues where the municipality should strive to make an impact. Politicians are eager to play the role of ombudsman and to point to gaps between aspirations and actual performance. It appears that performance information is helpful in identifying and articulating such deviancies (Nicholson-Crotty, Theobald and Nicholson-Crotty, 2006). In a survey of Norwegian councilors, Askim (2007a) found that performance information was perceived as a key source of agenda-setting inspiration, second only to direct feedback obtained through face-to-face interaction with the local population.

Furthermore, politicians search for performance information to determine the causes of problems and to forecast the consequences of new policies (Askim, forthcoming). For every issue on the municipal agenda, administrators prepare case documents with background information and suggestions for decisions. To get a fuller picture of alternatives and consequences, however, councilors search for supplementary sources of information. This is what Cyert and March (1963) call "problemistic search."

Politicians also use performance information as ammunition in ongoing debates. According to the US Government Accountability Office (2005b: 19), elected politicians can and do use performance information to support or reject political positions in debate. Askim and colleagues (2008) show that about eight out of ten Norwegian municipalities used information obtained through inter-organizational benchmarking in debates that had started prior to the benchmarking. And Askim (2007b) shows that most Norwegian councilors say they use performance information in debates, and that it is useful for reaching decisions.

The case for skepticism

Many have argued however that politicians make little use of performance information. For example, Pollitt (2006c) claims that politicians obtain information mainly by talking to senior officials and political colleagues as opposed to reading performance reports. Ter Bogt (2001; 2003; 2004) has shown that Dutch aldermen make little use of performance information for assessing the service production for which they are accountable; they prefer meetings and consultations with civil servants. Ingraham claims that performance information "rarely crosses the aisle in policy debates and becomes the foundation for core policy decisions" (2005: 394). Several theoretical approaches can explain such low use of performance information.

First of all, not all agency theorizing gives cause for optimism about the usefulness of performance information in politics. Agency theorizing can often be skeptical because of attribution problems. Agency theory stresses that principals – in this case politicians – are unlikely to emphasize performance information when it is difficult for them to clearly determine the relative contribution of an official, an agency or a program to measured performance (Greve, 2003; Talbot, 2005). This problem is likely to be persistent in an organization like a municipality, because generally, interdependencies between a department, other departments, and the department's environment cause "noise"; hence, such noise makes it difficult to determine whether one or more agencies may have contributed to performance and, moreover, it is difficult to determine whether factors beyond agency control also contributed (Askim, 2004).

Another attribution-type reason for skepticism arises from the fact that while the electorate judges politicians on policies and programs, most performance measurement routines are directed towards measuring the performance of organizational subdivisions. A likely reason for this "division bias" is that performance measurement routines are usually designed by CEOs and CFOs, whose primary concern is to control their subdivisions (Kleven, 2002). Some scholars assume that politicians' behavior is mainly geared towards maximizing their chances of re-election. These scholars may argue that performance information's inability to let voters judge politicians gives reason for skepticism about the usefulness of performance information: unless politicians can use performance information to win votes, they will not use it at all.

Many scholars who are skeptical about the prospects of performance information's utilization in politics draw on political behavior theory. Some emphasize that political decisions are difficult to predict because they arise from a complex mix of factors such as knowledge about the past, values, interests, and knowledge about future prospects and challenges (March and Olsen, 1976). One argument that gives rise to skepticism about the usefulness of performance information is that politicians are susceptible to so-called temporal myopia – they focus on the future and therefore tend to overlook the past (Downs, 1957; Levinthal and James, 1993). Therefore, politicians have little regard for the experiential learning they can gain from reading performance reports. They are keen to set targets, but normally "not so keen to evaluate degrees of goal attainment," says Naschold (1996: 10).

Furthermore, politics includes not only fighting over what goals to set for the future but also fighting over how to interpret the past (Talbot, 2005). Parties in power tend to overemphasize successes while parties in opposition tend to overemphasize failures. Consequently, we can speculate that politicians representing parties in power will emphasize performance information only when it portrays the incumbent regime's performance as a success; and vice versa: those representing parties in opposition will emphasize performance information only when it portrays the incumbent regime's performance as a failure. Hence, the prospects for similar interpretations of performance information are poor. The scope for biased interpretations is facilitated by the fact that organizations often make multiple measurements to assess attainment of an objective. Sometimes two or more measures return diverging indications of goal attainment. In such cases, politicians will often make divergent interpretations of performance and advocate divergent ways forward, depending on which performance measure they prefer (Nicholson-Crotty, Theobald and Nicholson-Crotty, 2006).

A final political behavior-type reason for skepticism concerns coalition building. Building and maintaining coalitions is an ever-present part of political power struggles, and it constrains organizations' ability to learn from performance information. A constraint emphasized by organizational learning theory stems from coalitions' tendency to produce many ambiguous and internally conflicting goals. According to Cyert and March (1963), individuals have goals; collectives do not. A collective can agree on goals only by forming a coalition that is large and strong enough to enforce agreements in the short run. Collectives like Norwegian municipalities are normally run by coalitions of parties that have loyalties to different constituents. Some coalition partners may have loyalties to citizens who want higher quality services at lower costs. Other coalition partners may have loyalties to central government agencies that want the municipality to allocate attention and resources to their respective policy areas. Still other coalition partners may have loyalties to constituents like vocational associations that want shorter hours and more pay. To satisfy its constituents, each coalition partner makes "side payments" in the form of goals, because by setting goals responsive to the needs of a constituent, a party signals willingness to work for that constituent's interests. As a result, municipalities often end up with a long list of internally conflicting goals, expressed in various planning documents. Such complex goal structures reduce the polity's prospects for making effective use of performance information (Greve, 2003).

Exploring the middle position: what explains differences in how performance information is used?

So far the chapter has reviewed broad arguments for and against performance information's usefulness in political decision making. In this section we explore a position between these two polar views; we review arguments that lead us to expect high and low use under certain circumstances. We cover literature on the impact of personal background, formal roles, political ideology, polity characteristics and policy sector.

Personal background

One personal background characteristic apparently determining how politicians and other governmental decision makers assemble, process and use performance information is that of their education. Existing research is inconclusive; some say education levels do not matter; for example, Moynihan and Ingraham (2004) in their study among agency leaders in US state government. Others say higher education has a positive effect. For example, Johnson and colleagues (1995) found that highly educated staff members are more likely to use performance information than staffers who are less educated. The explanation usually offered is that people with advanced degrees and training are skilled at handling large amounts of formal, numerical or technical information; skills that enhance the ability to collect, interpret and use performance information. This echoes a broader argument that higher education enhances politically relevant skills (Verba, Kay and Brady, 1995). Still others say education has a negative effect. For example, in the case of Norway, Askim (forthcoming) has found that utilization of performance information is lowest among the best-educated councilors. The explanation offered is that councilors will seek and emphasize performance information when they are unsure what to do – when values, ideologies and already-possessed information fail to resolve their decision dilemmas. The best educated are not inclined to be unsure what to do; they already possess (or think they do) the knowledge they need to make decisions.

A second personal characteristic of interest is a politician's political experience (Moynihan, 2005a). Some have served several terms in office, others are serving their first. How does experience affect the use of performance information? Again, research is inconclusive. Some argue that highly experienced politicians have good abilities to interpret and make use of information because they are more efficient readers of the large volumes of case documents and hence can more efficiently use time and interpret information. Furthermore, due to their superior knowledge of their polity's history and due to their broad networks both within and outside the political body, they are better positioned than less experienced politicians to interpret performance information by comparing it against previous trends and the workings of other organizations. Others say experience has a negative effect on performance information use.

Melkers and Willoughby (2005: 188) found in a study among administrative executives in US local government that the longer one's employment in government, the less one used performance information. Similarly, in the case of Norway, Askim (forthcoming) has found that councilors' utilization of performance information decreased with their experience. The explanation offered is that inexperienced councilors are more receptive than experienced ones to use performance information because for the inexperienced, performance information is among the information types they have unlimited access to. Moreover, inexperienced councilors search for performance information because they are, on average, more insecure than political veterans when faced with decision dilemmas and insecurity leads to search for information.

Role characteristics

Do politicians' formal roles in the polity affect their use of performance information? Few have researched this question, but there are reasons to believe that frontbenchers use performance information differently than backbenchers, and that politicians representing parties in power use it differently than those representing parties in opposition. Frontbenchers and in-power politicians – those situated closest to the apex – have access to a broader and deeper information base than backbenchers. As insiders, those at the apex are given access by administrative executives to exclusive information in closed formal and informal meetings (Jacobsen, 2003; Mouritzen and Svara, 2002). Furthermore, they are primary contact points for citizens and interest groups. They are also the ones being invited to conferences, seminars and study trips, thereby having the best opportunities to obtain information relevant to their roles as politicians.

Two arguments follow from this starting point. One assumes that backbenchers and politicians in opposition are keenly aware of the informational advantages which insiders have and therefore take steps to improve their access to information. Therefore, the further away from the apex the politicians are, the more they see the need to make the most of the information they do have unlimited access to – including the performance information they are given in performance reports and that which they obtain themselves. Consequently, one can expect backbenchers and politicians representing opposition parties to make more use of performance information than do frontbenchers and councilors representing parties in power, respectively.

The alternative argument holds that closeness to the power apex gives politicians access to greater amounts of information, which in turn gives them superior interpretive skills to, if so inclined, interpret and use performance information. Consequently, one can expect frontbenchers and politicians representing parties in power to be the ones who make the most use of performance information. In a survey of Norwegian councilors, Askim (forthcoming) found support for this notion: backbenchers used performance information less than frontbenchers did.

The same study did not find support for the expectation that the variables "in power" and "in opposition" influence councilors' use of performance information. One possible explanation is that the dynamics of information use simply do not create division along party lines. Alternatively, the roles "in opposition" and "in power" may condition councilors' performance information utilization when combined with other factors. As suggested below, future research should test whether within-polity competition increases utilization among those in power and whether within-polity conflict increases utilization among those in opposition. Testing should also be done to determine whether the very message that performance information carries leads politicians representing parties in power and politicians representing parties in opposition to use performance information differently. One can imagine that those in power are most inclined to use performance information when it portrays the incumbent regime's performances as successes; and vice versa, those in opposition are most inclined to use performance information when it portrays the incumbent regime's performances as failures.

Political ideology

Politicians from all parties have the same incentives to use performance information (to control agents, get feedback about policies, etc.), but use may still vary according to party affiliations. First, because of the content of parties' political ideology. Some say performance management is a politically neutral practice, but many have argued that it aligns better with some ideologies than with others. Some hold that socialists (left-wing and liberal parties) are most receptive to performance information. They argue that in public management reform, nonsocialists (right-wing and conservative parties) tend to trust the market rather than the public sector, and therefore tend to advocate contracting out and privatization. Socialists, on the other hand, are less antagonistic toward public sector provision. They tend to believe that the public sector can be improved from within, through learning. Consequently, they may use performance management to implement solutions within the traditional scope of public services, and to combat efforts to implement the radical NPM reforms favored by right-wing regimes. This expectation has received some empirical support. A study of Norwegian municipalities showed that socialist regimes are more likely than non-socialist regimes to measure performance (Johnsen, 1999b). Askim and colleagues (2008) found that nonsocialist regimes learn the least from benchmarking.

Others hold that nonsocialists are most receptive to performance information. They argue that performance measurement, a practice often associated with NPM, will be championed by right-wing and conservative parties, and hence that councilors representing such parties will make more use of performance information than those representing left-wing and liberal parties. Evidence is inconclusive on this point. In a survey of Norwegian councilors Askim (2007b) found a weak tendency towards higher utilization among right-wingers than among left-wingers, but statistical testing revealed that these differences most likely represent statistical coincidences rather than substantial differences. Communist councilors (RV) are the exception; their utilization was significantly lower than everybody else's (Askim, 2007b).

The low utilization among communists leads us to the second reason to expect a relationship between party ideology and utilization of performance information: perhaps it is not the content of party ideology (socialist vs. non-socialist) that matters, but the strength of the party's ideology. In general, and all else being equal, we can expect utilization of information in decision making to be highest among those who are in doubt about what to do (see above, on education). Politicians affiliated to parties with a highly integrated and structured belief system are typically not in doubt; their ideology resolves most decision dilemmas. Such parties are usually to be found on the flanks of the political landscape. Future research should test this expectation.

Polity characteristics

A politician's performance information can be assumed to depend not only on personal background, roles and political ideology, but also on factors associated with the polity or organization within which he or she works (Johnsen and Vakkuri, 2006; ter Bogt, 2001; Vakkuri and Meklin, 2006). First, political regime stability may influence the utilization of performance information. A stable regime has vested interests in past performances and hence an incentive to learn from them. A new regime, on the other hand, may want to start with a clean sheet and may thus be less interested in learning from its predecessor's performances. This expectation has received scant empirical attention.

However, in a study of municipal benchmarking in Norway, Askim and colleagues (2008) found a significant relationship between regime stability and learning outcomes. They speculate that maybe regime stability is associated with high levels of benchmarking-induced learning only when benchmarking portrays past performances as successes. One reason to expect such contingency is that incumbent regimes can be expected to have more vested interests in successes than in failures; another reason is that regimes are most eager to emphasize information when it improves their chances for re-election.

Second, levels of political competition within the polity may influence the utilization of performance information. Competition can be considered high when many parties are represented in the polity and when political blocks are equal in size. Views differ on how political competition affects the utilization of performance information. Some hold that a low-competition environment is most promising, because it facilitates fact-oriented discussions. Others hold that a high-competition environment is most promising because a marketplace of ideas is more likely to work when there is competition (Bretschneider et al., 1989). Recent Norwegian evidence supports this notion. In the above-mentioned study of municipal benchmarking, Askim and colleagues (2008) found that municipalities were most likely to take benchmarking experiences into account when many parties competed to influence policies. The explanation offered is that competition creates greater risks that badly performing parties will lose power. Such risks give parties in power incentives to improve polity performance, and they know that using performance information is a potent improvement strategy.

Third, levels of political conflict within the polity may affect politicians' utilization of performance information. Some political bodies resemble cozy clubs, while others resemble war zones. Conflict levels are often influenced by competition levels, but interpersonal, historical and contextual factors also play a part. Therefore, high-conflict environments can be found even where competition is low, and vice versa. High conflict levels can be expected to increase performance information utilization because resorting to neutral facts may untangle decision processes that have stalled due to fierce ideological, inter-party or interpersonal differences. Furthermore, high-conflict environments increase the chances that opposition parties employ performance information in their efforts to embarrass the parties in power, especially when polity performance is poor.

Finally, many have argued that the use of performance information increases with polity size. Positive associations between polity size and performance information utilization have been found not only at the local level (Poister and Streib, 1999) but also at state (Moynihan, 2005a) and national levels (Lægreid, Roness and Rubecksen, 2006b). Various explanations have been offered. A larger polity means more service users, more activities and more employees; in short, more to be accountable for. Keeping direct oversight becomes more difficult with increased polity size. Arms-length control based partially on performance information, by contrast, fits politicians in large polities well. Performance information is easily used by politicians to heuristically evaluate large numbers of departments, managers and programs.

Furthermore, "information use is not a discrete event in isolation; instead, it is only one stage in an interrelated set of stages" (Rich and Cheol, 2000: 180). Hence, exposure to performance information over time can be expected to enhance one's ability to make informed use of it. Large polities have large professional administrations that collect, frame and provide large amounts of information for politicians. Politicians' skillful use of such an information base can under some circumstances develop their cognitive skills and abilities to use performance information.

Policy sectors

Many claim there is reason to expect systematic differences in performance management practices between policy sectors (Jacobsen, 2006; Meyer and Rowan, 1977; Moynihan, 2005a; Pollitt, 2007b; Van Dooren, 2004; van Helden and Johnsen, 2002). Some have attributed this expectation to historical institutionalism, which emphasizes that working methods and cultures structure the way organizations respond to new challenges (Hall and Taylor, 1996). Most, however, have attributed the expectation to contingency theory, which emphasizes sector-specific differences in tasks (Carter, Klein and Day, 1992). Many have developed typologies of tasks and argued that each type can be expected to be associated with a certain level or type of performance information utilization. Some promote task dichotomies. For example, Johansson (1995) distinguishes between hard and soft tasks, and Greve (2003) distinguishes between more and less complex tasks. Several scholars have suggested a two-by-two typology based on the assumption that tasks differ according to whether activities and their results can be observed (Macintosh, 1985; ter Bogt, 2003; Wilson, 1989). Neither typology has so far been proven superior to the others in terms of explaining differences between policy sectors. A likely reason for lack of fit is that most governmental sectors are difficult to characterize according to typologies based on tasks, since most sectors comprise several tasks, some of which are "hard" and others which are "soft," some complex and others simple, and some observable and others unobservable (Van Dooren, 2006).

Recent local government research has produced some less ambitious, though still important lessons. First, municipalities in Norway appear to draw less on performance information and lessons from benchmarking when making decisions about education services than when making decisions about elderly care services (Askim, Johnsen and Christophersen, 2008). Possible reasons include stronger resistance from teachers than from nurses. Second, survey evidence from Norway shows that utilization of performance information is higher among councilors working with elderly care, administrative affairs and educational affairs than among councilors working with cultural affairs, technical services, and planning and commercial development (Askim, 2007a). High utilization among politicians working with administrative affairs has been found elsewhere too. Based on survey evidence from Dutch local government, ter Bogt (2004) shows that aldermen with responsibilities for administrative affairs make particularly active use of performance information. His explanation is that the content of this policy sector is internally oriented and not too politicized in character. Low utilization among politicians working with technical affairs is more surprising in light of existing research (Greve, 2003; Johansson, 1995). In the Norwegian case, the finding might partly be explained by the fact that decision makers' exposure to performance information has been somewhat lower in this sector than in certain other sectors. In education and elderly care, for example, central government has made significant efforts to produce and communicate valid and reliable performance information.

Discussion

The preceding section reviewed arguments that lead us to expect high and low use under certain circumstances. We now discuss how this review reflects on the broad arguments for and against performance information's usefulness in political decision making. First, the review strengthens the (previously rather weak) case for optimism. We have seen that politicians use performance information to set decision agendas, to map out consequences of alternative policies, to signal rationality, and to win debates. Second, the chapter uses established social theories to carve out a middle position between the optimists and the skeptics. Political behavior theory is often portrayed mainly as a source of skepticism. But in reality, it proves to be a source of interesting explanations for why performance information is sometimes used and sometimes not. For example, evidence shows that utilization is greater under stable political regimes than under unstable ones. Furthermore, agency theory is often portrayed mainly as a source of optimism. But in reality, this theory too is a source of explanations for differences in use. For example, it helps explain why performance information utilization is lower among the top brass than among those who suffer most from information asymmetry, like inexperienced and uneducated councilors, and backbenchers. To historical institutionalism and political behavior theory, this latter finding suggests a surprising prospect: performance management reforms reduce information asymmetries and thereby level out the playing field within municipal councils.

This chapter argues that the most important question to answer for social scientists interested in performance management is not "Why all this measurement if the information is not used by politicians?", but rather "Who makes use of performance information, when, and for what purposes?" Existing research has provided some answers to these questions but much remains to be done. As indicated above, I believe that future research should test especially how the interplay of situational and stable factors affects the utilization of performance information.

Conclusions

Many scholars have demonstrated that organizations keep measuring even though leaders make limited use of the performance information. Many call this a paradox (Johnsen and Vakkuri, 2006). Agency theory's solution to the paradox is that leaders know that most subordinates will behave as they should simply because of the possibility that their performance is being evaluated by leaders. In other words, knowing that someone "up there" might be watching will often be sufficient to restrain agents from behaving contrary to their principals' interests. Therefore, decision-makers' reluctance to dedicate their precious time to actually reading performance reports may not be so surprising (Hood, 2007a; Loft, 1988). Another resolution of the apparent paradox is offered by sociological institutionalism. Its key premise is that an organization's behavior can be interpreted as attempting to seek legitimacy in its environment. Organizations are not content to know that they perform well; they also want to be perceived as "good" by peer organizations, clients, voters, overseers and other environmental actors. Adopting performance management is a sound strategy if environmental actors see performance management as an indicator of "goodness" – being modern, rational, goal-focused, effective,and willing to learn (Brunsson and Olsen, 1990). Consequently, instrumental use of performance information is not so important; the mere adoption of performance management tools enables managers and politicians to signal to their environments that their polity is being run in a rational, efficient, transparent and results-oriented manner, and that they hold bureaucrats accountable for their performance (Feldman and March, 1981). Some view politicians' tendency to overlook the past as "irrational"; others put a positive spin on it. One example of the latter is Halachmi (2005). He says politicians know that by dwelling on the past, they may lose a proper perspective with which to gauge the future – a future that may be very different from the past. Another example is March, who says decision makers are sometimes well advised to "divorce the information structure from the decision structure," since tight links between information and its uses increase decision makers' vulnerability to manipulation by their information providers (March, 1987).

This chapter has reviewed reasons for skepticism and optimism about performance information's usefulness in political decision making, and factors that may condition its usefulness. However, some may question the significance of high and low performance information use. Does its utilization in decision making mean that performance information strongly influences policy outcomes? On the one hand, we know from evaluation theory that being exposed to a piece of information does not necessarily imply that one is a slave to it Politicians invariably weigh information from, for example, external interested parties, managers, and performance reports against factors such as available sources, statutory requirements and their own preferences (Lowndes, Pratchett and Stoker, 2001; Rich and Cheol, 2000). On the other hand, we know from psychology that the stimulus that directs attention will often influence the conclusion reached, as it directs attention towards selected aspects of the situation, to the exclusion of others (Simon, 1976). I argue that its use for agenda setting and argumentative purposes means that performance information increases municipalities' decision-making capacity – independent of its influence on decision outcomes (Hartley and Allison, 2002; Huber, 1991; Moynihan and Ingraham, 2004).

9
UK Parliamentary Scrutiny of Public Service Agreements: A Challenge Too Far?

Carole Johnson and Colin Talbot

This chapter turns its attention to the issue of how performance information is and isn't used by the United Kingdom's parliamentary scrutiny committees involved in scrutinizing government activity. Whilst performance management is largely rooted within the technocratic administrative arena, there is a growing trend towards the possibility, at least, that performance information could be used as one source of data for the purposes of supporting the democratic polity (Pollitt, 2006b). The case of the Public Service Agreements (PSAs) discussed below is, ostensibly, one example where there has been the intention to support the democratic use of performance information. The findings may lend support to Pollitt's assertion that politicians, if interested in performance information at all, are interested in broad brush data only. They appear not to be engaged by the prospect of carrying out detailed scrutiny. However, the government itself has not given the PSA policy the precedence it deserved and may be partly responsible for the lack of scrutiny that PSA policy received.

Most advanced democracies have some "separation of powers" between the executive and the legislative branches of government. A core role for the legislative branch is to scrutinize the activities of the executive branch. Traditionally, scrutiny has observed new policies, draft legislation and budget estimates, mainly focusing on potentially contentious issues. However, in recent years there has been a trend by the executive branch of government to publish various types of performance information about its own activities and those of the wider public services in a number of OECD countries (OECD, 2005; Talbot, 2005). This movement has become so marked that some analysts (and advocates) have come to refer to it as "outcome-based budgeting" or even "outcome-based governance" (van der Molen and van Rooyen, 2001).

The role of parliamentarians in outcome-based budgeting appears to be limited as they struggle to adapt to systems of government by performance as opposed to government by inputs. Data from 27 out of the 30 OECD member countries (OECD, 2005) demonstrates that 88 percent make performance data available to the public (and hence the legislative branch). However, in only 19 percent of the cases do politicians in the legislative branch use performance information for decision making, and this falls to 8 percent for the budget committees. This report suggests problems with data quality, readability and relevance are the main factors which discourage the use of performance information. In a recent review, Pollitt (2006b) argued that the use of performance information by parliamentarians is at best "patchy." Other research by one of the authors on Japan's *Government Policy Evaluation Act* (GPEA, 2001) suggests similar results. Van Dooren and Sterck (2006), echoing the OECD report, found that legislative politicians in Australia oppose outcome-based budgeting because the outcome indicators established are too abstract. Members of Parliament are expected to appropriate spending items to outcomes that lack purposeful definition, for example, an outcome might be defined as "a safer Australia." Therefore outcome-based budgeting, as practiced, can create a paradox, whereby rather than strengthening the scrutiny role, it erodes the power of scrutiny because the outcome indicators are meaningless for budgeting purposes.

This chapter reports on research focusing on the role of the UK legislative branch in scrutinizing performance data, in particular the PSA data which represents a form of outcome-based budgeting. It asks, how have politicians adapted their approach to scrutiny in response to this innovation in performance reporting?

The PSA policy

PSAs were introduced in 1998. They represent an important innovation for several reasons:

- They represent the extension of performance management to Central Government departments
- They are used to inform the Spending and Comprehensive Spending Review processes (Johnson, 2007)

- Scrutiny by Parliament was, initially at least, encouraged. PSAs thus represented a "fundamental change in the accountability of government to Parliament and the people" (Chancellor of the Exchequer, 1998a); a particularly significant point within a system where accountability to parliament is weak.

Furthermore, in the 2007 spending review process, PSAs were said to have "played a vital role in galvanizing public service delivery" and "driving major improvements in outcomes" (www.hmtreasury.gov.uk).

Since its inception, the PSA system has undergone development (HM Treasury, 2007). It remains correct to identify the process as in essence a "contract for the renewal of public services" designed to force change in the status quo regarding service production (Brown, 1998). An example of the objectives and targets used within the PSA system is provided below:

> Objective 1 – Tackling disadvantage by reviving the most deprived neighbourhoods, reducing social exclusion and supporting society's most vulnerable groups.
> Targets – Tackle social exclusion and deliver neighbourhood renewal, working with departments to help them meet their PSA floor targets, in particular narrowing the gap in health, education, crime, worklessness, housing and liveability outcomes between the most deprived areas and the rest of England with measurable improvement by 2010.
>
> (HM Treasury, 2004)

Abstract outcomes are thus monitored via specific performance indicators over time and are used collectively to determine the degree to which the objective has been met. Reported twice yearly, the PSA data has the potential to provide important informational leverage for Parliamentary scrutiny.

Crucially, PSAs are part of the broader spending review process and represent a novel element through which spending is (purportedly) linked to performance by government departments. The PSA policy presented Parliament with an opportunity to vigorously scrutinize the activities of government. Significantly, during a period of policy proliferation as New Labour sought effective policies through experimentation, one might assume that this would have led to greater debate about what government should or should not fund.

In the parliamentarian's favor, scrutinizing PSAs may never have been easy. The degree of commitment from the government to engage Parliament in scrutiny appears to have faltered early in the process. The phrase "Parliament and people" was soon replaced with the "public" and the "people" (Chancellor of the Exchequer, 1998b). There is also evidence that Parliamentary scrutiny would not be altogether welcome as the Treasury argued the system was new and "needed time to bed down" (Treasury Committee, 1999).

Like all policies it suffered from teething problems. Analysts questioned the claim regarding the fundamental nature of the PSA system. James (2004) concludes that the practical application of the system fell far short of the rhetoric and both ministers and senior officials have given less importance to PSAs than the formal policy suggests.

Furthermore, the National Audit Office, in two studies of PSA data quality, concluded that a significant number of PSAs were either not being reported on at all or were not fit for purpose – specifically 20 percent in 2005 and 18 percent in 2006 (Comptroller and Auditor General, 2005; 2006). In their 2006 study, the NAO concluded only 30 percent of PSA reporting was fully "fit for purpose," with disclosure or systems issues affecting a further 47 percent. Nevertheless, neither of these arguments are viable reasons for Parliament not to engage in this process. In fact, they would lead to the opposite argument that something was going awry, usually an open invitation for scrutiny to focus its spotlight on a topic.

Parliament and its scrutiny role

Parliamentary scrutiny represents one way in which governments can be held to account for their actions (McGee, 2002). The power of scrutiny by any one particular legislature relates, amongst other factors, to the degree to which the separation of powers is institutionalized within the constitution. The scrutiny role of the UK Parliament has never been particularly strong due to the separation of powers relying on convention. The United Kingdom, unlike the United States for example, lacks a clearly defined constitution outlining the respective powers of the two houses of Parliament *vis-à-vis* the Executive. Over time, there has been a gradual extension of the powers of the Executive which has exacerbated the power imbalance (Commission on the Scrutiny Role of Parliament, 2001; Norton, 1998).

Attempts to strengthen Parliament's ability to scrutinize have been a recurring theme. In 1979, departmental select committees were created in an effort to shadow the work of particular government departments. This is considered a significant innovation which potentially helps redress the Parliamentary–Executive power imbalance.

Further reforms were made by the New Labour government from 1997 onwards, through its "modernizing" agenda. Part of this agenda focused on the means by which Parliament holds ministers to account. Whilst such "modernization" has been described as largely "administrative," some changes have had the potential to increase the effectiveness of the scrutiny role. Two changes are considered important here, one is the increase in general resourcing and the other is the introduction of the core tasks.

The core tasks, introduced in 2002, outline what each select committee should aim to scrutinize each year. They do not usurp the right of committees to set their own agenda, a right viewed as essential to the power of committees, but they are intended to add value by broadening the scope of work carried out by committees. This responds to the criticism by the Liaison Committee (the committee of committee chairs) and others that whilst, in general, "the committees have done a great deal of valuable work [...] their full potential has still to be realized." Importantly, they had failed to carry out thorough financial scrutiny, preferring to focus on policy issues (Liaison Committee, 2002).

The core tasks concept emanated from the Hansard Society's *Commission on Parliamentary Scrutiny* (Hansard Society, 2001). The principle underlying them was to promote the "balancing of inquiries between administration, finance and policy" (Kelly, 2004: 4). It thus included recommendations on Expenditure and Performance. One of the core tasks specifies that select committees should "examine the department's Public Service Agreements, the associated targets and the statistical measures employed and report if appropriate" (Liaison Committee, 2002: para. 13).

Although not compulsory, the core tasks were intended to be influential and committees were asked to report against the core tasks in an annual report. Thus within the system of scrutiny in the UK Parliament there has been, since 2002 at least, a strong steering towards scrutinizing performance information emerging from the PSA system. This steering by the liaison committee to encourage select committees to scrutinize PSAs added a push factor to the pull factor originally, albeit weakly, stated within the policy itself.

The scrutiny of PSAs

Traditionally, scrutiny has operated through fairly in depth inquiries on specific policy topics, as outlined above. Committees are permanent, they are specialist, have members from all political parties and are supported by highly skilled clerks and expert aids. They have the power to call witnesses to give evidence. Data and evidence is also collected from government departments and other bodies. Parliamentary committees can have a significant impact on the policy process if their work is timely and well disseminated.

The lack of financial scrutiny has to some extent been addressed by the recently established Scrutiny Unit who have been actively supporting committees to play a greater part in facilitating debate around budget estimates (Committee Office Scrutiny Unit, 2007). However, the degree to which committees are also scrutinizing performance has been overlooked, therefore how far Parliament has adapted to the "fundamental shift" in accountability, supposedly opened-up by the introduction of PSAs, commands empirical enquiry.

The research reported here relates to three studies: an original scoping of the work of three cross-cutting select committees in relation to performance; a content analysis exercise of seven departmental select committees over four years, and a postal survey of MPs and committee clerks across all the UK select committees. This is intended to measure attitudes to the scrutiny of performance. Together these three sources of data provide a fairly comprehensive picture of UK Parliamentary interest in PSAs.

Evidence from the cross-cutting select committees

The Public Accounts, Treasury, and Public Administration Committees were selected because we expected that they were involved in scrutinizing government "performance policy." We utilized their reports on performance together with the author's experience of acting as a Parliamentary advisor on performance issues. Evidence from the three "cross-cutting" committees is mixed and does not fully accord with their formal roles and how they may have adapted to the accountability system on performance.

The Public Accounts Committee (PAC) is charged with scrutinizing "input" decisions, that is, government spending. Given this remit and the shift from managing by budgets to managing by performance, this committee ought to demonstrate the biggest change in its activities. PAC is also the reporting committee for the Comptroller and Auditor General and the National Audit Office (NAO), and therefore is supposed to examine their value for money studies of economy, efficiency and effectiveness in the way that government departments and other bodies use their resources.

In reality, the PAC has paid little attention to PSA policy. We may have expected them to have focused some attention on the relationship between departmental objectives, the PSAs and the outcomes achieved in performance terms of public bodies and their parent departments. However, there are very few references within the reports to PSAs at all. The report *Managing Resources to Develop Better Public Services* (Public Accounts Committee, 2005) is a notable exception, but even here PSAs are only one factor among many and the discussion is minor.

This situation is slightly odd as the PAC do scrutinize most NAO value for money reports. The NAO has taken a substantial interest in performance measurement in government, with the publication of a number of reports, two of which focus on PSAs specifically but none have been part of PAC enquiries (Comptroller and Auditor General, 2005; 2006).

The Treasury Select Committee has been fairly active in scrutinizing the policy of the Treasury towards PSAs. It has held hearings after each Spending Review and the publication of the PSA data (in 1999, 2000, 2002 and 2004) at which a panel of experts, Treasury officials and finally the Chancellor himself have been examined. Each time, critical reports and recommendations for improving both the Spending Review and PSA processes have been produced.

Early in the life of the Spending Review/PSA system, the committee produced a specific report on the PSAs (Treasury Committee, 1999). They also made some subsequent fairly strong recommendations about the need for scrutiny by Parliament, supported by external analysis, of the PSAs:

> We remain strongly of the opinion that the assessments of departments' performance against their PSA targets should be the subject of external review, by a body accountable to Parliament, such as the National Audit Office.
>
> (Treasury Committee, 2001)

Later reports on the Spending Reviews and PSAs (2002, 2004) paid significantly less attention to PSAs. Arguably, the early attention was partly due to their novelty and partly to the fact that the first set of PSAs in 1998, were published separately five months after the Spending Review and were subject to separate Treasury Committee scrutiny sessions. In subsequent iterations (2000, 2002 and 2004), Spending Reviews and new PSA sets were published simultaneously and covered within the same hearings and reports.

The most substantial piece of work on the "measurement culture" in government has been carried out by the Public Administration Select Committee in their 2003 Inquiry *On Target? Government by Measurement* (Public Administration Select Committee, 2003). This was a relatively large inquiry by UK Parliamentary standards, and the report includes a detailed analysis of PSAs across all departments prepared by a committee specialist.

The general thrust of the report was for a more consultative, flexible and audited system of performance measurement. The government's (belated) response was to try to kill the report with warm words, some neat side-stepping and one or two stern rejections. In general, government claimed to be already addressing most recommendations, but closer inspection reveals their actions remained consistent with those for which they were criticized in the report. For example, many days of work have focused on gaining flexibilities in the reporting requirements and targets for local actors to allow them to tackle issues on the ground in more appropriate ways, but few new flexibilities have been granted (Department for Communities and Local Government, 2006).

Evidence from the seven departmental select committees

Seven departmental select committees, that is, those that focus exclusively on a single department were reviewed for their activity on PSAs including: Defence, Education, Health, Home Affairs, Work and Pensions (DWP), the Office of the Deputy Prime Minister (ODPM now Communities and Local Government, CLG), and Environment, Food and Rural Affairs (DEFRA). They were selected because of the levels of public spending and political salience of their departments and this may have encouraged committee members to pay attention to PSA reporting and management. The findings relate to four Parliamentary years covering the period 2002–6. This period was selected for several reasons:

- PSAs were well established and four sets of PSA data existed.
- The "core tasks" encouraging scrutiny of PSAs were in place.

- The performance of public services was politically salient due to the government's emphasis on delivery.
- Select committees had begun to receive extra resources and support for their work, for example, from the recently established Scrutiny Unit.
- The National Audit Office produced several reports which potentially could have facilitated greater scrutiny of performance (Comptroller and Auditor General, 1998; 2000; 2001; 2005; 2006). The evidence available prior to the 2002/3 Parliamentary year is patchy, in part due to less rigorous reporting of activities. The few references found to PSA scrutiny before 2002/3 are at a minimal level.

Data for the analysis was gathered from published documents. Two types of documents were used: the *Committee Annual Reports* which provided the committee's own account of work conducted during the Parliamentary session and scrutiny reports resulting from inquiries which potentially held the committees' analyses and recommendations regarding PSAs. We focused on formal reporting because of the significance of this in communicating Parliamentary scrutiny.

The table summarizes our analysis of the numbers of PSAs, and the type and depth of scrutiny to which they were subjected by the departmental select committees. First, we estimated the number of PSA objectives and targets for which performance information might be available to committees. Counting PSA objectives and targets is not easy, because they have often been written in ways which effectively combine several targets in one (Comptroller and Auditor General, 2001). Furthermore, recently some performance requirements previously described as PSA targets have been restated as standards in the government's quest to appear to be reducing the numbers of targets. Our estimates may therefore be a little higher than the departments' own figures where provided. However, PSAs often overlap in the third year of the spending review periods (PSAs are set for three years, but revised every two years) and so our estimates of "live" PSAs remain conservative since we have not included these. Table 9.1 shows that substantial numbers of PSA objectives and targets are set for departments.

We also record the number of PSA objectives and targets which the committees claim to have scrutinized in their annual reports. The total number of PSAs for the seven departments during the period was 344 but the number scrutinized was just 75, representing less than one-quarter of the total. Whilst the breadth of scrutiny of PSAs varies between committees and between scrutiny periods within committees,

Table 9.1 Analysis of departmental select committee scrutiny of Public Service Agreements

Departmental select committee	Year	No. of PSAs in existence (our estimate)	No. of scrutinized PSAs	Type of scrutiny		Depth of focus on PSAs in report
				Evidence session	Inquiry/ report	
Defence	02/3	7	1	0	1	None
	03/4	7	5	1	3	Substantial scrutiny in 1 of 3
	04/5	6	1	1	0	N/A
	05/6	6	General	1	0	N/A
Education	02/3	17	1	1	0	N/A
	03/4	17	General	1	0	N/A
	04/5	23	2	1	1	None
	05/6	19	General	3	3	Minimal scrutiny in 1 of 3
Health	02/3	14	General + 2	Q/naire	1	Minimal scrutiny
	03/4	14	General + 1	1	1	Substantial scrutiny
	04/5	13	General + 1	1	1	None
	05/6	13	9	3	2	None
Home Affairs	02/3	20	General + 1	1	1	Minimal scrutiny
	03/4	20	General + 5	3	1	Substantial scrutiny
	04/5	7	General + 1	1	2	Substantial scrutiny
	05/6	7	4	4	1	Substantial scrutiny
DWP	02/3	10	General + 5	1	2	None

Table 9.1 Continued

Departmental select committee	Year	No. of PSAs in existence (our estimate)	No. of scrutinized PSAs	Type of scrutiny		Depth of focus on PSAs in Report
				Evidence session	Inquiry/ Report	
	03/4	10	General	1	0	N/A
	04/5	19	4	1	2	Substantial scrutiny
	05/6	19	8	3	3	Minimal in 2 and substantial in 1
ODPM	02/3	9	General + 2	1	2	None in one and minimal in one
	03/4	9	General + 1	2	1	Substantial scrutiny
	04/5	10	General	0	1	Minimal scrutiny
	05/6	10	General	0	1	None
DEFRA	02/3	12	General	0	1	Minimal scrutiny
	03/4	12	9	1	8	None
	04/5	14	5	1	7	None in 4 and Substantial in 3
	05/6	14	7	1	6	None
Totals		344	75	35	52	Substantial = 13 Minimal = 8 None = 31

Source: Based on analysis of Select Committees Publications, House of Commons, www.publications.parliament.uk

we conclude that the level of scrutiny remains low – most PSAs remain unexamined by Parliament.

We also focused on the depth of scrutiny given to those PSAs examined by the committees since a qualitative assessment may help to offset any lack of quantity. Of the 75 PSAs mentioned in the "annual" reports, 52 were claimed to have been the partial subject of inquiries leading to published reports (i.e., not just evidence sessions). Therefore, out of the 202 reports published by the seven committees during the review period, 52 potentially contained discussion of the PSAs, which appears to be a substantial number. However, closer examination of these reports shows that most (31) have no specific mention of PSAs in the body of the report (as opposed to evidence sessions), meaning that although they formed part of the evidential base for the inquiry, they were not considered sufficiently important to be included in the final report itself. Of those that did contain PSA references, eight contained what we qualitatively assess as minimal scrutiny (i.e., PSAs were mentioned in relation to one or more aspects); and 13 contained a substantial amount of text focused on a discussion of one or more PSAs (i.e., one or more PSAs were mentioned on a number of occasions and sometimes in more than one place).

Whilst the previous discussion has highlighted the broad picture, there are of course variations in the different committees' approaches. For example, the Defence and Education Committees have done relatively little by way of PSA scrutiny overall. The Committees of Health; Environment, Food and Rural Affairs; Work and Pensions; and Office of the Deputy Prime Minister display a rather variable pattern of scrutiny between the different topics addressed. The Home Affairs Committee has given more sustained attention to the PSAs, together with their special report on target setting (Home Affairs Select Committee, 2005). Nevertheless, much of their yearly commitment to scrutiny remains in the form of evidence sessions.

There also exist differences in the views of committees regarding the value of performance management, measurement and targets. The Health Committee is active in supporting greater collection and collation of data and investment in data systems to more adequately secure good healthcare. This is particularly clear in areas of healthcare which have hitherto been under-resourced such as maternity and sexual health services. They are keen to set targets in addition to performance indicators to help drive up standards, although they recognize the perverse outcomes which occur at times because of the attention given to politically salient targets. By contrast, the Defence and Home Affairs Committees were more critical of the quality of targets and their centrally determined imposition. In response, they called for greater emphasis on localism and consultation in target setting. There is no particular pattern, though, between expressed views and practice as the Home Affairs Committee were amongst the most proactive in the area of performance scrutiny.

These variations have not been subject to in-depth inquiry and there are a number of factors that could influence outcomes. We do know that the chairs of the committees play a very influential role in how they operate and the quality of the relationship between department and committee could affect a committee's ability to carry out scrutiny. Some hints as to what shapes committees' thinking around performance reporting is perhaps provided within the responses to the survey reported below.

Evidence from the survey of committee attitudes

The analysis of select committees' scrutiny and reporting on PSAs produces a very mixed pattern but overall it is neither comprehensive nor systematic. The question is obviously why this should be so. We draw on the results of a survey which intended to find out why select committees were reacting in this way to the PSA system. The results are based on a sample size of 54, which represents roughly a quarter of the select committee's staff and at least one response was received from 17 out of the 18 committees.

The key claim by government, that the PSA system represented a fundamental shift in accountability, was not supported by MPs responding to the survey. They agreed, but only marginally, with the statement that PSAs were an "important instrument of government policy," whilst they marginally disagreed that they had "significantly changed the way government accounts for itself to parliament."

When asked about the quality of PSA data, MPs were neutral about whether it was "easily accessible" or "easily understandable," but more skeptical about whether it was "sufficient to judge performance" or "reliable and accurate" or "useful for the intended purpose." MPs were also skeptical about the degree to which PSA data was seen as "accurate and fair" outside of Parliament and similarly in answer to the question about the degree to which the government had encouraged Parliamentary scrutiny.

MPs on the Foreign Affairs Committee also criticized the policy, particularly the "one-size fits all" approach which encouraged the PSA targets to be focused on "outcomes" regardless of appropriateness:

> The Foreign and Commonwealth Office's (FCO) PSA targets are too reliant on outcomes, it is difficult for the FCO to do more than influence; targets drawn up in terms of inputs/outputs would be more relevant and more useful.

Another respondent from the Education Committee questioned the way PSA targets were arrived at:

> The problem with PSAs is the lack of information about the way in which they are arrived at. Why have a target for 50 per cent participation in Higher Education? The Department for Education and Skills was unable to offer a convincing explanation. It has proved very difficult to have any sort of useful dialogue [...] with the department.

In relation to their own response to the scrutiny of PSAs, select committee MPs felt they ought to be doing more to "report regularly" on PSAs, but were not enthusiastic. One MP commented that:

> PSAs are one tool – but not the only way in which select committees can hold the executive to account.

Despite the fact that scrutiny of PSAs are emphasized in the core tasks, respondents regularly responded that their committee paid little attention to them as the following quotes demonstrate:

> PSAs rarely come up in our select committee evidence sessions with user groups/permanent secretary/ministers.
> To the best of my recollection PSAs have never been mentioned in the select committee in the whole of the last 12 months.

MPs and clerks felt they did not have sufficient resources to carry out systematic scrutiny and needed more help from the NAO. Whilst the latter view recorded the highest positive response, not all MPs think that NAO involvement would be worthwhile and think it may impact on the resources directly available to committees.

A further view was expressed regarding the need to embed the core tasks and scrutiny of performance and other administrative issues more generally through training for new MPs:

> Virtually never mentioned in the committees I am on, could do with some more awareness raising. Not mentioned in training for new MPs on committee work – yet another item I will add to the list when seeking to improve induction for new MPs.

These findings reinforce the examination of select committee practice as evidenced in their reports and proceedings. Taken together, these analyses can only lead to the conclusion that PSAs are not scrutinized broadly and of those that do get mentioned, they are mostly tangential or a relatively small part of reports. This certainly does not add up to scrutiny of "output or outcome-based government" if PSAs are the main vehicle for reporting achievement. The Home Affairs Select Committee's exceptional approach serves only to highlight just how unsystematic scrutiny is concerning performance.

Conclusions

This chapter has outlined how one performance policy has failed to encourage scrutiny by UK parliamentarians despite its potential relationship to future budget decisions. Like other research in this area, the opportunity to seize influence for democratic purposes has not materialized. There are some similarities between these findings and those of the OECD (2005) and Van Dooren and Sterck (2006). Our findings concur with these on the issues of accuracy, quality and relevance. Our findings concur with them on the issues of accuracy, quality and relevance, although other reasons were also stated, in particular: inadequate resourcing and that government had failed to convince Parliament that success against the PSAs was actually important for future spending decisions.

The invitation to scrutinize was not particularly influential and the attempt to institutionalize performance scrutiny within the core tasks by Parliament itself appears to have had only a minimal impact on the levels of actual scrutiny. In their recent report on financial scrutiny, the Scrutiny Unit allude to the weak institutionalization of the core tasks (2007: 12) stating that "there is no systematic mechanism for parliamentary scrutiny of the spending review." The qualitative responses to the survey highlight that committees resist restrictions on scrutiny topics even though they often felt more should be done on performance. Nevertheless, the system has almost certainly encouraged what scrutiny there is and the allied innovation of annual reporting by committees now allows regular and systematic reporting. This could be developed further, but at least the gaps in the breadth of scrutiny that occur are now transparent.

It may well be the case, as the MPs clearly think from our survey, that the government itself does not take the PSAs seriously. But is this really a valid reason for parliamentarians not to take it seriously? Parliament uses all sorts of data to hold the executive to account, much of which may not be intended by government for such purposes, and PSA data is another possible tool whether government wants it to be or not.

The lack of resources and institutional support are issues. The lack, especially, of expert resources remains an issue despite substantial increases in resources for select committees. Representatives from the Scrutiny Unit recently acknowledged the difficulties for MPs in scrutinizing the government especially on technical matters without the support of experts. In the United Kingdom, Parliamentary committees do not have the direct support of the NAO in the way that, for example, the US Congressional committees have direct access to the NAO equivalent, the Government Accountability Office (GAO). Nor do they have the equivalent of the Congressional Budget Office. On a more promising note, there are some changes here, although quite minor. The NAO has recently been involved in supporting the Scrutiny Unit and the Foreign Affairs Select Committee has requested that they carry out a *value for money* study on the British Council (a QUANGO). Traditionally the NAO has worked solely for the Public Accounts Committee.

Nevertheless, what select committees scrutinize is a matter of choice, something which they value, and they appear to choose topics for their inquiries in much the same way as they have always done. Whatever the constraints, through institutional rules and resources, select committees do conduct a large volume of high-quality work, producing numerous reports every year as our figures above demonstrate. They clearly choose not to focus on regular, systematic and detailed scrutiny of PSAs and remain wedded to the more traditional episodic "critical incident" approach noted by analysts (Commission on the Scrutiny Role of Parliament, 2001). This would suggest that both formal and informal institutional restraints are very powerful brakes on change, although change may occur incrementally.

These findings raise some fundamental issues about the move towards "government by performance" or "governance by outcomes" advocated by policy makers and some academics. If (and this is a large supposition) the executive arms of governments really are changing their policy making practices to be based more on outputs and/or outcomes rather than inputs, then traditional forms of scrutiny which focus on inputs (budget and actual spending) would need to adapt to this change. The evidence from the UK case suggests that such adaptation is difficult for the legislative branch to achieve. This could create a substantial democratic deficit if the two branches of government are operating different modes of evaluating policy – one based on performance and the other on traditional inputs- and process-based accountability.

There is a danger of creating less accountability if the executive change to alternative forms of policy formation and action while Parliament continues its current approach to scrutiny. The findings from this research and others (James, 2004) suggest that this has not occurred in the past because the executive has not, thus far, really implemented "government by performance" along the lines of its own rhetoric. If it did Parliament would be wise to respond more appropriately than has been the case thus far. Given that the comprehensive spending review in 2007 squeezed public expenditure, there might be those in government and the Treasury who see value in actually using the PSA system. Parliamentarians may need to think again about their priorities for scrutiny. On balance it would seem that it is Parliament rather than the executive which is currently most challenged by the PSA and other performance policy reforms.

10
Performance Information and Educational Policy Making

Åge Johnsen

We do not know a great deal about the way performance information is used in public policy in modern democracies (Pollitt, 2006b). Nonetheless, there lies a great potential for decision makers to use performance information to assess and enhance efficiency and effectiveness, as well as to provide feedback to stakeholders in the political system about the need for policy innovation. The tools that generate performance information include the use of performance indicators (PIs), performance audits and evaluations. This chapter focuses on the use of performance indicators as a means of informing public policy.

Accounting and management scholars are often inclined to see performance measurement as a strategic instrument for top-management only. In that view, the main function of performance management is to use the PIs tightly coupled to objectives in order to control an otherwise stubborn or inefficient bureaucracy. Performance information, for instance in the form of Balanced Scorecards or target regimes, is in that case used for implementing formal strategies based on objectives. This mechanistic, top-down view on performance management in public policy may be too normative and simplistic (Johnsen, 1999a; 2005). It may do public policy a disservice if that notion remains as the main characterization of performance management. In order to better understand the use of performance information in public policy, we need descriptive (positive) studies of politics and management.

This chapter analyses the use of performance information in public policy, with educational policy for primary schools in Norway under the former centre–right coalition government (Bondevik II, 2001–5) as a case. The policy of measuring educational outcomes, participating in international measurements such as the Program for International

Student Assessment (PISA), ranking schools and the publication of the results, were (and to some degree still are) contested issues in the government's educational policy. The case points to the fact that measurement does not dispose public policy from its conflicting interests and often tenacious underlying problems. This implies that both policy and the performance information arouse conflicts and are subject to trade-offs. It is therefore attractive to study the problems of performance measurement and management in established democracies. Just like policies, well-functioning performance measurement models may not be success stories but rather – and on the contrary – paradoxical and seemingly problematical.

This chapter is outlined as follows. The first section presents a life cycle framework for analyzing experiences with performance management in public policy. The second section gives an overview of important issues in Norwegian educational policies. The third section analyses the Norwegian case, using the life cycle framework of performance management. The final section discusses and concludes the analysis.

The life cycle of performance management practices in public policy

We define performance management in the public sector as the measurement, comparison and reporting of PIs of efficiency, effectiveness and equity with the intention to improve rational decision making in administrative and political processes (Johnsen, 2005). Performance management may consist of target systems, ranking systems or intelligence systems (Hood, 2007a).

Performance management is an often contested issue (Carter, 1991). It is understandable that some stakeholders resist it because of, for instance, increased measurement costs. Others may find more transparency a threat rather than a relief. In this sense, it could be perfectly rational to resist or postpone performance management reforms. In many of these cases however, resisting measurement and avoiding transparency is dysfunctional and blocks the potential benefits that often accrue late in the programmes. In order to make the best out of it, it is important for researchers, managers and policy makers to understand the politics of performance management.

In our analysis, we use a life cycle framework to study the politics of performance management (Carter, 1991; Johnsen, 2005; van Helden, Johnsen and Vakkuri, 2007). This cycle consists of five stages: design, implementation, use, impacts and evaluation of performance management models. The five stages framework builds on the notion from information economics that performance management is used rationally when the benefits exceed the costs (Mayston, 1985). These benefits and costs could vary over the model's life cycle as well as between different stakeholders. In this respect a large part of the costs may stem from maladoption in design, resistance in implementation, perverting behavior and dysfunctional effects. Typically, the costs will be higher than the benefits in the early stages of the life cycle, hence, there may be a tendency to resist and abort performance management before the major benefits materialize. There may also be a tendency in research and practice to focus on the costs rather than on the benefits. A life cycle approach may add consistency to the analysis of performance management and its politics by looking at the costs and benefits beyond the design and implementation stages.

Design

In the design stage, performance management systems are devised. Central questions in this stage are, for example: how should the measurements be conceptualized? Should contingencies and processes, as well as outputs and outcomes be measured? How often should measurements take place, and how shall the data be collected? Should all information be made public in order to facilitate transparency?

A performance management model will be conceptualized differently depending on the designer. Economists commonly label the performance management model a production model, political scientists an effect model, organization theorists an input–output model, and managers a value chain. The basic feature of many of the performance management models is that they visualize the involvement of stakeholders in some more or less well formulated policies and objectives. Many of the models also visualize that the measurement of performance is concerned with efficiency, effectiveness and equity. This list may be extended by adding concepts such as transparency, reliability and accountability. In order to manage these issues it is necessary to measure inputs, processes, outputs and outcomes (Bouckaert and Halligan, 2006; De Bruijn, 2002; Jackson, 1988). On a general level, the performance model is applicable to programmes, services and activities (Talbot, 2005).

In order to be decision-relevant some public sector performance management systems use targets. Target systems are controversial in public management (Hood, 2006). Nevertheless, in educational policy they seem to have a positive impact on performance. According to Boyne and Chen (2007) the presence of targets for pupils' exam results positively improved school performance. Even though there are many open questions regarding the impacts of targets, it remains to be seen whether this finding will affect educational policy.

The issue of whether to make performance information public is controversial. If policy making is a reserved matter for such actors as professionals, specialists and standing Parliamentary committees, the performance information does not need to be made public. If, on the other hand, policy making is also about educating and informing the public at large (March and Olsen, 1995), then there is a need for making performance information public.

Implementation

Typical questions in the implementation stage include: Will the system be introduced top-down or bottom-up? Should the implementation encompass all or only select services? Should the PIs be tightly or loosely coupled to objectives (see also Chapter 3 by Lægreid, Roness and Rubecksen)? Should implementation be conducted alone or in cooperation with others in projects and networks? Should external consultants be used, or should the management rely on or develop internal competence and capabilities? Should performance measurement be mandatory?

The process of generating acceptance and commitment is an overwhelming challenge even in experienced countries such as New Zealand and the United States (Halachmi, 2005; Norman, 2002). A failure to get acceptance may easily lead to paralysis or ritualism and cause problems in the subsequent stage of the life cycle. Paralysis may be the result of uncertainties regarding basic questions such as: Who are the major stakeholders? Who are the legitimate decision makers? From design and implementation studies, we know that management commitment is important (Cavalluzzo and Ittner, 2004; de Lancer Julnes and Holzer, 2001); and from management by objectives studies, we learn that participation from employees and middle-management is also important (Drucker, 1976; Likierman, 1993). Berman and Wang (2000) found that the organizational capacity to engage many stakeholders affected the implementation and use of performance measurement. Top and middle management, employees and stakeholders all need to be involved. Therefore, some degree of bottom-up and top-down processes seems to be warranted.

A persistent problem is to mandate performance measurement when some stakeholders' experience is that the cost exceeds the benefit. Halachmi (2005) argued against mandatory performance measurement, but without mandatory systems it would be difficult to obtain policy evidence since, in particular, the laggards will want to opt out. For the same reason, a strategy of making the public sector open and transparent with PIs will fail if measurement is not mandatory.

Use

Performance information is said to provide information that documents efficiency, effectiveness and equity, and that improves transparency, reliability and accountability. It is therefore difficult for policy makers to understand the resistance from professionals and unions against PIs. Equally puzzling for them is the apparently low interest in the use of performance information. This disillusionment often results from the absence of a cost benefit analysis of the uses. Some relevant questions in this stage are: How is the information going to be used? Who should collect and analyze the information? How can managers, politicians and citizens use performance information more intensively?

Benefits and costs are not confined to one way of using performance information. For example, Behn (2003) listed eight managerial uses: evaluating the performance of a public agency; controlling subordinates; budgeting public spending on programmes, people, and projects; motivating line staff, middle managers, nonprofit and for profit collaborators, stakeholders, and citizens to improve performance; promoting an agency relative to political superiors, legislators, stakeholders, journalists, and citizens when the agency is doing a good job; celebrating accomplishments that are worthy or important; learning what is working or not; and improving things that need to be done differently.

A benefit from making the information public is that organizations are pressured to assure that the data are valid, reliable and comparable. A counter argument is that by making information public, the incentive for gaming becomes stronger (de Bruijn, 2002; see also Radnor in Chapter 6). Gaming will, however, be mitigated when stakeholders scrutinize the data that runs counter to their interests. The problem of gaming could further be reduced by decoupling the PIs from objectives or the financial incentive systems, at least at the individual level.

A comparison of performance management systems in local government in the Netherlands and Norway found that the number of indicators was reduced over time (van Helden and Johnsen, 2002). This finding corroborates Carter's (1991) finding that during the implementation stage, the number of PIs often is reduced. This tendency could indicate that the PIs' quality is often low in the design stage and that some of the PIs have to be discarded or modified during the implementation and use stage. This finding may also indicate that extensive performance management systems are complex and costly to use and maintain once they shift from assessments off the cuff to rigorous PI systems. Therefore, the number of PIs often has to be reduced and focused on the most decision-relevant processes, outputs and outcomes.

Impacts

After a performance measurement system has been put into use, claims of costly measures, data with low reliability and validity, and critical reports of perverting behavior (De Bruijn, 2002) and dysfunctional effects (Smith, 1995) will emerge. The loudest voices will come from stakeholders and their lobbyists who perceive themselves as losers from policy changes. In this stage, the question is how to maintain a legitimate and cost-effective performance measurement system?

Public information about performance may have incentive effects for low performing organizations to adapt in a decentralized way as opposed to a centrally planned way (Johnsen, 2005), a trait that many – and particularly liberal – governments could favor. However, the policy of making PIs public, and to explicitly or implicitly use benchmarking and ranking, may be felt as threatening to some stakeholders, such as professions or unions. On the one hand, these management tools may be compatible with professional norms and interests – also professionals want to reduce uncertainty and address ambiguity. Performance information can be used to put issues on the agenda and to facilitate decision making (Askim, 2007a), which could improve performance and provide innovation. On the other hand, the professionals may claim that they want to discuss within their professions and with the government directly. PIs are seen as an intrusion of professional integrity (a point also made by Van de Walle and Roberts in Chapter 13). Therefore, performance management could increase the level of conflict in the polity.

PIs tend to lose their capacity to differentiate. Organizations alter their behavior in order to perform – or at least they make it appear as if they perform – as good as the best in the class. As a result, the PI no longer shows variation between organizations. This is the "running down" of performance measures (Meyer and Gupta, 1994). The solution is to replace these indicators with new measures that again introduce variability. Llewellyn and Northcott (2005) found, however, that performance is not always improved as some units for various reasons manage their performance to become "average." In this case, the impact on the indicators is the same. Although there is no improvement, variability decreases and PIs run down.

When the PIs run down, the performance management system needs to be redesigned. However, in order to be able to monitor efficiency and effectiveness over time there is a need for keeping some of the run-down PIs as comparable time series. Time series that currently show little variance need to be maintained in case the underlying performance again becomes a management issue. These maintenance tasks take resources from developing new and more salient measures. Maintaining the performance measurement system therefore requires a trade-off between many demands and costs.

Evaluation

Major evaluations of performance management systems can be seen either as a distinct stage in the life cycle or can be incorporated into each of the other stages. For example: in the design stage, there may be an evaluation of the system before a decision to go forward with implementation. The implementation stage may encompass pilot projects before full-scale implementation. The use stage may incorporate self-evaluation or independent evaluations in order to take the decision to continue, redesign or abort the system. Evaluation is not only about formal procedures, but also about public and scientific discourses. Evaluation, either as part of other stages or as a final stage, has its own costs and benefits that need to be incorporated in a total assessment of all costs and benefits.

The performance management literature gives many examples of perverting behavior and dysfunctional effects, but the overall or net impact of performance management on public policy may still be positive. It could be the case that negative effects, for instance the costs that professionals such as teachers have in relation to increased administrative burdens by filling in forms and reporting (Sangolt, 2003), are concentrated and hence more evident. Therefore, they may get more attention than positive effects that often are dispersed over many individuals and organizations in the society and over a long time. The positive impacts may be split in major effects such as effectiveness, accountability and policy innovation.

The case of educational policy making in Norway

The impact of educational reform on daily practice is a controversial issue. The pedagogical activities in the classes are often decoupled from administrative and institutional reforms (Weick, 1976). T. Hernes (2005) has identified four ideal type organizational responses to NPM reforms, and this chapter applies these potential responses in the subsequent analysis: (1) The first type is paralysis – the inability to take action or implement new reforms; (2) The second type is ritualistic decoupling – adaptation without implementation. If performance management is implemented and used unwisely, "politics" may contribute to paralysis or ritualistic decoupling; (3) The third type is loose coupling – which means a partial adaptation and implementation; (4) The last type is called organic adaptation, and this is cultural and interactive adaptation relative to existing professional communities. The underlying idea in organic adaptation, in contrast to formal adaptation, is that reform elements such as performance management systems have to be adapted to local circumstances in order to avoid paralysis, decoupling and loose coupling. Hence, mere mechanistic copying of a reform element may not be a desirable or ideal reform response.

Educational policy in Norway traditionally fitted the consensual and corporatist decision-making tradition, dominated by the ministry and teachers' unions (Bergesen, 2006). The Norwegian school system was perceived as comprehensive and produced almost exclusively by the public sector, which provided an equal education of high quality for all pupils regardless of social background and residence in the country. However, since the 1980s, this dominant perception and rhetoric has been challenged. Educational policy and the measurement of schools' performance became a contested issue.

In the late 1980s the OECD criticized Norwegian educational policy for lacking evidence on pupils' and schools' performance and for losing control after major decentralization reforms in the 1970s and 1980s (Ministry of Education and Religious Affairs, 1989). The OECD was worried that evaluation and use of exam results was to a large extent left to the local teachers, without the educational authorities being able or willing to create standardized tests and national evaluation (Horntvedt and Matthiesen, 1993). When economists analyzed the educational policy and proposed reforms for improving the performance of the Norwegian school system in the late 1980s and early 1990s (Friestad and Robertsen, 1990; NOU, 1991), however, these proposals were met with massive condemnation from many in the teachers' unions. Economists who in the 1990s and early 2000s wanted to study school performance using grades as output measures were not granted access to the grade data by the educational authorities.

During the 1990s the government implemented a mandatory local to central government reporting system (KOSTRA) that also encompassed some PIs for primary and secondary education. A former Minister of Education from the Labor Party, Gudmund Hernes, initiated Norway's participation in PISA. The publication of the first data from PISA was a major event in Norwegian educational policy and got massive media and political attention. The first PISA statistics from 2000 were published shortly after the centre–right Bondevik II government took office in the autumn of 2001. The statistics showed that Norwegian primary schools were underperforming in important educational fields such as literacy, maths and sciences, and social inclusion, even though the Norwegian school system was relatively resources intensive. Furthermore, the situation in the classrooms was often noisy and many felt that disciplinary problems were not adequately taken care of. The good news was that most pupils and teachers thrived in their daily activities.

In response to the criticism, the centre–right government's educational policy emphasized improving the pupils' basic skills in literacy, mathematics, foreign language, sciences and digital competence (St.meld, 30 (2003–4)). The Parliament met this educational reform with almost consensual approval. The PISA statistics underscored the new education consensus of the late 1990s, focusing more on basic educational skills. This focus traditionally had been the main argument in the Conservative Party's educational policy. Some parties had divergent views on how the performance information should be used, however. The policy of measuring, ranking and publication of school performance aroused resistance from the socialist parties, the teachers' unions and pupils' organization, as well as from some academic circles.

After the 2005 national election a centre–left (red–green) coalition government was formed, consisting of some of the parties that had been the most critical of the previous government's performance management policy. Although the new government pledged to change this policy, the new red–green government has continued the basic content of the educational policy as well as the Conservative Party's traditional critique of school performance. However, the red–green government did abolish publication of schools' mean grades and the ranking of schools (Bergesen, 2006).

The stages of performance management in the educational policy making

The following sections analyze performance management in the case of the Norwegian primary school educational policy, using each of the five stages of the life cycle model.

Designing the performance management system

Traditionally, the educational authorities have measured information on pupils, classes, teaching hours and schools (as well as costs) in order to compute average costs and estimate marginal costs. These data were (and are) required amongst others in budgeting decisions. In the public discourse on the new educational policy in Norway, the most controversial issues were the main objectives of education, whether and how to measure outputs, whether performance information on grades should be published and the schools should be ranked, and whether more private schools should be allowed. The political discourses not only facilitated the design of the performance management system, but also revealed the parties' positions and policies to the electorate. Thus, one benefit in the design stage is that by discussing the measurement of performance, the political parties reveal their policies and the electorate is better able to make informed choices.

The Norwegian performance management systems have largely been designed as intelligence and ranking (benchmarking) systems without including objectives and targets. In order for the performance information to fulfill its many roles, there was a need for different measures (Behn, 2003). A balanced measurement system was designed, encompassing structural features (input), pedagogical activities (processes) as well as pupils' test scores and grades (outputs). The inclusion of contextual factors prevented decision makers from claiming comparability across time and services when there is no comparability (Halachmi, 2005). The performance information therefore reported adjusted mean grades per school, controlling for the pupils' social background.

It is not self-evident that all performance measurement systems that have been designed should be implemented directly by the government. Performance is also monitored by political parties, interest groups, competitors, users and the professionals themselves (Hirschman, 1970; McCubbins and Schwartz, 1984). However, school performance is multi-dimensional and ambiguous. Leaving the measurement of school performance outside the realm of public policy would therefore have resulted in the absence of valid and reliable PIs. The design, implementation and use of such non-mandatory performance measurement systems by individual stakeholders would have been a very costly enterprise.

Implementing performance management

The implementation of the policy of measuring and ranking schools' performance led to a heated debate. Teachers' unions saw a hidden agenda of introducing market liberalism in the public school system.

This ideological turn in the debate caused problems since it mobilized hostility among some professionals' and pupils' organizations – in this case even long before implementation of the system started. The result of this process was partly ritualistic decoupled performance management in schools. Moreover, it resulted in a potential loss of votes amongst teachers for the governing parties. Therefore, it might have been useful in the implementation stage to start with some training and pilot projects in order to formally buffer these activities from the traditional administrative routines (Johnsen, 1999a). This kind of decoupling is not necessarily hypocrisy or double standards (Brunsson, 1989). These processes could be open and transparent for all interested stakeholders to see. One possible implication of piloting is that problems and resistance increase the likelihood of paralysis or ritualistic decoupling. In order to avoid this uncertainty, the government quickly moved to implementation (Brunsson, 1985). This strategy later caused problems in some of the measurement instruments (i.e., literacy) (Fevolden and Lillejord, 2005).

Initially, there were tensions between the political leadership of the Ministry of Education and the teachers' unions. The Minister of Education was a high-profiled liberalist (i.e., right-wing), while the leadership and many members of the teachers' unions were sympathetic to the left. However, the relationship between the Minister and the unions improved during the implementation stage, partly due to constructive discourses and cooperation on the content of the educational policy that the performance information provided.

A cost benefit analysis of the implementation stage makes clear that the development, piloting and testing of the systems requires many resources in addition to the political costs of exposure to conflicts. The benefits mainly stem from learning through the process of testing and piloting.

Using performance information

After the Norwegian Ministry of Education in 2004 declared their intention to publish the pupils' average examination scores for every primary school, some teachers sabotaged measurement by leaking the tests before the exams (Bergesen, 2006). In particular, the policy of conducting national tests and the ranking of schools aroused much resistance, especially from the political left. The major pupils' organization even encouraged pupils to boycott the national tests, even though the policy of conducting these test was democratically approved by a large majority in Parliament.

Cooperation with many other OECD countries in PISA was an important support for the government. When stakeholders criticized the measures for being unreliable, or that Norway was a special case beyond comparison, the government could point to standardized measures and the participation of other comparable states, such as Finland and the Netherlands in the PISA project. Finland, in particular, received much attention since the country got very good results, is comparable in size and is a Nordic country. In this way, it became more difficult for the opposition and other critical stakeholders such as the teachers' unions to claim a lack of evidence for low performance in the Norwegian school system (Bergesen, 2006). Hence, the government could use the PIs to withstand criticism on its educational policy. Political-administrative factors do have a profound impact on whether a system is used or whether it leads to paralysis or ritualistic decoupling.

Another critique from the teachers' union was doubt whether the performance information provided sufficient information for local action (Bergesen, 2006). Therefore, it was argued that the performance information is useless. Moynihan (2005b) offers a solution for this difficulty (see also his chapter in this volume). He argued that performance information can only be actively used when learning forums are established. These forums should analyze and act upon the information. Learning forums may provide an important factor in the use stage, facilitating loose couplings or organic adaptation and preventing paralysis and ritualistic decoupling. In municipal benchmarking in Norway 2002–4, the primary education networks achieved less organizational learning than health care networks (Askim, Johnsen and Christophersen, 2008). Teachers tend to be hostile towards performance management. Learning forums may be an important factor facilitating and explaining the use of the information and the impact of performance management. Developing learning forums at school level is until now a lacuna in Norwegian educational policy.

Impacts of performance management

The design, implementation and use of performance management often shift the balance of power in the polity. Traditionally, the Norwegian governance system was corporatist. Interference from other stakeholders due to public discourses on performance information does not fit with this corporatist model, since it reduces the unions' influence on public policy. Bergesen (2006) argued that before the centre–right Bondevik II government came to power, the Ministry of Education used to consult the teachers' unions before issuing policies. These traditions come under pressure. Although several stakeholders endorse this trend, the unions regard the policy of transparency as an intrusion into professionals' discretion. Therefore, making information available in the public realm is seen as a trade-off between introducing more performance management and transparency, versus traditional professional control and corporatist cooperation.

PIs seldom give answers – they do not function as "dials" metering the state of an issue. Rather, they function as "tin openers" (Carter, 1991) that indicate which boxes of problems different stakeholders ought to scrutinize more closely. There appears to be some truth in the slogan that "what gets measured gets done." Certain indicators function as incentives, and people and organizations adapt. For example, the first PISA statistics from 2000 documented that Norwegian pupils' performed badly in literacy, mathematics and sciences. The statistics from 2003 documented a further deterioration in sciences. Furthermore, performance varied systematically between the pupils depending on socio-economic factors. This finding contradicted the traditionally strong value of equality, and challenged the comprehensive school model – a school for everyone with no groups excluded. The debate following this publication was a major impetus for the centre–right government, as well as the subsequent red–green government, to reform the pedagogical content of the Norwegian school system. There is now a wide consensus between the political parties as well as in the teachers' unions that the Norwegian school system needs to focus more on improving basic educational skills (Olsen, 2006). Performance information clearly did facilitate policy innovation.

The motive for reforming the educational system in Norway was present for a long time – the relatively high use of resources has been known since the 1980s (NOU, 1991). The PISA statistics, however, provided the opportunity when it documented the low scores on literacy, mathematics and sciences. This perceived crisis gave the socialist parties an opportunity to renew and rejuvenate their policies. Socialist parties traditionally have a strong electoral base among teachers, and thus are reluctant about dramatic public sector reforms. The performance information from PISA on the Norwegian primary schools' bad performance opened a "window of opportunity" for reform (Paulsen, 2005).

Big reforms and radical changes on the macro level of society may reduce analytical capacity and comparability on the micro level. People may be preoccupied with implementing reforms without having the capacity to evaluate the reforms or to analyze and maintain reliable statistics over time. As a result, it may be difficult to assess whether the new reforms did in fact increase efficiency, effectiveness or equity. Nevertheless, this negative side-effect may be unimportant relative to the positive effect of identifying important issues to improve. The primary school sector in Norway may have experienced a "reform fatigue," but this fatigue stems largely from the many structural reforms since the 1980s that (unfortunately) haven't been accompanied by adequate performance measurements until recently.

Evaluating the educational performance management system

Performance information that helps politicians and other policy makers in expressing their views, get relevant evidence as feedback, and makes policy and society transparent, may be conducive to open and democratic discourses and processes (Popper, 1966). These political deliberations facilitate effectiveness because of their ability to inform policy decisions about the social benefits and costs of policy and policy failure. For example, inadequate literacy skills, as revealed by the PISA indicators, evoke high social costs for individuals as well as for society.

An ideal evaluation of the impact of performance management in the case of educational policy in Norway, for example the impact of joining PISA, would be based on before and after measurements of educational policy and school performance, as well as comparisons to a control group of countries not participating in PISA. Such evaluations, however, have not been conducted. What we can ascertain is that there is now a public discourse on social exclusion and pedagogy in Norway (Telhaug, 2007a; 2007b) that probably would not have taken place so intensively without the provision of performance information. The influence of this discourse on future policies may be substantial. It might further settle the shift from the traditional corporatist model to a more open form of policy making.

Discussion and conclusions

Rational actors may seek knowledge about the society to inform decision making, as well as to legitimate past decisions. Therefore, the efforts of the former centre–right and current red–green coalition governments to manage the educational policy by performance information seem laudable. A key question is, however, whether and how the information is used. The case of performance information in the Norwegian educational policy elucidates some aspects of this issue.

A somewhat paradoxical notion in the literature is that many actors demand performance information but seldom use it, even when there is ample supply. A common explanation is that politicians and managers use information for ritualistic purposes since systematic data collection is said to signal rationality. Another explanation asserts that people will ask for more information than they can use because they do not know how and when they are going to use the information (Feldman and March, 1981). The information needs to be on the shelf in order to be picked when a problem arises. As a result, much information is not used. A third explanation for the supply and demand paradox has to do with the quantitative nature of PIs. It is argued that politicians prefer to use rich information such as provided by personal conversations, face-to-face contacts and informal meetings, rather than formal information such as that provided by PIs (Daft and Lengel, 1990). The political system is complex with a division of labor and specialization (Thompson, 1967).

Some Parliamentary committees – typically the public accounts, finance and relevant standing committees – might be able to handle the technically demanding performance information. A lay person would often not understand all the complexities involved in using performance information in a meaningful way and therefore has to trust more knowledgeable colleagues and specialists (Ezzamel et al., 2008). This work echoes Anthony Downs's (1957) classical economic theory of democracy. His explanation was that politicians would only use the information if it was decision-relevant and cost-efficient relative to other information with regards to re-election. Most performance information concerns the past, but elections concern the future. Therefore, politicians focus on budgets and programs, which they often regard to be the most cost-efficient and decision-relevant information. A potential conclusion from politicians' seemingly low use of performance information could be that performance management for public policy is futile. It is seen as ritualistic decoupling, rhetoric and symbolic politics. The Norwegian case, however, does not support this view.

A study from Norwegian local government documented that politicians use performance information relatively often (Askim, 2007a; see also Askim in Chapter 8 in this volume). It should be noted that Norwegian local and central government authorities have put much effort into the development of different performance management systems since the early 1980s. Even if politicians do not use PIs as much as many would have hoped for, we have to ask whether it is the politicians' task to do so. Developing, reporting, scrutinizing and monitoring performance is a common task for the many lobbyists, political advisors and accounting and auditing experts. The majority of the politicians would often only be concerned with the information in special cases or where major deviations occur. In other cases, politicians are briefed based on performance information, maybe even without recalling that the information stems from formal performance management systems. Therefore, performance information may be used more, and at a more advanced level, than is often assumed.

The Norwegian case highlights two issues. First, relevant information is available but central actors (in this case leftist political parties, the teachers' unions and the pupils' organizations) do not want to use the information. This implies that politics and interests are important for understanding performance management in public policy. Second, low performance gets most of the attention and this in spite of the "learning from best practice" rhetoric. In public management, as opposed to business management, there is a tendency to "learn from bad performance." In the public sector, avoiding low performance that could result in "naming and shaming" could be as strong an incentive as performing well. There might not be any strong incentive in performing "best" because the "winner" hardly "takes it all" in public management. It may rather be that "the loser loses it all." For many public services avoiding low performance, by achieving a certain basic or average level of performance for specific (often vulnerable) users and clients, could be more important than achieving a high level of service. Therefore, in public policy and management, it may be more important to avoid being "bad" than being "best." In order to understand the emphasis on bad performance and the incentives it creates, several complementary perspectives may be useful.

A system perspective explains that, in a self-regulating system, one would focus on negative or positive deviations. Any feedback on big deviations from the normal, or expectations of such deviation, would eventually trigger actions to balance the system. The system perspective may in this way explain the focus on deviations but not the emphasis on bad performance.

A media perspective with a focus on political communication might point to the fact that media and voters find it easy to react to negative performance. Dramaturgical tools of the "media society," such as making a story dramatic, personalized and conflict ridden (Hernes, 1978) are, as it were, created for bad news. For public administrators and politicians, avoiding unduly negative attention may, therefore, be a better career or re-election strategy than trying to stick out as high performing.

Third, a political–administrative perspective may explain why it might be easier for the administration and government to agree on – or at least to admit the responsibility for – low performance, than for identifying or taking the credit for high performance. For the Opposition, there is not much reward in identifying high performance. It is exposing and blaming low performance that may eventually bring the Opposition into the ministerial seats after the next election. In some instances, it is also important for the ruling government to identify bad performance. Bad performance could reframe a problem in such a way that the government could motivate, mobilize and legitimate change (Brunsson, 1985). Hence, focusing on performance below par may pay off both for administrators and for politicians who want change.

The main conclusion is that performance management is important for public policy because it informs public discourse. The history, institutions and practices of public policy vary between countries. The national culture as well as the educational policy in Norway has traditionally emphasized equality. Norway has often had minority and/or coalition governments, but the ruling parties have had divergent educational policies. The emphasis has therefore often been on formulating policy and implementing reforms. Managing performance may therefore have slipped into the background until PISA and other statistics made the performance public and the need for policy innovation urgent.

Even though stakeholders use performance information selectively according to their ideologies and interests, its contribution to public deliberations is important for democratic societies. Performance information may enhance transparency, improve decision making and facilitate policy innovation. At the same time, the analysis of performance management in five stages shows that the performance management life cycle is in itself subject to politics, as is the policy that the performance management was supposed to inform in the first place. The use of the life cycle framework can provide a better balance in analyses of the costs and benefits of performance management systems than is often the case because it takes all stages into consideration.

Hopefully, this chapter has given food for thought for researchers and policy makers. The purpose has been to analyze how performance information is used in public policy. In conclusion, we do not want to contribute to a fatalist conception of performance management – far from it. Even the efforts to resist, boycott and sabotage performance measurement, as well as the widespread tendency to use relevant performance information selectively in lobbying, are evident signs of a system that is used and working. The impact of performance management on specific policies and their long-run outcomes, however, needs further research.

11
Rational, Political and Cultural Uses of Performance Monitors: The Case of Dutch Urban Policy

Dennis de Kool

The New Public Management was a catalyst for monitoring activities in the public sector (Bouckaert, De Peuter and Van Dooren, 2003; Mayne and Zapico-Goni, 1997; Vedung, 1997). The Netherlands is no exception with amongst others a drug monitor, an integration monitor and a traffic mobility monitor. These monitors track policy-relevant developments in a systematic and periodic way. Although monitoring of policy processes is quite common in the public sector, the utilization of these monitors remains under-explored (Poister, 1983; Vedung, 1997). In the current mode of monitoring, rational assumptions are dominant (De Kool and van Buuren, 2004). This chapter argues that besides the rational approach, we need cultural and political perspectives for a better understanding of the utilization of monitors.

This chapter analyzes the utilization of information generated by monitoring activities within Dutch Urban Policy (Grotestedenbeleid or GSB in Dutch). Dutch Urban Policy has been monitored since 1995 by means of the Dutch Urban Policy Monitor (Jaarboek GSB in Dutch). Both the national government and the cities participate in this monitoring activity. This chapter, first, looks at the characteristics of Dutch Urban Policy and the accompanying monitoring program. It then distinguishes between theoretical approaches to utilization of monitors and the critical factors for utilization of monitors that these theoretical approaches suggest. Finally, it uses the case of the Dutch Urban Policy Monitor to draw conclusions about the (lack of) utilization.

This case study consists of a document analysis of Dutch Urban Policy, the Dutch Urban Policy monitor, reports of national–local government meetings and 36 semi-structured interviews with key actors within the Dutch Urban Policy program (De Kool, 2007). Stakeholders (civil servants and politicians) at the national level (several ministries), the local level (cities) and other relevant actors have been interviewed. Respondents and documents from five different cities have been selected, two big cities (Rotterdam and Utrecht) and three medium-sized cities (Haarlem, Den Bosch and Dordrecht).

Characteristics of Dutch Urban Policy and the accompanying monitoring program

In this section, I will first explore the notion of monitoring. Then I will discuss the role of monitoring within Dutch Urban Policy.

Monitoring

The rise of New Public Management is one of the most remarkable international trends in public administration (Hood, 1991). Important elements of NPM are the emphasis upon outputs and outcomes, transparency, accountability, performance measurement and service quality (Hood, 1991; Pollitt, 2003). This development has resulted in the expansion of performance measurement systems such as bench-marking, auditing and monitoring (Bouckaert, De Peuter and Van Dooren, 2003; Mayne and Zapico-Goni, 1997; Poister, 1983; Power, 1999).

Monitors have the following five features (Engbersen, 1997; Verweij, Goezinne and Dijkstra, 1995):

- Monitoring is a systematic activity. That means that monitoring activities are not ad hoc or incidental, but repeated activities that use more or less standard research methods and indicators to measure developments.
- Monitoring is a periodic activity with a repetitive character.
- Monitoring is focused upon developments. The assumption is that there are at least two measurement moments, t (0) and t (1) that can be compared.
- These developments are policy relevant; there is a connection between monitoring and the policy process.
- Monitoring results in a description. Generally, this description comes as a report. Sometimes, the findings become part of a database.

Based on these characteristics, monitoring will be defined as *the systematic and periodic observation and description of policy-relevant developments*. The information generated by monitors can feed into the different needs of policy makers and politicians. Empirical research has shown that policy monitors fulfill one or more of the following functions (De Kool and van Buuren, 2004):

- *Signaling*: monitoring enables policy makers and politicians to look for relevant policy developments and trends.
- *Steering and accounting*: monitoring enables policy makers and politicians to gather information in order to assess whether the produced outputs (policy results) or outcomes (policy effects) of a policy program require different interventions; and to account for the achieved results.
- *Learning*: monitoring facilitates "first loop" and "second loop learning", in which the feedback of actual results can lead to a re-assessment of the efficacy and efficiency of policy interventions, as well as to a re-assessment of the assumptions which lay behind a policy program (Argyris and Schön, 1996).
- *Communicating*: monitoring supports the agenda setting between relevant stakeholders in a policy sector, through the provision of a transparent and accessible common information pool.

Dutch Urban Policy

The socio-economic situation of the big cities in the Netherlands has deteriorated since the 1960s. In order to change this situation, the Dutch government initiated the Dutch Urban Policy program in 1994. The policy goals were the improvement of the livability, safety and economic vitality of the big cities in the Netherlands (Verweij and Goezinne, 1996). The Ministry of Home Affairs has been responsible for the coordination of the program (Ministerie van Binnenlandse Zaken en Koninkrijksrelaties, 2004b). In the beginning, the program included only the four largest cities (Amsterdam, The Hague, Rotterdam and Utrecht – the so-called "Big 4" or G4). In 1995 and 1996, 21 medium-sized cities joined the program, followed in 1999 by another five cities. Sittard-Geleen joined the program in 2006. Today, 31 big cities are part of Dutch Urban Policy. The development of Dutch Urban Policy has gone through three stages. Table 11.1 shows the main characteristics of Dutch Urban Policy in the three successive periods.

Table 11.1 Main characteristics of Dutch Urban Policy

	First period 1995–9	Second period 2000–4	Third period 2005–9
Phase of development	"Pioneering"	"Developing"	"Maturing"
Covenant	"One size fits all"	Tailor-made	Tailor-made
Basis of covenant	Action plans were based on the covenant	City vision and long-term development programs	Long-term development programs
Basis of financial allocation	Projects	Specific Purpose Grants	Broad Special Purpose Grants
Process goals	• Degree of integration • Decentered approach • Measurable results	• Degree of integration • Decentered approach • Measurable results (outcomes) • Partnerships	• Degree of integration • Decentered approach • Measurable results (outputs) • Partnerships • Less bureaucracy
Role of monitor	Research	Policy document	Integral report
Number of involved cities	4 => 25	25 => 30	30 => 31

First period (1995–1999)

In the first "pioneering" period, the national government signed a covenant with the four largest cities, in which they agreed on the main policy priorities – that is, labor, education, livability and care and safety (Verweij and Goezinne, 1996). For each of these themes, they decided on measurable results. On the basis of this covenant, the cities had to produce action plans, in which the cities formulated "what" they would do (results) and "how" (projects). These action plans can be seen as the predecessors of the long-term development programs in the second and third period (see discussion below). The national government allocated financial resources to projects based on these plans. Since 1995, policy developments in the 30 cities have been reported annually in the Dutch Urban Policy Monitor (Jaarboek Grotestedenbeleid in Dutch). The formal object of the Dutch Urban Policy Monitor is "to generate insight into the annual progress of the social, physical and economic developments and the policy of the 30 cities, based on the agreed goals and the measured indicators that are related to these policy goals" (Ministerie van Binnenlandse Zaken en Koninkrijksrelaties, 2004b: 13, own translation). This means that an important intended function of this monitor is to make relevant developments in the cities transparent for all the parties involved in the Dutch Urban Policy. The emphasis was on signaling (Ministerie van Binnenlandse Zaken en Koninkrijksrelaties, 2002: 7).

Second period (2000–2004)

In the second "developing" period, the national government signed tailor-made covenants with each individual city, instead of a one-size-fits-all agreement with the Big 4. The action programs and projects were supplemented by the so-called long-term development programs (Meerjarige Ontwikkelingsprogramma's in Dutch). These programs contained measurable goals and performances. During this period, the attention was primarily directed at policy outcomes (effects). Modest attempts have been made to make a causal connection between outcomes and policy efforts. In these policy documents, equal partnership relations between national government and the cities are emphasized. The policy has been divided into three so-called "pillars": a physical, an economic and a social pillar. Although the ministry created three pillars to intensify policy coordination, the financial allocation structures were based on many specific-purpose grants, each with their own way of steering and accounting. The Ministry of Housing, Spatial Planning and the Environment was the co-coordinator of the physical pillar; the Ministry of Economic Affairs coordinated the economic pillar and the Ministry of Health, Welfare and Sports was prima rily responsible for the coordination of the social pillar. Since 2002, the consulting firm Ecorys has been carrying out the annual monitoring on behalf of the Ministry of Home Affairs. In the new monitoring design, more attention is being given to policy results (both input, output and outcome). Besides signaling policy outcomes, the functions of learning and even evaluation become more important. Apart from this "general" monitor, there are specific monitors within the pillars too. The monitor Urban Renewal (monitor Stedelijke Vernieuwing in Dutch) monitored progress within the physical pillar. The Benchmark Municipal Entrepreneurship (Benchmark Gemeentelijk Ondernemersklimaat in Dutch) has the same function for the economic pillar. The monitor of the social pillar has never been developed.

Third period (2005–2009)

In March 2005, the national government and the cities have signed new "performance" covenants for the third "maturing" period, which are based on the new long-term development programs of the cities. In contrast to the second period, the main focus is not on outcomes (effects), but on output (results). First, it was argued that exogenous factors hindered the attribution of outcomes to policy initiatives. A second reason is that it was found impossible to determine whether outcomes had been realized, since they could not be formulated in concrete measurable indicators (Ministerie van Binnenlandse Zaken en Koninkrijksrelaties, 2004a: 14). In the new system, cities will potentially have to reimburse some of the grants at the end of the covenanting period if they do not reach agreed performances. A third reason for reducing the number of outcome indicators was the bureaucratic overload which was created by the multitude of specific arrangements with their own demands for rendering accounts.

Several initiatives have been taken to reduce the monitoring bureaucracy. Different specific subsidies and their accountability mechanisms have been combined into three "Broad Special Purpose Grants" (Brede Doel Uitkeringen or BDUs in Dutch): (1) physical; (2) economy; and (3) social, integration and safety. In this way, the national government intends to reduce bureaucracy and stimulate integrated policy making on the local level. Another way of reducing the administrative burden is a lower frequency of monitors. Instead of annual reports, only three monitors will be published in the third period of Dutch Urban Policy. One monitor in 2005 (zero-measurement), a second report in 2007 (mid-term review) and the final report in 2009 (final measurement). Not only will the frequency be reduced, but also the number of monitors. It is the aim of the Ministry that one integrated monitor will generate information in a single integrated process. This should reduce administrative burdens (Ministerie van Binnenlandse Zaken en Koninkrijksrelaties, 2004b). The integrated monitor will have two functions during the third period. First, to signal the progress of output agreements as stipulated in the performance covenants and, to a far lesser extent, signal a limited number of outcomes. Second, the monitor will have to support the steering and accountability process (Ministerie van Binnenlandse Zaken en Koninkrijksrelaties, 2004b: 53–4).

Theoretical approaches to utilization and critical factors

I will discuss three approaches to monitoring and utilization, a rational approach, a political approach and a cultural approach. These three perspectives are not mutually exclusive. For each approach, I discuss the meaning of monitoring, the meaning of utilization, and critical factors for utilization.

Rational approach to monitoring and utilization

The rational approach to monitoring highlights the goals of governmental policies. The policy process is conceptualized as a series of subsequent stages (Hoogerwerf and Herweijer, 1998). The policy is seen as a rational plan and the collection of information is seen as fact finding in order to improve the effectiveness of the policy (process).

Utilization means that "facts" generated by monitoring improve policy making. The rational utilization approach is based on several assumptions. The first assumption is that utilization is a goal-oriented (decision-driven) process (Weiss, 1977). The information needs of the (potential) users are expected to be clear, unambiguous and rational. The second assumption is that the role of the information source is clear: monitors serve as providers of facts. This information is used to identify possible policy alternatives and support decision-making processes *or* can result in argued choices not to use the information. The third assumption is that utilization is a linear process. Within the logic of consequentiality (March and Olsen, 1989) actors behave in a predictable way: the policy cycle starts with a problem, then information is collected and used to solve the problem, and finally policy choices are made. The fourth assumption is that information is used in a direct way (Beyer and Trice, 1982; Dahler-Larsen, 1998; Weiss, 1977). The rationale is that data from monitors are used immediately to improve policy programs.

The rational approach suggests several critical factors for utilization. The first is the reliability of monitors (Dahler-Larsen, 1998; Weiss and Bucuvalas, 1980). The second critical factor is the relevance of monitors. The third critical factor is the goal orientation of monitors. This factor assumes a policy theory (Hoogerwerf and Herweijer, 1998). The fourth critical factor is the usefulness of monitors (Hanney et al., 2004; Lindblom and Cohen, 1979). Table 11.2 contains the critical factors and indicators. The expected utilization of monitors within the rational approach can be formulated as follows: the more reliable, relevant, goal-oriented and useful monitors are, the higher the utilization of monitors.

Political approach to monitoring and utilization

The political approach highlights the (conflicting) stakes of the involved actors. The policy process is approached as an arena in which actors

Table 11.2 Critical factors and indicators of rational utilization

Rational utilization approach	
Critical factor	**Indicator**
Reliability	Information is unambiguous, valid and/or grounded
Relevance	Information is complete and/or actual
Goal-orientation	Monitor is grounded in policy theory
Usefulness	Policy goals and indicators of monitors are connected and/or supply and demand of information are in balance

fight for power. The policy is seen as a negotiated outcome in a political struggle. Within the political approach, information generated by monitoring is seen as a powerful resource, which can be strategically (mis-) used to protect the specific positions and interests of the various stakeholders (Bekkers, 1994; Feldman and March, 1981).

Within the political utilization approach, monitors are potential sources of power and are used to defend the interests of the involved actors. The political utilization approach is based on several assumptions. The first assumption is that policy goals are not given, but related to the individual positions and stakes of the involved actors. Actors only use information to favor their own positions (Pfeffer, 1992). The second assumption is that actors are not rational but political. Within this political context, information that does not serve the needs of actors is ignored or manipulated (Pfeffer, 1992; Stone, 1997). The third assumption is that utilization is not a linear, but an unpredictable process. Because of the different strategies of different actors, the exchange of information has an unpredictable and dynamic character. Not only the positions, but also the preferences of the actors may change. The same goes for the perceived strategic value of monitoring information. The fourth assumption is that information can be misused, or used in manipulative or selective ways. *Misuse* is the deliberate withholding, ignoring or distorting of information (e.g., information that is unfavorable to the actor). *Manipulation* means to deliberately create confusing images. Using fictitious numbers in statistics is an example (Stone, 1997). *Selective utilization* means that only information that maintains or strengthens the position of the actor(s) is used, while other information is strategically ignored (Pfeffer, 1992).

Utilization in the political approach depends on the availability of accessible and trusted data with a small distance to established interests. The first critical factor is access to monitors. Getting and maintaining access to information generated by monitoring is a potential source of power (Pfeffer and Salancik, 1978). The second critical factor is trust. Developing trust between actors is an important condition to guarantee the exchange of information (see also Koppenjan and Klijn, 2004). Actors that are not committed to monitoring may react by concealing information. The third critical factor has to do with the interests of the potential users. Information is more likely to be used when it is not counter-intuitive and when it supports the interests of the actor (Weiss and Bucuvalas, 1980). Policy makers are likely to ignore information that is not in accordance with their stakes and preferences (Weiss and Bucuvalas, 1980). The fourth critical condition is the level of competition between the different information sources. Policy makers can make use of competing sources of information (Lomas, 2000: 144). Therefore, monitors have to compete with other potential sources of information. Table 11.3 summarizes the critical factors and indicators.

Cultural approach to monitoring and utilization

The cultural approach highlights the ritual dimension of policy making. The policy process is approached as a theatre, in which different actors

Table 11.3   Critical factors and indicators of political utilization

Political utilization approach	
Critical factor	**Indicator**
Access to information	Information is available to the actors
Trust	Actors have a positive image about the intention of other actors
Interests of potential users	The monitor is in line with individual and/or collective interests
Competing information sources	The monitor is perceived as the most important source of information

play their roles. Within this approach, monitors are seen as sources of meaning that give both sense to the activities of the involved actors and a way to express common language and direction (Dahler-Larsen, 1998; Beyer and Trice, 1982).

Within the cultural utilization approach, monitors are sources of meaning and are used to express common grammar and direction. The cultural utilization approach is based on several assumptions. First, utilization of information is related to institutionalized patterns of expectations of potential users. These patterns are shaped by organizational norms. The second assumption is that information from monitors serves as a source of sense making. Within this perspective, monitors are seen as "social constructions that make sense" (Weick, 1995). Information gathering and utilization can be symbols of modernity, rationality, efficiency and effectiveness, and devices of "good" management. Monitors offer a way of showing conformity to shared norms of rationality and progress (performance improvement). The third assumption is that the utilization process follows a rather congruent path. This has to do with the cultural-institutional setting in which actors operate. This setting results in specific norms and acceptable ways of acting. Actors act according to the logic of appropriateness (March and Olsen, 1989). The fourth assumption is that utilization in some cases could be a mere symbolic expression, which means, for example, that information is used to legitimize decisions already made (Vedung, 1997) or to *display* authority, symbolize proper management and control, represent competence, inspire confidence and reaffirm social virtue (Feldman and March, 1981).

Utilization of monitors within the cultural approach depends on the meaningfulness, recognizability, and interactive character of monitors, and the connection of monitors with existing frames of references. The first critical factor is meaning. Within the cultural approach (collecting) information has a value in itself (Feldman and March, 1981). For that reason, monitoring becomes a goal instead of a means. The second critical factor is recognizability. It is important that the policy concepts and problems are recognized and shared by the actors involved (Beyer and Trice, 1982). The third critical factor is frames of reference (Weiss, 1980) Every actor has specific habits and routines. For this reason it is important that monitors match these existing practices. The fourth critical factor is interaction. Interaction during monitoring activities can create a common language and shared experiences (Fidler and Johnson, 1984). Table 11.4 summarizes the critical factors and indicators.

Table 11.4   Critical factors and indicators of cultural utilization

Cultural utilization approach	
Critical factor	**Indicator**
Meaning	Actors are concerned with monitoring
Recognizability	Monitor expresses shared problems
Frames of references	Monitor is connected to existing practices
Interaction	Monitors support interaction and collaboration

What does the case of the Dutch Urban Policy Monitor tell us about the (lack of) utilization?

In this section, I will interrogate the theoretical framework with empirical findings from the Dutch Urban Policy case. I will systematically discuss the rational, political and cultural approaches.

Rational utilization of the Dutch Urban Policy Monitor

The theoretical assumption of rational utilization is: the more reliable, relevant, goal-oriented and useful monitors are, the higher the utilization of monitors. In the perception of the national government, the monitor is sufficiently *reliable*. However, some cities criticize the lack of robust indicators in the monitor; for example for safety, because this issue is being measured at present in different ways by the cities. The cities also complain about the lack of robust indicators within the social pillar of the policy program. Nevertheless the cities recognize that it can be very difficult to find adequate policy indicators. Expressed doubts about the methodological quality and the reliability of the information can have rational reasons, but political reasons as well (see political utilization).

The respondents do not agree about the relevance of the monitor. Some cities state that the monitor has too much the character of a "telephone book." However, cities also expressed the need for more local information at the district level. City officials have conflicting ideas about the extent of the annual yearbook. Some local respondents stated that the size of the yearbook is too large, while other local respondents expressed the need for more detailed information (preferably on a district level). Generally, city officials are more interested in the main lines while the civil servants prefer more detail.

The national government acknowledges that some blind spots exist, for example information about the accessibility of cities. A rational explanation is that actors were unable to formulate adequate indicators to measure these themes.

The respondents give double signals about the *currentness* of the monitor too. On the one hand some respondents state that the frequency of the monitor is too high for signaling (developments in cities are slow) – "There are no big changes and developments in the space of one year" (interview). On the other hand, the frequency is too low for steering. The monitor is published in autumn, which is too late for it to play a role in the local planning and control cycle. The cities, however, indicate that most of the information is already known before the report is published.

The respondents from the Ministry of Home Affairs highlight the importance of a strict *goal-orientation*, with clear and concrete policy goals before a monitoring system can be developed. These goals should be SMART (specific, measurable, acceptable, realistic and time-bound). However, reality shows that most of the policy goals are not clear and concrete. The general goal for the first period was to improve the livability, safety and economic vitality of the cities. The covenant only states that the goals will be made more explicit when possible. The second period is focused on nine (general) outcome goals. In the third period these goals have been limited to five outcome goals that have been translated into many output indicators.

At the start of the Dutch Urban Policy, the link between policy goals and indicators was very weak, which affected the *usefulness of the monitor*. The national government recognizes, though, that the indicators in the monitor sometimes did correspond to the policy goals. This makes translation of information to policy difficult. Since 2002, more attention has been given to policy results and policy learning. However, the Ministry of the Interior and Kingdom Relations highlights the fact that direct utilization is not the aim of the monitor, because of the programmatic character of Dutch Urban Policy (long-term focus). Furthermore, the monitor has a strong focus on presenting information on an aggregated level ("totals"), while cities prefer getting information on a local and district level ("details"). It is difficult to meet these needs with a single instrument.

The significance of the monitor for rational utilization seems to be limited. The main use seems to be that national departments and politicians get information about policy developments in the cities. The Dutch Urban Policy Monitor is hardly used for steering activities for several (rational) reasons. The first reason is the lack of clear policy goals. The second reason is the invalid connection between some policy goals and the indicators in the monitor. The third reason is that monitors do not provide explanations for developments. The local civil servants use the monitor as a reference book (passive utilization) for their local reports. The lack of interest of local politicians is striking.

Political utilization of the Dutch Urban Policy Monitor

The political approach expects utilization under the following conditions: the more accessible, the more trust; the smaller the distance with vested stakes and the more important monitors are for the fulfillment of the own tasks, the higher the utilization of monitors.

The *access* to the Dutch Urban Policy Monitor seems not to be problematic for most of the actors involved. Generally speaking, the annual yearbook is distributed widely. Most of the interviewed actors are familiar with the annual monitor report, especially the civil servants. Some local politicians were less acquainted with the monitor, but this has more to do with a lack of interest in the "national" monitor than with a lack of access. In terms of access to intergovernmental platforms, all involved parties are participating. The founding cities had some reservations about the access of new cities, because they feared that broadening Dutch Urban Policy could result in fewer funds for the individual cities, given that the total budget is fixed.

Policy documents of the Ministry of Home Affairs highlight that Dutch Urban Policy is a new intergovernmental practice, a co-production in which mutual understanding and *trust* is very important (Ministerie van Binnenlandse Zaken en Koninkrijksrelaties, 2004b). However, the national government admits that intergovernmental monitoring can increase distrust. Most of the cities approach intergovernmental monitoring activities as a signal of distrust. Monitoring obligations are felt to run counter to the level of intergovernmental trust. However, this does not mean that cities are against accountability and monitoring. The cities have the impression that some ministries have more trust in local capacities (e.g., the Ministry of Home Affairs, the Ministry of Agriculture, Nature and Food Quality, the Ministry of Public Health, Welfare and Care and the Ministry of Economic Affairs) than other ministries (Ministry of Social Affairs and Ministry of Justice).

In Dutch Urban Policy, the stakeholders have different *interests*. The coordinating Ministry of Home Affairs has interest in an effective and integrated Dutch Urban Policy. For this reason, this ministry needs information to get insight into the progress of the Dutch Urban Policy. The Dutch Urban Policy Monitor has to fulfill this national need for information. The national government also needs information on how the national funds were spent: "Our ministry wants to check to what extent the policy goals have been met and tries to get an aggregated picture of the Dutch Urban Policy-cities together" (interview).

The other ministries focus more on the progress within their own policy domain and therefore are more skeptical about a cross-cutting monitoring device. Ministries do not want to give up on their own information and financial channels with the cities. They do not want to lose control over their policy domain. Therefore, it has been difficult to cluster financial flows. The topic of clustering financial flows has already been on the political agenda since 1987. The development of the Broad Purpose Grants in the third period can be seen as an important step forward. For this reason the departments want "their" indicators in the monitoring program.

The cities' interests lie with getting (extra) financial resources, getting information about the progress within their own city (on the level of districts), modest monitoring systems (as few indicators as possible), more policy space (decentralization), low administrative burdens and no double accounting practices. The cities have no interest in getting insight into the progress of the Dutch Urban Policy in general, although there is a modest need to make comparisons with other cities. The cities have also been a strong supporter of Broad Purpose Grants, because it means more flexibility and fewer administrative burdens. However, different cities have different interests (G4 and other cities for example). Cities are competing for national Dutch Urban Policy resources. Different interests can also be found between politicians and civil servants. Most politicians are interested in the general picture, while policy departments and local civil servants are more interested in details (both quantitative facts and qualitative analyses). The different interests also become explicit in the discussion about the translation of the general policy goals into concrete measurable indicators. As stated before, this (strategic) discussion about the content and number of indicators takes place in the developing stage of the monitors.

Both the cities and the national government obtain their policy information from different sources, so monitors have to *compete* with other sources of information. For the national government, the goal of the annual monitor (and different sectoral monitors) is to provide and obtain information about the progress of the Dutch Urban Policy.

As a result, the cities perceive this monitor as a "national" instrument that is more valuable to the national government than to cities. Furthermore, the cities state that "local" sources of information are better connected to the local policy practices. For this reason, cities prefer their "own" sources of information, such as local monitors, local management reports and so on. This information is more detailed and considered more meaningful. Competing sources of information, for example the "Stedenatlas," seem to have a competitive advantage for the cities. The local policy programs are the primary points of references. The goals and agreements made within the frame of the Dutch Urban Policy are placed within the local policy frames and not the other way round. On the national level, we also see a competitive advantage of "specific" departmental information for the ministries at the expense of the "general" Dutch Urban Policy monitor. Both the cities and the ministries prefer their own information channels which, therefore, makes the monitor less strategically important to them.

The *political significance* of the Dutch Urban Policy Monitor is limited, although there is some variety according to the interests of the involved actors. The most important political function of the monitor is strategic learning. The national government uses the positive results in the monitor to support its claims of success (and to attribute negative results to external factors). The cities use the information in the monitor selectively to support their requests for more national resources.

Cultural utilization of the Dutch Urban Policy Monitor

The theoretical expectation of the utilization of monitors within the cultural approach is: the more meaningful, recognizable and interactive the character of the monitors, and the better the connection of monitors with existing frames of references, the higher the utilization of monitors.

In terms of *significance*, it is very important that information generated by monitors is connected to the existing level of knowledge of the potential users. Local politicians especially lack specific knowledge about the Dutch Urban Policy. Some of them were even unaware of the existence of the monitor. This demonstrates that they primarily focus on local information. Local civil servants are better informed about the monitor, although they attribute more significance to their "own" local sources of information. The monitor is perceived to be too abstract – even for local civil servants. On the national level, most policy departments attribute more significance to their own sectoral policies and regulations. National politicians attribute more value to oral information (personal communication). Finally local aldermen are more interested in the main lines and general results, while research departments are more interested in details and methodology.

The document "Deltaplan" (1994) in which the G4 have formulated their common problems and challenges was an important shared framework. By introducing the Dutch Urban Policy, the national government gave a signal that they *recognize* the concerns of the cities. The monitor has played a role in the development of a common agenda. Nevertheless the big cities perceive problems differently than the other cities. The G4 claimed that their problems are more serious than those of the smaller cities. The national government recognized the singularity of the cities by signing unique covenants with each individual city.

There seems to be a *disconnection* between the national and the local frames of reference. The extent and range of the monitor has been reduced over time, partly on the request of the cities. In addition, attempts have been made to foster policy learning founded on the basis of the monitor. The Ministry of Home Affairs is also aware of some symbolic issue. From 2003, the name of the Ministry of Home Affairs is no longer mentioned on the cover of the yearly report, to express that the monitor is a common instrument. However, the perception of the cities remains that the monitor is a national instrument that does not accommodate local needs. For the cities, the districts are the primary point of reference. Moreover, Dutch Urban Policy is an integral part of the broader local policy. The local practices and policy programs are the first point of reference for the cities. Finally we can observe differences between the cities. The big cities are better equipped for monitoring activities than the smaller cities.

From the beginning the national government has highlighted the vital importance of good *interaction* with the cities. The communication strategy was aimed at the creation of a common bond between the national government and the cities. Respondents from the national government state that the Dutch Urban Policy has increased intergovernmental interactions. These interactions have a positive influence on collaboration (Expertgroep Brinkman, 1998; Ministerie van Binnenlandse Zaken en Koninkrijksrelaties, 1998). Local civil servants confirm that collaboration has been intensified. Both the national government and the cities have become aware of a mutual interdependence.

The cultural *significance* of the Dutch Urban Policy Monitor is broad and diverse. The most important cultural function of the monitor for both the national government and the cities is that this instrument stimulates intergovernmental interactions. The actors use the monitor as a starting point for intergovernmental dialogue.

Conclusions

In this chapter, I studied the *utilization of the Dutch Urban Policy Monitor* by using three approaches to the utilization of monitors. The utilization of the monitor as proposed by the rational approach is limited. Although there is not much discussion about the reliability of the monitor, it lacks goal-orientation because most of the policy goals are not concrete. Moreover, the monitor is hardly used for steering activities. The main rational use is by national departments and politicians, who use the Dutch Urban Policy Monitor to get information about relevant policy developments in the cities.

The political dimension reveals some additional insights into the use of the monitor. In general the monitor is seen as a sign of distrust in the capacities of the cities. The monitor primarily serves the interests of the Ministry of Home Affairs, which wants to be informed about policies in the cities. The monitor, however, has a weak competitive position *vis-à-vis* other information sources. The most important political function of the monitor is strategic learning. The national government uses the positive results in the monitor to support its claims of success (and to attribute negative results to external factors). The cities use the information in the monitor selectively to ground their requests for more national resources.

The cultural approach suggests that monitors are sources of meaning, and used to express common grammar and direction. The monitor of the Dutch Urban Policy only modestly fulfills this function, because actors are more involved in their own monitoring activities. The monitor is not perceived as a common research instrument. The monitor did, however, stimulate the development of a common policy agenda. The most important cultural function of the monitor, for both the national government and the cities, is that this instrument stimulates inter-governmental interactions. The actors use the monitor as a starting point for intergovernmental dialogue.

It is important that all actors involved see the monitor as a joint effort that will assist them in achieving the goals of the Dutch Urban Policy, and not as a control mechanism enforced upon them by the national government. Actors should not primarily focus on punishments (risk perception of monitoring), but on learning (challenge perception of monitoring). This attitude requires a certain level of trust. The research demonstrated that in order for monitoring instruments to be effective, we cannot confine ourselves to rational expectations and solutions. We also need to take political interests and cultural factors into account.

12
Reporting Public Performance Information: The Promise and Challenges of Citizen Involvement

Alfred Tat-Kei Ho

Today, performance measurement is a widely accepted tool of government management in the United States. At the national level, the George W. Bush administration has adopted the *Performance Assessment Rating Tool* to integrate performance measurement into strategic planning and budgeting (Breul and Moravitz, 2007). Many US state and local governments and professional organizations also have their own initiatives to promote performance measurement, "results-oriented" management, and public performance reporting (Berman and Wang, 2000; Jordan and Hackbart, 1999; Melkers and Willoughby, 2001; Poister and Streib, 1999).

So far, many of these reforms have been primarily driven by the executive branch or public managers, and to a lesser extent by policy makers and legislators who want to see more accurate and reliable performance information for planning, budgeting and program management purposes. The general public is seldom involved in designing and using performance information. This managerial orientation in performance measurement reforms is totally understandable given its historical roots. Since the turn of the twentieth century, the concept of performance measurement has been advocated by the professional management community as a tool to improve managerial efficiency and cost-effectiveness (Hatry and Fisk, 1972; Ridley and Herbert, 1938; see also Van Dooren in Chapter 1). From an early emphasis on output, workload, and cost-efficiency, to the recent focus on effectiveness and outcomes, performance measurement has often been pursued from the perspective of managers (Ammons, 1995; Hatry, 2006; Walters, 1998).

However, in the 1990s, there were growing criticisms of the "technocratic" focus and "instrumental rationality" of public management reforms among the academic community. While cost-efficiency and effectiveness are still important principles of public administration, many scholars argue that the government is different from a business and citizens are more than customers. Therefore, public sector reforms should pay attention to other fundamental values, such as democracy and equity, and the public should be more involved in decision making (Dawson and Dargie, 2002; Deleon and Deleon, 2002; Kettl, 2002)

The broadened thinking about public management reforms has begun to stimulate a new movement in the United States that advocates greater citizen engagement in performance measurement. For example, the Alfred P. Sloan Foundation, which has been funding many state and local performance measurement initiatives for the past two decades, has begun to fund initiatives to encourage citizen participation in performance measurement (Sloan Foundation, 2007). Also, the Governmental Accounting Standards Board, which sets financial reporting standards for many state and local governments in the United States, has released specific recommendations for government officials who are interested in working with citizens to develop and use performance measurement (Governmental Accounting Standards Board, 2003). The National Academy of Public Administration also encourages this line of thinking. In its report, "A Government to Trust and Respect," it states:

> Government programs are improved and civic trust is substantially alleviated when government agencies reach out to engage citizens directly in agenda setting, program development, and policy implementation. Agencies that do this soon learn that citizens have much to add, that they are important repositories of experience and ideas. [...] The agencies of government have an obligation – a critically important obligation – to keep the American people informed of their activities, their accomplishments, and their failures. [...] Local and state-based initiatives in which nonprofit groups, business leaders, and/or civic organizations are providing independent, but non-adversarial assessments of government performance toward citizen-driven prioritized outcomes are increasing. We encourage the continued development of such projects at all levels of government.
>
> (National Academy of Public Administration, 2007: 21–6)

This new focus in performance measurement reforms inevitably leads to several important questions. First, why is public engagement important in performance measurement? Second, how can the public participate meaningfully and effectively in the design of performance measures, an effort which tends to be technical and managerial in nature? Third, do citizens really carry a different perspective and contribute different thinking to the exercise of performance measurement? Finally, how does citizen participation impact the use of performance information by government officials? How does it impact policy debates or managerial decisions?

The purpose of this chapter is to answer these questions by examining a case study in the United States. In the following, I first examine the rationales for public engagement in performance measurement and why it is important for government officials to think beyond bureaucratic boundaries. Then I present a case study of Des Moines, Iowa, to illustrate how community activists can play an active role, and how government officials may build a partnership with citizens in performance measurement. Finally, based on the case study, I evaluate the impact and challenges of public engagement in performance measurement.

Rationales for, and challenges in, engaging the public in performance measurement and reporting

Many government officials today face the challenge of building public trust in the institution of government and explaining to the public how taxpayers' money is put to use. In the United States, for example, 57 percent of Americans agreed that "when something is run by the government, it is usually inefficient and wasteful" (Pew Research Center for the People and the Press, 2003). Many have also lost their trust in the capacity of government to be fair and responsive to the needs of ordinary citizens, to spend money effectively and efficiently, and to resolve policy problems (Baldassare, 2000; Hibbing and Theiss-Morse, 2001; 2002).

This is partly why many government officials today are interested in performance reporting. By documenting what public programs have accomplished and how taxpayers' money is spent, many public officials hope that they can demonstrate accountability to the public and rebuild public trust in government. However, an irony in the current practice of performance measurement and reporting is that the public is seldom involved even though performance measurement is intended to be a tool of public accountability. Many public officials often give very little thought to what the public wants to know about the "performance" of government. Even less consideration is given to how performance should be reported to the public. As a result, even though performance measurement is widely practiced by many government agencies, many performance reports are circulated only within managers' offices. If the reports are made available to the public, they are usually poorly formatted for public consumption – they can be several inches thick, the content may not connect to issues that citizens care about, and the presentation often makes it difficult for many ordinary citizens to find what they are interested in knowing.

This lack of public involvement and input in performance measurement and reporting creates several potential problems. First, without an effective oversight and public engagement process, citizens will have to rely heavily on the "professional judgment" of public managers to determine which performance results should be reported and how. This creates a potential principal–agent problem in which managers (the agents) may not fully disclose the true performance picture to the public and their elected representatives (the principal). For example, in studying the history of the job-training programs funded by the Job Training Partnership Act of the United States, Courty and Marschke (1997) find that case managers tend to manipulate the outcome measurement of these training programs. They often report program successes more immediately (e.g., the percentage of trainees who get employed) and delay the report of failures (e.g., the percentage of trainees who remain unemployed at the end of the training program), hoping that the failed cases may show improvement later. This kind of principal–agent problems is often found in the public sector and can be especially acute when program goals are ill-defined, managers have a lot of discretion, and monitoring and verification of performance by external entities is limited (Dixit, 2002; Lynn, Heinrich and Hill, 2001; Propper and Wilson, 2003; Wilson, Croxson and Atkinson, 2006).

Second, even if managers are sincerely interested in using performance measurement to hold their programs accountable to the public, they may easily be trapped by their own blind spots and fail to see beyond what they have been routinely doing in program delivery and planning. The public can therefore provide valuable input to help managers see beyond traditional managerial concerns and understand better the fundamental values of public services from the citizens' and the user's perspectives (Heikkila and Isett, 2007). For example, in a study about the "values" of city hall to a community in the state of

Massachusetts in the United States, Smith and Hunstman (1997) find that citizens care not just about the efficiency issue in processing their requests, but also about the time burden on the public in preparing for service requests. Issues such as where to get government forms, how to fill them out, and how and where to submit the forms can be frustrating to many citizens who may not visit the city hall often. However, government officials tend to ignore these aspects of "performance" and measure only the efficiency and effectiveness in processing the forms once they are submitted by citizens.

Third, no matter how sincere and objective a public manager is in designing and executing the exercise of performance measurement, cynical citizens and critics of government programs are likely to view the performance measurement and reporting effort as a mere public relations gimmick. This problem was reflected in the Netherlands experience in the 1980s. Despite the highly publicized reforms known as the Tilburg Model of performance management and budgeting, many voters were still discontented or indifferent with the government because the reforms were driven totally by administrators, and citizens were seldom engaged to address policy issues and concerns from their perspectives (Hendriks and Tops, 2003). The experience forced reformers to put greater focus on the external environment and the role of citizens (Schedler and Proeller, 2002).

Lack of public buy-in also creates another problem – elected officials may become less motivated to give a lot of attention to the information generated from performance measurement. As a result, they may not use such information in policy making and program oversight. This problem can be illustrated by the George W. Bush administration's US federal performance budgeting reform known as the *Performance Assessment Rating Tool* (PART). Despite diligent efforts put into the exercise, Congress has largely ignored the results of the PART in policy making and budgeting because they have not been engaged in developing the tool and have not seen any significant constituency buy-in to the measurement results (Posner and Fantone, 2007). This experience shows that even if performance measurement can produce highly scientific, reliable, and valid performance information, it may still lack the necessary credibility in the political process if the public and major stakeholders are not involved.

Furthermore, by not involving the public, government officials lose a valuable opportunity to educate citizens and engage them in dialogues about the costs of service delivery and the complex challenges faced by government agencies. Ebdon and Franklin (2004) show that communicating with citizens and engaging them more directly in decision making can increase citizens' understanding of the government's funding needs and the complexities and challenges faced by government agencies. Berman (1997) also shows that cities tend to have less cynical citizenry if they engage the public more, and Berman and Wang (2000) show that citizen participation can help build stronger public trust in government.

These potential contributions are especially important in today's fiscal environment, in which government agencies are asked to do more with less. How to prioritize resources and tasks becomes a critical managerial challenge. Public involvement can help refine the focus and efforts of performance measurement, as public input can guide managers' decisions on what aspects of the program are most important to the public and what data should be collected first given the limited time and resources. Even if public officials may decide to collect performance data on program input, output, effectiveness and cost-efficiency for internal managerial purposes, they can differentiate the data more carefully and become more effective in communicating government performance and the value of government programs to the public.

Finally, public engagement in performance measurement is a way to tap into the talent and expertise of the community. In citizen committees or public meetings, citizen participants from different walks of life and from different socio-economic and educational backgrounds may suggest new perspectives and different solutions to the performance challenges faced by officials (Lukensmeyer and Torres, 2006). As a result, public officials may gain new insights on how a program's effectiveness and efficiency can be improved.

Hence, there are many practical reasons and benefits for government officials to involve citizens in performance measurement and reporting. At the same time, one cannot deny the presence of several challenges and barriers in doing so. First and foremost, it is important to overcome the fear and distrust of government officials toward citizen involvement. Government officials may view citizens as apathetic, uncommitted and incompetent (King, Stivers and Box, 1998; Rosenbaum, 1978). What may make the situation worse is the fact that many government officials only interact with the public when citizens are dissatisfied with public services and file complaints and grievances. These negative interactions are likely to reinforce officials' belief that citizens are cynical and unreasonable and cannot be trusted to give advice and make decisions (Yang, 2005).

Another barrier to engaging the public in performance measurement is cost. Civic engagement requires staff time to go to meetings and follow up on citizens' requests and suggestions. It may also involve various meeting costs, such as venue rental, *per diem* reimbursement for participants and hiring of meeting facilitators. There are also opportunity costs involved – one minute or one dollar spent in public meetings is one minute or one dollar less to deliver public services.

Moreover, even if public officials are willing to spend extra time and resources to support public engagement in performance measurement, there is still the question of whether the public has sufficient interest and motivation to participate in public meetings that examine government performance. After all, performance measurement is supposed to be a routine data collection exercise and many performance measures may be concerned with the technical and mundane details of the operation of a program. Many ordinary citizens who are not familiar with the concept of performance measurement may have difficulty in articulating how the "performance" of a government program should be measured in a quantifiable, reliable and valid manner. Furthermore, many citizens are time-pressed with personal, family and work responsibilities and may not be willing to volunteer their time to attend public meetings about measuring government performance.

Finally, recruiting the "right" citizen representatives is always a tricky question for public officials (Sirianni and Friedland, 1995). Many local elected officials, such as mayors and city council members, may not oppose the idea of public engagement because citizens may provide needed expertise for the government. However, citizen involvement imposes interesting governance questions: How much power should be delegated to these citizen volunteers? Are they simply advisors to the elected representatives, or should they have substantive decision-making power? How should these volunteers be recruited and selected? Should they be openly recruited from a community, or should they be selected and appointed by the elected body of the government, such as the city council? How should the elected representatives align their interests and priorities with the interests and concerns of these citizen volunteers?

These questions are important considerations for elected officials and the answers depend on the political situation of a particular community. In general, citizen volunteers should play an advisory role only and should never replace elected officials or professional managers in program decision making. In communities where politics is relatively stable and citizens are quite satisfied with the quality and level of public services, elected officials may feel less threatened by citizen participation.

As a result, they may be more receptive to the idea of recruiting citizens more openly to get more diverse and representative opinions from the community. Also, they may be more willing to give these volunteers greater oversight and agenda-setting power in evaluating program performance. On the other hand, if city politics is more unstable and divisive, the general public is generally dissatisfied with government services, and mass media is highly critical of the existing leadership, there is more political risk in exposing government performance problems further. As a result, elected officials may want to have a more "controlled" setting to get citizen input and may hesitate to give citizens too much discretion and information in performance measurement.

Hence, how a community wants to approach citizen participation in performance measurement depends largely on the political environment, the attitude of elected government officials toward citizen participation, and the risk aversion of elected officials in exposing government performance problems to the public. In the following, I use a case study of the city of Des Moines in the state of Iowa to illustrate how government officials may choose to balance these concerns and what benefits and challenges they may face in collaborating with citizens in performance measurement.

A case study of the Des Moines citizen-initiated performance assessment project

Background of the project

The city of Des Moines is the state capitol of Iowa, which is near the middle of the United States. The city itself has a population of about 200,000 and is located in a metropolitan area of about 450,000 people. The city government has a professional manager, about 2,000 employees, and a seven-member city council. It is responsible for a wide range of services, including police and fire protection, sanitation services, parks and recreation, infrastructure maintenance and construction, traffic control and parking, an airport, housing, community development and social services, economic development initiatives and libraries. The annual budget of the city is about $300 million dollars.

Between 2001 and 2004, the city of Des Moines and a team of researchers from Iowa State University, University of Iowa, and the Iowa League of Cities received funding from the Alfred P. Sloan Foundation to implement an experimental project known as the "citizen-initiated performance assessment" (CIPA) project, in which public officials and citizen representatives jointly developed performance measures and used them to evaluate the performance of public services. The city of Des Moines was among nine cities that decided to participate in the project. Des Moines was chosen because, first, it was willing to fully support and participate in this experimental project and, second, it was very similar to many mid-sized cities in the United States and so its experience could shine light on other cities' development in performance measurement.

Several factors motivated the city officials of Des Moines to support and participate in the project. First, city officials in Des Moines were very interested in performance measurement. The then city manager, Eric Andersen, wanted to introduce the tool to city departments to improve the efficiency and effectiveness of services. The city had also joined the comparative performance measurement project by the International City/County Management Association (ICMA), which had more than 200 US and Canadian cities sharing performance data with each other for benchmarking and performance comparison with similar-sized cities, and had been collecting many performance measures for a number of years.

Hence, before the launch of the CIPA project, the city of Des Moines already had some experience in performance measurement. The reason why city management was interested in the CIPA project was because even though they had the performance measurement matrix from ICMA, they were not sure whether the national measures had any significant meaning for local residents and whether they were measuring the "right" indicators that citizens really cared about.

Also, the city management believed that citizen participation could be a motivator for city departments to support the performance measurement initiative. If city employees realized that the performance measurement exercise was not just "one more idea" from top management or some national professional organizations but also something that local residents wanted, city staff would be less likely to resist the idea and would be more cooperative in the data exercise.

Citizen participation might also get the city council to pay closer attention to performance measures. While the city manager and the professional staff were enthusiastic about performance measurement, it was unclear how the elected council members would react to it. Since elected officials were always sensitive to voters' opinions, having citizens' support for performance measurement could help managers justify why the city should spend money and staff time to measure performance of programs. Also, citizens could be the necessary "political shield" for managers if performance results were less satisfactory than expected. If the city's performance was not so positive, some elected officials might put pressure on professional managers not to continue the exercise. This was the time when managers needed citizens' help, who could argue before the city council why performance measurement should continue and why data integrity and consistency were needed to help improve the quality of city management and policy making in the long run.

Recruiting and selecting citizen representatives

A key question for the city manager was whom the city should recruit to participate in the CIPA project. These citizens needed to be representative of the diverse interests of the city. Also, they had to have political credibility before the city council and the public so that the city management could feel comfortable accepting their recommendations. After some internal deliberation, the city officials decided to work with Des Moines Neighbors, which was an umbrella organization for the 51 neighborhood associations of the whole city. The organization was very active in local politics and played an important role in policy advocacy before the city council, training of grass-root leaders and volunteers, and coordination of local campaigns and neighborhood events. Since all city council members were familiar with the organization and some of them even received campaign assistance or endorsements from Des Moines Neighbors, the organization had the political legitimacy to partner with the city. Moreover, the city staff themselves had worked with Des Moines Neighbors closely before on several community development and neighborhood revitalization projects. Given these long working relationships among the city council, the city government and Des Moines Neighbors, the partnership was a natural development.

With the successful alignment of all the major political interests, the city council of Des Moines officially passed a city resolution to launch the CIPA program in 2001. A core working group, known as the "citizen performance team," was formed that included 10 to 12 volunteer representatives from Des Moines Neighbors, one representative from the city manager's office, and one city council member. Occasionally, the city manager himself also attended some of the meetings and participated in some of the key discussions with neighborhood representatives.

Working with citizen representatives to select
performance measures

The working model of CIPA is shown in Figure 12.1. Once the performance team was formed, the performance team began a discussion on what service areas they wanted to focus on and measure. Many topics

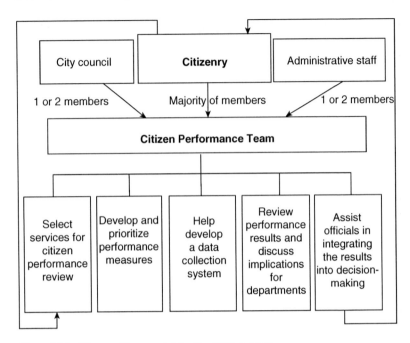

Figure 12.1 The working model for the CIPA project

had been proposed, including the use of tax incentives, economic development and job creation programs, and public safety. To help the performance team gain more insight into citizen priorities and primary neighborhood concerns, a town hall meeting was conducted in January 2002 in which about 100 neighborhood leaders and community organizational representatives participated and discussed various neighborhood and community concerns in small groups. Researchers and students from Iowa State University and the University of Iowa provided technical assistance and facilitated some of the discussion to help clarify and focus the opinions expressed in the meeting. After the meeting, a survey was also conducted among neighborhood leaders to further refine the focus of the CIPA project.

Based on the results of these efforts, the CIPA performance team finally came to a consensus that the project should measure the performance of "nuisance control" – that is, the government's efforts in reducing graffiti, mosquitoes, illegal dumping, abandoned housing, junky yards, teenager loitering, and air and noise pollution. These were the issues that citizens could experience and relate to daily, and so the performance team believed that citizens should be more informed about the efforts and results of these government policies and programs.

Once the team selected nuisance control as the focus topic, the performance team discussed why these nuisance issues emerged in certain neighborhoods and what the city government and residents needed to do to address the concerns. From the discussion, the critical issues of each policy topic came out naturally, and the performance team used them to develop performance measures. For example, in discussing odor control, the performance team members were very interested in knowing where the problems had been, how well the city responded to complaints and service requests, and whether the problems were resolved and the residents were satisfied with the current air quality in their neighborhood. In discussing illegal dumping, such as abandoned furniture and other nuisance items, the performance team members again were very interested in measuring where the problems had been and how quickly the city responded to resolving the problems. Discussions like these were used to highlight citizens' concerns, which were then used to develop performance measures for the respective services and departments.

After the measures were finalized, city officials began the data collection process. Since a lot of the performance measures requested by citizens were related to the number of nuisance complaints, the geographical location of the problems cited, and the city government's response time to service requests, the city government's service request computing system known as the "Citywide Citizen Response System" (CCRS) was a primary source of performance data. In addition, the city contracted out to researchers at Iowa State University to conduct sampled surveys about residents' satisfaction with various city services and their perceptions of the quality of life in their residence areas. Small-scale surveys of neighborhood organization leaders were also conducted to measure their satisfaction with neighborhood conditions and to solicit suggestions for improvement.

Reporting to the city council and the public

After the city officials collected the data, they reported internally first to the citizen performance team so that they could consider the results and suggest recommendations to the city staff on how various city services could be improved. The performance team and Des Moines Neighbors also realized that they had to engage the city council proactively because ultimately, the city council was responsible for making policy and budgetary decisions and telling city departments what they should do to improve community conditions. Hence, when the performance measurement reports were ready, citizen representatives from the performance team and Des Moines Neighbors made special presentations to the city council and urged them to look into different policy issues reflected in the reports.

In addition, Des Moines Neighbors was instrumental in getting local newspapers and TV stations to cover some of the neighborhood activities of the CIPA project and to feature how citizen representatives and city staff partnered with each other to examine local nuisance issues. Although these media reports were quite incidental and were insufficient by themselves to generate sustained policy actions, they certainly helped raise the attention of elected officials about the CIPA project and some of the neighborhood concerns.

Finally, the city management made a special effort to report the performance results to the larger public. Since 2004, the city of Des Moines has been issuing a public performance report. Unlike many government reports, which are usually thick, data-intensive, and poor in graphical design, the Des Moines performance reports are only about 40 pages long, focusing on many quality of life issues that the performance team had expressed interest in, and giving only highlights of the city's efforts and accomplishments in these areas. To ensure that the report is easily accessible by the general public, hardcopies of the report are available not only at the city hall, but also in local libraries and major grocery stores. In addition, the report is downloadable on the city's website (www.dmgov.org/performance).

Assessing the impact of the CIPA project

Citizen input offered some unique perspectives on how the government should measure and report performance to the public. First, the types of measures that citizens are interested in are often different from what professional managers want to see for budgeting or planning purposes. For example, among the 34 measures suggested by the citizen performance team for different nuisance issues, 12 measures were related to complaints or problems cited and another eight were about citizen satisfaction with the community condition and the results of government actions to resolve the problems (see Figure 12.2). Also, seven of the measures were on response time. These three types of measures, which could be categorized as "intermediate outcome measures," composed the overwhelmingly majority (about 80 percent) of the total number of measures,

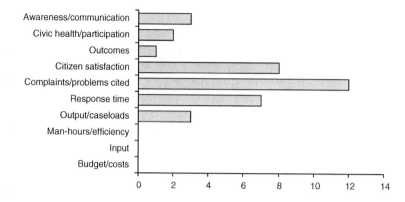

Figure 12.2 Number of citizen-initiated performance measures on nuisance control, by types

Note: The total number of measures generated by citizens is 34. The sum of frequencies in this table, however, exceeds 34 because a few measures belong to more than one category.

showing that citizens were most interested in knowing whether the government was effective and responsive in resolving problems and whether community conditions were improved. They did not care as much about the input of services, such as personnel or budget, or the cost-efficiency of the operations, such as cost per caseload. They believed those were the concerns and responsibilities of the managers, not citizens. They simply wanted the jobs to get done and any problems to be resolved.

A surprise to city management in the citizen discussion of performance measures was how much interest citizens had in measuring the awareness of various services and the effort of the government in communicating these services to citizens. For example, a number of measures were about the percentage of citizens who were included in the city's e-mail listserv and the percentage of citizens who were aware of various neighborhood activities and meetings organized by city departments. In performance team meetings, some citizens raised concerns about the "civic health" of the city and the fact that the general public was often unaware of some of the neighborhood issues and the responses of the city government in addressing those issues. They wanted to see more aggressive public communication efforts by the government as well as greater collaboration between Des Moines Neighbors, the city government and other community nonprofit organizations so that more citizens were better informed and could be more involved.

This was an aspect of "government performance" that Des Moines city officials had not thought much about before the CIPA project. City departments might be very effective and capable of getting their jobs done in a cost-efficient manner, but without communicating these successes to the public, they might have created an undesirable "performance perception gap." Through discussion with citizen representatives in the CIPA process, government officials also realized that they had to work more closely with neighborhood leaders to help citizens understand the public's responsibilities, the government's responsibilities, and how the two sides needed to collaborate more to improve the quality of life in a neighborhood. For example, garbage clean-up and maintenance and repairs of sidewalks in front of a property are the responsibilities of individual property homeowners. However, the enforcement of community hygiene and building codes is the responsibility of the government. Before CIPA, government officials thought of "performance" solely in terms of output and efficiency – how many complaints they received about these problems, how many cases they had to handle, and how fast they processed the complaints by issuing warnings and court orders. After CIPA, government officials broadened their understanding of "performance" by asking themselves these questions – how well property owners were informed of these neighborhood policies and how effective city officials were in collaborating with local leaders and neighborhood associations to encourage voluntary compliance with the city codes. These questions prompted officials to think about performance not just from an administrative process perspective, but also about from the perspectives of customer relations, communication and governance.

The citizen participants also suggested that many of the performance measures should be reported by neighborhoods. Performance measures at the citywide level might be useful to city officials who wanted to get an overall assessment of various departments for policy planning and budgeting purposes, but from a citizen's perspective, citizens were more interested in the performance of city services at the neighborhood level because that was their "reference point" – the place where they lived or worked at and could relate to more easily and directly when they saw the measurement results. Some of them were also strongly interested in knowing if there was any intra-jurisdictional equity in public service delivery. For example, they wanted to compare the response time of city departments to different nuisance complaints to see if there was any significant difference between richer and poorer neighborhoods and between different geographical locations. To these citizens, efficiency and effectiveness of services and social equity were inseparable concerns.

Citizen input through the CIPA project changed the way Des Moines officials reported government performance. Internally, they still had departmental performance reports to the city management and the city council to show the details of input, output, and cost-efficiency measures of various services and how well different departments accomplished their strategic goals. However, based on citizen input, the city developed a new initiative and developed a separate, streamlined performance report for citizens as mentioned above.

Moreover, the CIPA project helped the city manager's office rethink its neighborhood revitalization programs and code enforcement. First, city officials realized that they had to pay closer attention to how they communicated different services and policies to citizens. As a result, in its 2005 annual performance report to citizens, the city added a special section that explained the work of its Neighborhood Inspection Division and how it tried to work with citizens to combat nuisance problems. Moreover, based on citizens' ideas and recommendations, the city manager's office changed their neighborhood revitalization strategies slightly and reinforced a multi-departmental approach to neighborhood services. Instead of asking the police, planning and community development departments to deal with various neighborhood issues independently and separately, the city formed a small working team for each neighborhood under the revitalization program, each of which consisted of several departmental representatives so that they could think collectively about neighborhood revitalization issues, such as public area beautification, and make more coordinated efforts to deal with nuisance problems, such as graffiti, illegal dumping, and abandoned housing. The city also reported openly in its 2005 performance report which neighborhoods had rated nuisance control as "unsatisfactory" and set clear performance targets to improve the services.

Hence, the CIPA project had made some significant impact on the city's communication strategies and neighborhood development policies. However, its impact on other city services and the city council in general was less clear. First, CIPA was a collaborative initiative among the city government, Des Moines Neighbors and the universities in the region focusing on nuisance control issues only. It was an externally funded experiment that lasted only three years and was never expanded to other city services. After 2004, Des Moines Neighbors never pushed the city to expand the scope of the project. What increased the challenge was that in 2004, the President of Des Moines Neighbors, one of the key leaders instrumental in establishing the project, stepped down after two terms of office. Then in 2005, the city manager who was an enthusiastic supporter of the project also left and took a job in another city. With the leadership transition, the CIPA project was put on hold for two years and since then, it has not been able to regain its momentum. However, the city of Des Moines has continued to publish its annual performance report for citizens based on some of the citizen input from the CIPA project.

The case study of Des Moines illustrates the subtle political dynamics that arise if the public is engaged in performance measurement. First, the alignment of the support from elected officials, the city administration and major public stakeholders is critical if it is to be done in a partnership manner. Such alignment must strike a delicate balance among these three parties so that it will not too significantly threaten the authority and political interests of elected officials as well as the sense of job security among government employees.

Second, citizen input is likely to bring in new perspectives and new demands on the government. Hence, it is important to channel citizen input in a constructive way to help government agencies and their employees see it as "valuable insights" rather than challenges and condemnations so that citizen input can be used to bring improvement in government services and policies. How to do this effectively in a certain political and administrative setting requires good political skills and strong leadership at the very top level of a local government. The city manager, for example, is the most vital link between the elected officials and the public representatives. As shown in the Des Moines case, when this key player is gone, the partnership can tumble very quickly and easily.

Based on the Des Moines experiment, several key lessons can be drawn for other governments who are interested in engaging the public in performance measurement:

- A certain level of trust and mutual respect between government officials and citizen representatives is necessary before any engagement can be launched. If government officials believe that citizens are only there to complain, or if citizens believe that government officials will not sincerely listen to their concerns and report performance honestly, the collaboration will be likely to fail.
- Citizens often have a different perspective on performance measurement than managers do. Generally, they are less interested in input and output measures, and are more interested in outcomes and in citizen perception of service quality, responsiveness, customer services, intra-jurisdictional equity, transparency and effectiveness

in public communication. Hence, citizen input often broadens managers' perspective on "performance" and challenges them to rethink how they should communicate with citizens on service efforts and accomplishments.

- Despite the value of citizen participation, managers still need to manage and citizens cannot replace professional managers. Citizens expect managers to take care of technical issues such as finding ways to produce better services with lower costs and maximizing cost-efficiency of programs. Citizen input may contribute fresh ideas and new perspectives to management problems, but citizens ultimately will have to rely on, or collaborate with, government officials to implement the ideas.

- The point above also implies that citizen participation in performance measurement does not necessarily guarantee better services and more satisfactory performance. Citizen-initiated performance measures may highlight the concerns and critical issues of a program from the citizens' perspective, but the measures by themselves are insufficient to guarantee good management and greater public investment to improve services.

- A citizen–official partnership in performance measurement can also be highly fragile. It not only requires government leaders to take risks and make government performance issues more transparent to the public, but also community leaders to commit time and resources to support the project, participate in meetings, and work closely with government officials to learn about performance issues that can sometimes be highly technical and managerial in nature.

- The success of citizen-government partnership in performance measurement relies heavily on visionary and committed leadership. Without this foundation, the incentives in the current political and administrative environment are likely to make performance measurement an internal, managerial exercise because it is less risky, less time consuming, and less expensive.

Conclusion

In recent years, many governments have initiated performance measurement reforms and encouraged their managers to think more about and measure "outcomes" and "program results". Such an effort should definitely be applauded as it puts greater pressure on government officials to hold themselves accountable in spending taxpayers' money. However, what is often overlooked in these reforms is the question about who has the right and the opportunity to define results and outcomes. If government managers are left on their own to define "success" and "performance," there is a great risk of goal displacement in the principal–agent setting of government and the public interest may not be best served.

In this chapter, I used a case study of the "Citizen-Initiated Performance Assessment" project in Des Moines, in the United States, to show that citizens can indeed add a fresh perspective to government performance measurement and reporting. Through public engagement, government officials can learn from citizens what performance measures are most meaningful and important to the public, how best the government should communicate "performance" to taxpayers, and how the government may provide various services more efficiently and effectively from the users' perspective.

As Mathews (1999) argues in his book, *Politics for People*, the attitude that government officials can sit back and wait for complaints to come must change. This passive pattern of citizen–government interaction assumes that government officials are the decision makers and judges and that the public does not have much to offer. However, in the twenty-first century when citizens have more access to different sources of information about the government, and non-governmental groups can provide tremendous help to the government in solving public policy and community challenges, this attitude is not sustainable (Boyte, 2005). The government can no longer do everything by itself. Nor should it be allowed to evaluate its own performance without public input and insight. Therefore, it is hoped that the Des Moines case study in this chapter will serve as a stimulus to other communities who are interested in experimenting with different ways to engage citizens in performance measurement. It is only through public engagement that performance measurement can truly be a tool to hold government accountable for results that matter (Epstein, Coates and Wray, 2005).

13
Publishing Performance Information: An Illusion of Control?

Steven Van de Walle and Alasdair Roberts

We live in the age of quantified performance. It is no longer sufficient to believe that a public sector organization does its job well, in general terms; or that the professionals within that organization can be relied upon. We want data that will allow us to judge and compare the behavior of service providers. In the new millennium, the number of schemes designed to satisfy this demand for performance data has grown substantially. The growth of rating and ranking programs is one of the dominant trends in contemporary public services reform (see also Arndt, 2007).

As we will show, ranking and rating schemes can vary in structure; sometimes they are established by government alone, and sometimes by a mix of governmental and private organizations; other rankings are private initiatives. Their ostensible aim is to improve control over the performance of service providers. In some cases, control is exercised by central agencies, whose capacity to detect laggards is thought to be improved by such systems. Increasingly, control is also to be exercised by citizens, who are expected to use performance information to guide their own decisions about the choice of service providers (Coe and Brunet, 2006). The rationale for adoption of such systems seems difficult to challenge at first glance; they are often pitched as mechanisms for improving "transparency" and "accountability," concepts that are now so thoroughly entrenched in popular discourse that they have become banalities (Hood, 2007b).

Yet there are good reasons for being skeptical about rating and ranking systems (Hood, 2006; 2007a). There are several reasons why they will not be a clear spur to better performance by service providers. For example, performance measures may not grasp the key aspects of service production. That is, what is measured may not actually matter in terms of quality of outputs. Or measures may not be reliable; for example, it may prove easier for service providers to manipulate performance measures than to improve actual performance. Or providers may be incapable of taking steps necessary to improve performance, even when rating systems provide clear evidence of failure.

These are all producer-side difficulties. There are equally tenuous assumptions about the use of performance data by consumers of public services. Consumers may not pay attention to published data, or may not understand its true meaning. They may continue to rely on other considerations while making decisions about the choice of service provider, or may lack the capacity to make any such choice. There are, in short, many ways in which the "program logic" of rating and ranking systems – the bundle of assumptions about the causal links between publication of data and improved performance (Wholey, 1999) – may break down.

We must also be careful not to take an unduly narrow view of rating and ranking systems. They are not merely technical innovations, designed with the expectation that they may improve the quality of public services. Rating and ranking systems are also expressions of contemporary culture. They are part of the centuries-long drive toward rationalization of society (see also Chapter 1 by Van Dooren). The popularity of such schemes is also explained, in large part, as a response to growing anxiety about the loss of control over an increasingly complex and turbulent world (cf. infra). We hope that rating and ranking systems will help to restore sovereignty – either in the sense of government's control over a broadly dispersed bureaucracy, or the citizen's control of large and unfamiliar service providers. It is unclear, however, whether any such scheme could fulfill this larger goal. Rating and ranking schemes may serve only to provide the illusion of control.

The structure of rating and ranking systems

In this chapter, we define a ranking and rating system as a system that collects and tabulates performance data about a large number of organizations engaged in comparable work. The most common examples are schemes that aggregate data about public schools, universities and hospitals.

There are several critical points to be noted. First, these systems are often established in policy fields that have salience to powerful voting blocs – such as education and healthcare. It is conceivable that similar schemes *could* be established for prisons, welfare agencies and immigration services – and noteworthy that they are not. Second, performance information collected within these schemes is *quantitative* and *standardized*: organizations covered by a rating and ranking system are expected to provide numerical results that are calculated in the same way.

Third, these systems are applied within service delivery systems that are highly decentralized but which still share a large degree of commonality in terms of methods of work and outputs, such as schools and hospitals. If there is not a "large N" – that is, a large number of organizations – then the need for a highly structured system of comparison would not be clear. If the structure and work processes of each organization were also subject to tight central control, then there would be no point in comparing performance information, because the variations would have to be attributed to environmental considerations (e.g., the character of the population served) rather than decisions by management or staff in the service organization. On the other hand, if there is a large variation in character of work – if organizations are doing very different work – then the scheme fails, because apples cannot be compared to oranges. So these schemes thrive where there is a middle ground with both disaggregation but also rough conformity in production.

Fourth, such systems need not be government-run, or even designed by government. It is conceivable, for example, that a central government agency could execute the key steps in implementation of a rating and ranking scheme: the *specification* of data to be provided; actual *collection* of data; *manipulation* of data (meant in the benign sense, for example by the construction of rankings); and *publication* of results. However, there have been cases where government has been responsible only for the first and second of these tasks. Private actors have then obtained data from government overseers, sometimes through the operation of transparency laws, and then undertaken the tasks of manipulation and publication themselves (in some of these cases, government overseers may not have anticipated this outcome when they collected the data). There are also instances of wholly private schemes – for example, instances where media outlets have requested data directly from service providers, and undertaken the tasks of manipulation and publication as well. University rating schemes in several countries are built on this model.

Finally, rating and ranking schemes may rely on different sanctions to spur laggardly organizations. In the weakest version, a scheme may rely simply on the effect of disclosure alone. Embarrassment or political pressure might induce a provider to improve, even if they retain a monopoly over provision within a jurisdiction. A stronger version might rely on market pressures: consumers might act on published information by switching from a laggard to a high-performing organization. Finally, central authorities could impose their own sanctions, such as financial penalties or the threat of restructuring and closure, on laggards.

Reasons for popularity

There are several reasons for the growing popularity of rating and ranking systems. One obvious explanation is dramatically lowered cost of collecting and publishing data (O'Neill, 2002: 66). Improvements in information technology now make it easier to capture and aggregate data within organizations that are covered by these systems. The cost of transmitting that information to monitoring agencies, and of manipulating data to produce performance scores and rankings, is similarly reduced because of technological change. The internet has essentially eliminated the marginal cost of distributing ratings and rankings to a broad audience. In large part, this is a familiar story about the exploitation of new technologies to assert control over previously uncontested territory.

The explanation does not rest wholly on technological change. For political executives at the center of government, the need for better controls over highly decentralized delivery systems has also increased. Education and healthcare are expensive policy domains, and the cost of these services has tended to rise rapidly in relation to other goods and services (Baumol, 1997). Confronting tight fiscal constraints, political leaders have been reluctant to invest further in these sectors without good evidence that they are obtaining significant performance improvements as a result (Barber, 2007; Keegan, 2003). Performance monitoring becomes a mechanism for gauging return on investment, and persuading other players in the political process that increased expenditure is justified.

Political and economic changes in the advanced democracies have also encouraged the introduction of ranking and rating systems. In the sphere of politics, party identification among a broad mass of middle class voters has declined; consequently there is more competition for this group of voters, and increased attention by political leaders to issues – such as education and healthcare – that are important to them (Brownstein, 2007). The salience of education and healthcare has increased, and rating and ranking systems are helpful instruments in the political game.

The introduction of these systems is also eased because of their compatibility with broader cultural trends. In the last decade, tremendous emphasis has been put on the virtues of transparency in government operations, and on the citizen's "right to know" (Mason and Street, 2006). It is therefore difficult to resist demands for the disclosure of performance information, especially if the raw data is already collected as a matter of routine by internal administrative systems. Arguments about the dysfunctional consequences that may follow from disclosure, and from the creation of ratings and rankings, are no longer regarded as dispositive.

At the same time, great stress has been put on the right of citizens to have the power to choose among competing service providers. "The relationship between state and citizen has changed," former British Prime Minister Tony Blair told his party supporters in 2004, "People have grown up. They want to make their own life choices" (Blair, 2004). The American commentator Andrei Cherny says that Western governments are experiencing a "choice revolution" (Cherny, 2000). The choice revolution drives a demand for information about service providers: if citizens are to act as consumers, they need something equivalent to consumer reports – a function performed, in a simple way, by rating and ranking schemes.

Yet, the debate on whether to publish performance information is a highly polarized one with proponents and opponents weighing advantages and perverse effects. Some evidence suggests that citizens are not always in favor of publishing league tables, for example, in schools (Wiggins and Tymms, 2002) or in health (Marshall, Hiscock and Sibbald, 2002). Many professionals have expressed their doubts as to the value of ranking and rating systems in improving delivery. Countries have reacted differently to these evolutions, and practices range from a situation of "English exceptionalism," over a limited use or quasi absence of ranking and rating schemes, to an outright ban of publishing school performance tables (Boyle, 2007).

Producer-side difficulties with rating and ranking systems

Rating and ranking systems pose difficulties on both the producer and user side of public services. Public service providers struggle with the inherent tension in rating and ranking systems between transparency and improvement. The introduction of rating and ranking systems may also lead to various forms of dysfunctional behavior, such as gaming or cheating. This may be particularly likely when providers lack the capacity to make the more fundamental internal changes necessary to respond properly to signals provided by ranking and rating systems.

Tension between transparency and improvement

Transparency has generally been positively described as contributing to better governance (Hood, 2007b: 192). Yet there is a real tension between the publication of performance information for improving performance and for improving accountability. The assumption of an accountability–performance relationship "has attained the status of an institutionalized myth" (Dubnick, 2005: 378). Measurement plays a dual role: improving transparency, and making services effective (Noordegraaf and Abma, 2003; Van Dooren et al., 2006).

Rather than focusing their attention on actual improvement, enterprising managers may displace their effort to focus on the *appearance* of better service. Selective reporting then becomes an important marketing tool. Accountability may be replaced with marketing where dramatization may matter more than accuracy (Coe and Brunet, 2006). Karsten and colleagues (2001) found a tendency for schools to spend more on marketing and promotion in a ranked environment.

Other dysfunctional effects

Unintended and dysfunctional consequences of rating and ranking systems receive their fair share of attention in research. All the traditional dysfunctional effects of performance measurement apply to rating and ranking systems (Blau, 1963; Pidd, 2005; Ridgway, 1956; see also Radnor, Chapter 6 in this volume), and specific research has focused on the dysfunctional consequences of publicly available performance information in the health sector (Hamblin, 2007) and education (Karsten, Visscher and De Jong, 2001; van Petegem et al., 2005). Traditional dysfunctions include a tendency to focus on what gets rated or ranked, a focus on short-term results, and outright gaming and cheating (Hood, 2006; Bevan and Hood, 2006). Precisely because so much may be at stake with rating and ranking systems, gaming behavior becomes attractive (Wiggins and Tymms, 2002: 43).

Capacity to adapt

Rating and ranking systems are built on the assumption that information about performance will lead to an improvement of this performance because of the external pressure created by these systems (Elmore, 2007).

Failing organizations, however, often do not have the capacity to improve their performance (Jas and Skelcher, 2005). Under-performing schools, for example, simply may not have the capacity to respond to signals about failure, and rating their performance will do little to change this (Elmore, 2007: 8). Rating and ranking may even be counterproductive, because of the tendency to assume that bad performance is the result of bad will, self-interest, abuse or incompetence, rather than structural or environmental factors. Rather than assisting organizations to improve the quality of their services, the rating and ranking systems may have perverse effects on trust, and undermine the cooperation and goodwill necessary for improvement (cf. infra; see also Chapter 7 by Denhardt and Aristigueta).

User-side difficulties with rating and ranking systems

Ratings and rankings are published with the intention to support citizens in making informed choices. While there are not many assessments of the impact of publishing performance information, some of the evidence suggests that citizens do not always use performance information, even when it is available. In this section, we explore citizens' behavior in using rating and rankings systems, and the behavioral assumptions on which these systems are built.

Do citizens use performance information?

The limited amount of research on whether citizens actually use published performance information tends to be equivocal about its effects. Some research suggests that published performance information has a profound behavioral impact. The best example is that of parents in England, for example, moving house to live in the right school catchment area. School performance data is even used in house sales (Working Party on Performance Monitoring in the Public Services, 2005: 19). By contrast, research from the health sector has produced different findings. In a research review, Marshall and colleagues found that "most of the evidence (from both the United States and Scotland) suggests that when this information is published, the public does not search it out, does not understand it, distrusts it, and fails to make use of it" (Marshall et al., 2003: 141). Patients are not very knowledgeable about the performance situation of the hospital into which they have been admitted (Schneider and Epstein, 1998), and performance information generally has little impact on patients' decision making (Marshall et al., 2000: 62).

Reasons for non-use of performance information

When examining reasons for this non-use of published performance information, all the usual reasons for why information is not used in decisions resurface (Van de Walle and Bovaird, 2007). Consumers of services may be unaware of the information; or it may be considered to be too complicated, not timely or difficult to access. In the case of public service rankings, distrust should be added as an important factor. In the United Kingdom, it was found that many people were skeptical about the reliability of published health data (Mason and Street, 2006), and that many placed more trust in their own experience than in reported information (Marshall, Hiscock and Sibbald, 2002: 1281). The choice debate, however, tends to regard formal performance information as superior to other types of information. Yet, we know from the decision-making literature that other sources of information such as stories, anecdotes and narratives are very powerful. Where performance information is used by citizens, it does not replace other information such as hearsay or friends' recommendations, and anecdotal information remains critically important (Marshall et al., 2000: 61). But there is a more important reason why performance information is not always used instrumentally: the assumptions of the instrumental model may simply be wrong.

Behavioral assumptions: choice, and the citizen as rational decision maker

The central assumption behind the publication of performance information is that citizens will seek out performance information, interpret it, and make a reasoned choice between different public service providers (exit), or use the information indirectly by putting pressure on suppliers to improve their performance (voice) (Hirschman, 1970). The assumptions of this rational decision-making model, however, have frequently been challenged. The citizen as decision maker essentially suffers from the same deficiencies as the decision makers featured in the managerial decision-making literature: information overload, bounded rationalities, selective perceptions, misleading heuristics and so on (Tversky and Kahneman, 1982; Van de Walle and Bovaird, 2007). Rather than making informed choices, citizens may employ an inquisitorial search process, where they seek out information that confirms their already made choices.

Where choice is in theory possible, we see that citizens do not necessarily exercise this choice. Sometimes there may be very simple reasons for this. Schneider and Epstein (1998: 1641) give the example of patients who may have a very limited amount of time to decide on a surgeon or a hospital. In other cases, there are no such straightforward reasons why citizens do not exercise choice. In healthcare, for example, we find that patients continue visiting hospitals with higher mortality rates (Marshall et al., 2000: 63; Vladeck et al., 1988: 124), and that parents do not opt for the best possible schools for their children, even when they have the opportunity to do so.

A possible explanation for this behavior is that citizens may not be the rational decision makers the choice movement assumes them to be. Other factors than traditionally defined "best performance" may be important in selecting a public service, and qualitative research by Marshall and colleagues in health provision suggested that users were actually rather unconvinced about choice, some suggesting that "You don't change doctors like you change cars" (Marshall, Hiscock and Sibbald, 2002: 1281).

Scrutinizing performance information and making a choice based on this information is a demanding process, of which the outcomes are uncertain. Having to exercise choice may even make people less satisfied, and increase stress and anxiety, thereby challenging the idea that having choice is actually better (Schwartz, 2004). In addition, it could be argued that the choice agenda is not really about choice, because the range of alternatives to choose from is often pre-determined and sometimes extremely limited (Bauman, 1999).

The tight connection between rating and ranking schemes and the choice debate may give us a false message about accountability. While being framed as "empowering citizens," choice implies a shift of responsibility. A belief in market mechanisms leads to the assumption that citizens will solve the performance problem by using a different service, or by using exit and voice behavior. As such, promoting choice by publishing performance information is useful for policy makers who do not want to take decisions (a point also made by Marshall, Hiscock and Sibbald, 2002: 1281). While the model is in theory based on empowerment, what it may mean is: figure it out for yourself! (Schwartz, 2004). As such we are really dealing with a false accountability. Hacker argues this is exemplary of the risk shift that is occurring in society, whereby "giving" citizens more choice really implies a transfer of risk from collective actors to personal responsibility (Hacker, 2006). In other words, if citizens receive bad healthcare or if their children attend bad schools, then this should be interpreted as *their* responsibility. The citizen is to blame, by failing to properly exercise choice.

The informed citizen, choice and inequality

An additional complication with the choice model based on performance information is that more informed choices are not an option for all citizens. The use of formal performance information is clearly linked to a certain socio-demographic profile, because using performance information requires certain skills. Schneider and Epstein found that users of hospital performance reports tended to be younger and better educated (Schneider and Epstein, 1998), and Meijer (2007: 172) worried about the digital divide in the case of publishing performance information online. Publishing performance information and stimulating citizens to exercise personal choice based on this information may result in more inequality, because the performance information has a different impact on different groups. The rhetoric of empowerment and choice clearly does not apply to the poor, sick, or lower educated. It has been suggested that, in the case of health care, hospital report cards "may further marginalize the experiences of these groups who in any case are already underserved by the health system" (Davies, Washington and Bindman, 2002: 379). As a result, more information may increase inequalities: better educated people will change their behavior through consulting rankings, while others won't. Offering choice may then lead to the disappearance of commonness, because people have different experiences (Schwartz, 2004: 17), and to rising inequality.

Publishing performance information, rankings and the consequences of high modernity

As we have demonstrated in the previous section, the assumptions behind the use and publication of performance information are of a very rational nature. In this section, we argue that the main role of ratings and rankings is not simply to provide information to improve services or support managers and citizens in their rational decisions. Instead, we highlight the role of indicators and rankings in creating an *appearance* of control in complex environments. Indicators and rankings are not just managerial innovations but reflect ongoing processes of societal modernization.

Modernity, standardization, individualization and control

A statistical system and the development of administrative nomenclatures have been essential to the development of the modern state (Desrosières, 1998). States needed information, at first mainly for tax and conscription purposes, later for a wide range of administrative and welfare functions.

The word "statistics" as it was used in its original eighteenth-century sense "was a description of the state, by and for itself" (Desrosières, 1998: 147). In a sense, nomenclatures, measures, indicators and statistics allowed the state to know, to penetrate and to control society.

This "knowing" of society reflected a deep conviction that control and planning of society was possible through social engineering. Nineteenth-century social reformers worked on the assumption that you needed to know the facts in order to change them (Boyle, 2001: 69). Knowing society, however, as the development of nomenclatures and taxonomies reflects, requires a simplification of society – society has to be made legible (Scott, 1998). The core of such a simplification is the standardization of measures. Unified measurement facilitated control, and through the use of such standards, the administration of society through a decentralized system became possible. Scott (1998) gives the example of the standardization of local standards of measurement (such as length, weight, etc.) as a requirement for control, assessment, taxation and planning.

Standardization of measures for school and hospitals can be seen in the same light. The motivation for standardizing is also remarkably similar. Standardization is promoted not just as a method of enhancing control, but also of promoting justice and equity. Standardized weights and measures promoted trade, and helped to avoid deception in the transactions between sellers and buyers by weeding out a complicated and unintelligible system that was prone to abuse (Scott, 1998). Introducing rankings for schools and hospitals promotes equity by – theoretically at least – offering everyone access to the same standards of service, and a higher level of service overall.

The main characteristic of this process of modernization is atomization and individualization, not only reflected in the declining importance of group memberships, but also in how we look at reality. This process of modernization has been long in the making. One could date its origins back to the scientific revolution, with its search for ever smaller parts of reality and for general laws, and to the empirical philosophical tradition. Many of the powerful ideas about economy, government and society that still influence many policy makers today present society as an aggregation of self-interested individuals. The continuing influence of those ideas is remarkable given their origins in the late eighteenth and early nineteenth century. Sociologists, from their side, have observed this modernization in an increasing individualization and atomization of society in Western countries, reflected in decreasing family sizes, and disappearing traditions and communities

(Inglehart, 1997). A characteristic of this evolution towards atomization and individualization is that it has lead to systems and ideas that do not recognize joint arrangements and mutual dependencies.

Declining trust in professionals and a need for control

Professional authority and professional knowledge have come under attack, and citizens and policy makers no longer uncritically accept that professionals such as teachers or doctors are delivering a high-quality service. This has resulted in a crisis of professionalism (O'Neill, 2002; Pfadenhauer, 2006). Many tasks of government are very suitable to be performed by self-steering professionals, because the tasks cannot be properly specified in advance, and because the quality of the outcome cannot easily be judged afterwards (Wilson, 1989: 149). Unlike production-type organizations, where activities, outputs and outcomes can easily be specified and measured, schools and hospitals are highly complex systems where the assessment of output and outcomes is difficult because of the large degree of professional and organizational discretion (Pritchett and Woolcock, 2002). A bureaucratic organization of these institutions, based on Fordist principles is therefore less appropriate, because such systems cannot cope with discretion (Wilson, 1989: 149).

However, declining trust in professionals, by the public and by managers, rules out professional expertise as the main guiding principle for such complex organizations. Discretionary services cannot easily be controlled or steered, so a demand emerges for a guiding principle to replace professionalism. This principle, rating and ranking, is copied from the one used in production-type agencies, and requires procedures, detailed record-keeping, and so on (Wilson, 1989: 170). In the absence of trust in both professional standards and in self-regulation in these complex and decentralized systems, indicators and rankings have come to replace relations of trust and deference. For politicians, the use of numbers and rankings is a means for regaining control over their departments. The performance movement has for this reason been described as an attack on professional monopolies (Radin, 2006: 54), a challenge to professional standards and a corrosion of professional autonomy (Moran, 2003).

By transforming the complex acts of professionals (teachers, medical doctors) into (performance) numbers, it feels as if we can understand them. Indicators have created for policy makers and citizens an appearance or illusion of control. Ironically, while rankings have been hailed as methods for restoring accountability and trust, they also symbolize the disappearance of societies' trust in professionals.

Rankings and creating sense and order

This process of modernization, described above, is still continuing. Rather than being in a postmodern era, some would claim we have entered a period of high modernity, where the processes of modernization have become radicalized and universalized (Giddens, 1996). One aspect of this high modernity is a continuing abstraction, generalization, and atomization of society. Modernization is reflected in an increasing abstraction of reality. Direct information about public services from friends or family is replaced by abstract and mediated performance information. Performance information mediates between public services and citizens (Giddens, 1996: 102).

The increasing use of performance information is a logical consequence of this evolution, which may have started already with the Enlightenment. One could even claim that the fact that rating and ranking systems are used so intensively in the United Kingdom has to do with the country's strong tradition of empiricism in political philosophy. Countries and sectors where performance information is used intensively usually share very positivist assumptions of knowledge (Henkel, 1991: 121). Ranking public services brings order to the messy social world.

The task of imposing order on a complex reality is often difficult, as we see with regard to efforts to measure performance of schools and hospitals. In dispersed systems with unclear outcomes, establishing a feeling of control is difficult. The uncertainty, differentiation, and disappearance of trust in professionals create real coping problems. Bevan and Hood describe the use of targets as a method of exercising control in complex environments (Bevan and Hood, 2006). Performance information, and especially ranking, re-establishes an impression of control. Rankings thus serve as coping mechanisms, replacing the earlier trust in professionals. The declining trust in professionals has created a need for new trusted methods of exchange. The disappearance of trust in one expert system (that of professionals) required its replacement by other mechanisms or systems, or symbolic tokens (Giddens, 1996: 22). Trust rests in the abstract capacities of these tokens. Rankings reflect an attempt at providing such new tokens.

Rankings offer predictability and rest in a world full of risk. They respond to citizens' need to feel in control, and create an illusion of having the levers of change. In the context of the public sector, Pollitt has used the concept "hypermodernism" in relation to overly progressive and teleological beliefs in public sector reform (Pollitt, 2007a). People have a desire to have simple and abstract views of reality, and manicheistic summaries of this reality as reflected in an institution's situation at the top or at the bottom of a public service ranking answer to such desires (de Kervasdoué, 2007). They give citizens the possibility to act as actors in control and to act as rational beings and decision makers. Obviously, these symbolic tokens only create an impression of information and rationality.

While helpful illusions, rating and rankings systems, just like all symbolic tokens, come with an important drawback. A symbols system in high modernity requires no context to interpret, or so we like to believe. Citizens may come to adopt a belief that they can assess the functioning of individual schools and hospitals using ratings and rankings without knowing this individual school's or hospital's context. Public sector rankings decontextualize public sector performance. Disembedded knowledge replaces embedded knowledge about schools and hospitals because the latter is less formalized and thus harder to interpret (Townley, 2002). Rating and ranking systems have the advantage that they help us to hold performance conversations about the functioning of public institutions by creating a common standard of conversation, but by doing so they also obscure a great deal of this "reality." The functioning of public institutions and information about this performance may have become decoupled (Power, 1999). More knowledge may actually have contributed to ambivalence and uncertainty and thus less control, not more (Giddens, 1996).

Rankings and accountability: risk avoidance and scapegoating

When a school or hospital is victimized because of its low position in certain rankings, the disembedded nature of performance knowledge in the rankings makes it difficult to interpret the reasons for this low position. Our need for control incites us to blame someone for this position (Beck, 1992). It is not without reason that some have equated new forms of accountability through performance information with punishment (Behn, 2001: 3). We *need* to believe that something is wrong with the performance of this hospital or that school. Not doing so would mean challenging the rating and rankings system, which would be a direct challenge to our feelings of control. Blaming the school's or hospital's management is preferred over having our illusion of control dispelled.

This scapegoating is relatively easy precisely because of the disembedded nature of public service rankings. This disembedded, decontextualized, nature allows you to rapidly formulate an opinion about a certain school or hospital. The role of rankings as a common language and symbolic tokens makes a scapegoating approach preferable to a challenge to the ranking system because it keeps the illusion of control intact.

The future of ratings and rankings

Rating and ranking systems are recent innovations in governance, and often highly controversial. There is active debate about the meaningfulness of the data made available to the public, and about the effect that publication of data has on the internal operations of organizations, as well as the behavior of consumers. As we have seen, many of the concerns aired in these disputes are well-founded: there is good reason to wonder whether rating and ranking systems result in an overall improvement in the quality of public services.

Might we have grounds, then, to doubt that this will prove to be a durable innovation? Probably not. As we have tried to show, the deployment of rating and ranking systems is not simply a technical decision – that is, a mechanical question of "instrument choice" governed by a weighing of the benefits and costs that accrue from deployment of such systems. The drive toward adoption of these systems is also driven by larger cultural, political and economic forces, which continue to operate without regard to such narrow calculations of benefits and costs. We may seek to alter or amend these systems in an effort to improve the benefit–cost ratio, but the broad question of whether we will engage in the business of ranking and rating may already be settled.

Indeed, the controversy of such systems may eventually fade away, so that the business of rating and ranking becomes a familiar and accepted way of thinking about the governance of public services. There is precedent for this. There was a time, for example, when many of the concepts used to measure national economic activity – Gross Domestic Product, the unemployment rate, the inflation rate the balance of payments – were unfamiliar and deeply contested. Today they are taken for granted in everyday discourse, even though the conceptual difficulties that initially provoked controversy persist (Boyle, 2001: 43; Saltelli, 2007). Rating and ranking systems may be consolidated in the same way.

We would then find ourselves in a world in which the qualities of modernity – rationalization, standardization, the quantification of value – are further advanced. We might imagine that this constitutes a triumph of popular sovereignty. These systems will be justified as mechanisms for assuring better central control over dispersed bureaucracies, and better accountability of service providers to their customers. And citizens may feel that they have acquired some greater measure of control in a world otherwise characterized by great turbulence. But this impression of heightened control is likely to be misleading. The economic forces that generate uncertainty are much broader in their impacts. Moreover the multiple producer-side and consumer-side problems with rating and ranking systems are likely to persist, limiting their effectiveness in enhancing control over service providers, even in a narrow sense.

Epilogue: The Many Faces of Use

Harry Hatry

Previous chapters have discussed, from a variety of viewpoints, the usefulness of the information generated by performance measurement processes in government. This chapter extracts from these materials, and discusses, three major dimensions of usefulness. These dimensions include: first, technical features on which usage may depend; second, the variety of types of potential users, each of whom is likely to need somewhat different performance information; and, third, the major ways in which performance information can be used. Then the chapter identifies the very substantial limitations of performance information, a topic that has seldom been well articulated in the past. Finally, the chapter does some crystal-ball gazing, discussing the future of performance measurement and performance management, especially as it relates to their likely future usefulness.

As Van Dooren says in Chapter 1, "If we want to study success and failure of performance movements, we have to study the use of performance information."

The key technical prerequisites for use

We here identify five key "technical" elements that seem necessary for successful use of performance measurement information:

- **Validity of the performance indicators.** Do the indicators measure what is relevant and important about the particular issue or service?
- **Quality of the data.** Is the quality of the data collected for each of the performance indicators of sufficient accuracy?

- **Timeliness of the data.** Are the performance data collected and reported in a sufficiently timely fashion so the information is available when needed?
- **Analysis of the data.** Has at least some basic analysis been undertaken of that data to put it into meaningful form, such as by providing breakouts of the aggregate data and by providing legitimate comparisons so that users can interpret the extent to which the measured levels of performance represent good or poor outcomes?
- **Presentation of the performance information.** Is the information presented in a form that the user groups can understand and interpret and in a easy to read format?

It is this author's experience that typically each of the above basic technical elements is frequently violated at least to some degree. This has likely contributed to the highly restrained use of performance information, as the various authors of the previous chapters indicate. Often, the set of performance indicators and data presented in performance reports includes a haphazard set of information that intertwines indicators of outputs, workload data, internal process indicators, outcome indicators, and even at times input indicators. This tends to drown the basic outcome information in the sea of what may be secondary information. Many existing national and sub-national performance measurement systems provide such mixtures of indicators keeping busy officials from using it. (A number of chapters, such as Bouckaert and Halligan's, identify various aspects of this problem.)

In the past, little basic analysis has been presented to users, though this does appear to be improving, in part because of the availability of continually improving technology (such as mapping software) that can help with such analysis. We are not talking here about sophisticated evaluation efforts, but only such basic analysis steps as breaking out aggregate data of an outcome indicator by individual geographical locations (depending on the government level, these could be states/ provinces, regions, districts, cities, neighborhoods, etc.) or by other key demographic characteristics (such as reporting the outcomes for various age groups, income groups, gender, race/ethnicity groups, special disadvantage/handicapped groups, etc.). Such breakouts have commonly been neglected throughout the world in performance measurement. The other major component of basic analysis is to provide basic comparisons. Some comparisons are typically used, such as comparisons with previous years' performance (though time trend information is seldom presented). Less often found in performance reports are comparisons with targets set by the service program at the beginning of the year (such as sometimes presented in program budgets) and comparisons with other similar jurisdictions with similar programs.

Finally, the format in which the data presented to users has been far from optimal and sometimes terrible. Reports have often contained too much information, with the key findings buried somewhere in that information. Sometimes too many data are provided. Sometimes the labels for the performance indicators are very unclear so that users cannot really understand what the data represent. Too infrequently have the voluminous amounts of data collected been highlighted and summarized (using even such basic steps as highlighting key findings, perhaps by merely circling unexpected outcomes or highlighting them in color). And brief summaries that extract the major findings are surprisingly seldom provided.

These gaps particularly affect higher level officials and legislators. For example, legislatures are often criticized for a lack of focus on the outcomes of services they fund. Few legislators throughout the world regularly ask about past results or the expected future results of the programs and services they are asked to fund. However, a substantial part of the blame for this falls on the Executive Branch in not providing valid indicators (e.g., that information likely to be most relevant on the important outcomes of concern to the legislators and their citizen constituents) and summaries and highlights of the performance information. (See Johnson and Talbot's chapter for discussion of limited UK Parliament's use of outcome information.)

Types of potential users

What information is wanted will, of course, vary at least somewhat by the type of user, as well as the particular circumstances – such as whether a new program is being considered, whether its budget is being reviewed, whether problems have arisen that need quick attention, and so on.

A basic taxonomy would likely start with the type and level of organization. This includes whether it is a public body or a private non-governmental organization. At the government level differences in the performance information needed will, of course, depend on the level of government, such as a national/central, state/provincial, of local government.

Within each such level, there will almost certainly be the following key user groups:

a. The Executive Branch. The Executive Branch will typically have at least three sub-levels of users, including:
   - high-level public officials, including department/ministry heads and their deputies
   - mid-management officials
   - first-line supervisors and non-supervisory employees
b. Legislature
c. The public and media

It is well understood that these different categories of users are likely to be interested in varying degrees of detail. Also, within any of these categories, people can differ considerably in their interest in data, such as that coming from a performance measurement process.

Surprisingly, however, and probably not often recognized, is that the findings for most outcome indicators are likely to be of potential interest at all levels and for all these groups. For example, basic outcome indicators, such as crime rates, infant mortality rates, water and air quality indicators, school test scores and graduation rates, will be of interest and importance at all levels. The time it takes for citizens to get a public assistance check from their government is likely to be of concern all the way up the line, including to legislators and, of course, the media (especially if the response time is excessive). Indeed, such mundane indicators as citizen ratings of the courteousness of public employees when they respond to citizens requests for assistance can become of interest even to national public officials and legislators.

What can differ substantially is the coverage of the indicator. This will have considerable effect on the intensity of user interest. For example, parents and school officials will be quite interested in school-level test scores and dropout rates for their own schools. National education officials will tend to focus on nationwide data and not be interested in data on individual schools. National legislators will be particularly concerned about the collective data relevant to their own constituents. The basic outcome indicator is the same, but its coverage differs. Citizens will have some interest in national crime rates, but are likely to be intensely interested in the crime rates in their own neighborhood and community.

On the other hand, operating management inevitably will routinely need more information on outcomes, details not likely to be of sufficient interest to higher level officials to report regularly to them. For example, not likely to be normally reported to higher level officials are the names of individual businesses that failed safety or environmental inspections, nor data on such intermediate outcomes as the percentage of firms that agreed to correct the violations.

High-level OMB-type offices have increasingly been attempting to reduce the number of outcomes regularly reported to high-level officials, limiting the number of indicators that individual agencies can provide. While this may, or may not, be a good approach, it appears in at least some instances to discourage agencies from reporting other performance data for their own internal purposes. This is a side-effect of the problem, discussed later, that the "top-down," prevalent, approach to performance measurement has not been accompanied by adequately encouraging operating managers to use the performance data for improving their services.

In recent years, considerable emphasis has been placed internationally on getting citizen involvement and use of performance information. It seems that it is assumed that many, probably most, citizens will be very interested in such information and use it to press their governments into improving services. It seems clear that citizens are likely to be considerably more interested in information on outcomes than information they may have traditionally received, such as counts of outputs. As more such information is collected and reported by governments, this seems likely to lead to somewhat more citizen interest and possibly use of that information. However, what is not clear is the extent of citizen interest in such data, except for data that applies to their own individual circumstances, such as service outcomes covering their own neighborhood or other affinity groups. (See Ho in Chapter 12 for a discussion of citizen involvement in performance measurement.)

A taxonomy of uses

Not often recognized by public officials is the large variety of uses of performance information. Below is one such listing. See de Lancer Julnes in Chapter 4 for another, closely related approach to classifying categories of uses.

(a) **Accountability.**   Upper level officials want evidence as to what the services being provided are achieving. This has probably been the major thrust in pushing performance measurement, both in developed and developing countries. Countries receiving funding support from the multilateral and bilateral funding organizations have been under pressure from those funders to provide such information. While considerable lip service has been given to using the information to help improve services, the emphasis appears to have been on getting information to show what has been accomplished. For developed countries, the mandate for performance measurement has usually come from elected officials in the legislature or executive branch of the governments. Few operating departments/ministries appear to have taken it upon themselves to introduce performance measurement.

(b) Budgeting. Performance information can be used in budgeting processes for basically three purposes:

- Development/preparation of the budget
- Justification of the budget proposal
- To fulfill the requirements of the upper-level officials

Unfortunately, few documented examples appear to exist of the use of budgeting and outcome information for justification and preparation. The exception has been the use of output data (such as the number of lane miles/meters of roads constructed or repaired and the number of clients served by a program). This has likely occurred because of the much closer link between costs and outputs. The production function between outcomes and outputs and, thus, between outcomes and costs, is usually not well known and therefore not of much use in rationalizing budgets. For example, what is the cost to improve customer satisfaction with a particular service by ten percentage points?

(c) Improving services. This category involves a large number of sub-uses, each of which is aimed ultimately at improving the service. These include the following:

(c.1) Raising questions/identifying problems. This use has sometimes been identified as being the major use of performance data, particularly outcome data. Questions can be raised at any level of the government about outcome data. Outcomes that are unexpected, whether unexpectedly bad or good, can readily become the subject for any official, or legislator, to ask "Why did this occur?" The questioning has the potential for stimulating attention to finding out why the problem occurred and to attempt to make changes to improve future outcomes.

Officials may wish to question disappointing outcomes but also where the program has done particularly well, both to make sure that the information is correct and possibly also to see whether what was done successfully can be transferred elsewhere or should continue to be supported. As Johnsen points out in Chapter 10, performance indicators seldom give answers but function as "tin openers," encouraging stakeholders to scrutinize issues more closely.

(c.2) Identifying training and technical assistance needs. This use appears to be rare but provides an opportunity for most government services. This use is likely to be most appropriate at the lower levels of a government agency. At the lowest level, outcome information could be broken out both by individual office and, sometimes, by each individual service worker, such as the outcomes of caseworkers in a variety of health and human services agencies where the individual employee has considerable responsibility for individual clients. This use can potentially be appropriate for almost any service – for example, in identifying technical assistance or training needs for individual offices responsible for water or air pollution inspections or for employees working on eligibility determinations on public assistance applicants.

(c.3) Motivating employees to improve service quality. A number of variations in this approach exist. Some governments at the various levels have played with approaches for tying pay to performance. It is not clear that monetary approaches are successful and they may even be counterproductive in causing dissension from employees who do not trust the way awards are made. This appears to have occurred because, usually, the final decision on awards is based on the judgment of a supervisor. What has seldom been attempted is awards based primarily on more objectively predefined outcomes, and where the employees involved agree that the process is fair.

Non-monetary awards, however, may have considerably more potential in the public sector. They may have motivating power without accompanying dissension. Askim notes in Chapter 8 that "we just know that most subordinates will behave as they should simply because of the possibility that their performance is being evaluated by leaders." Not widely used are recognition awards for public employees who have been members of teams, groups or offices that have produced especially good outcomes. Such awards are inexpensive and can be given to many employees, perhaps for either high levels of performance or for considerable improvement from past performance. Such awards can be used by governments to celebrate successes, helping to balance the often negative viewpoint of citizens about the public sector.

(c.4) "How Are We Doing?" sessions.   In this approach a higher level official holds regular meetings with his or her staff, perhaps after each performance report has been received, to go over the report's findings. At the meeting, the successes and the failures are identified, reasons for these are explored, and perhaps initial plans made for improvements (this approach can also be considered a form of motivational approach).

A major form of this approach has begun to sprout in the United States in what has been called the "Stat" movement. It began in the New York City Police Department, spread to many other agencies in New York City's government and then to the city of Baltimore in the form of its "CitiStat" program. A number of other local and, recently, state governments such as Washington and Maryland have begun to adopt variations. In this approach, a department head, mayor, governor or other key officials meet regularly with individual agencies to go over a series of statistics on that agency's performance. Most applications thus far have included not only outcome information but also output and process information, such as staff absentee rates. (The initial efforts in New York City focused primarily on outcome information such as crime rates. However, some other governments have tended to focus more on internal processes.) This approach appears to be quite attractive to many in upper management and appears likely to spread widely, certainly in the United States.

(c.5) Performance contracting.   One of the first real uses of outcome information in the United States has been its introduction into contracts with private for-profit businesses. This approach has also been applied to nonprofit organizations. The first such applications included providing bonuses and penalties to the contractors for completing road construction on schedule – whether ahead of, or behind, schedule. A key element is to make sure that the contractor has a significant amount of influence over the outcome indicators included in the contract. Such agreements have been used in solid waste collection, employment training programs (in which the contractor or grantee are paid at least in part based on success in getting unemployed persons into employment), and success in finding adoptive parents for children. Such contracts are probably possible in most government services. However, the contract clauses need to be worked out very carefully and provision needs to be made for obtaining accurate outcome data.

(c.6) Showing the distributional/equity affects of services. Outcome data broken out by categories of citizens, as discussed earlier, will indicate whether some subgroups of citizens have not been achieving the same outcomes as others. Such information can be used to affect allocations of public resources.

(c.7) Providing information for in-depth evaluations of a service. Some governments periodically undertake in-depth evaluations of selected services, particularly those for which problems have been raised. Such evaluations often can use existing performance data from the performance measurement process as a major source of data. Similarly, examination of performance data can indicate if a service or program needs a more in-depth evaluation.

(c.8) Learning/problem solving. Aside from immediately being used to improve services, the exploration of performance data can provide programs with insights into what is working and what is not working. Moynihan believes that agencies can engage in "goal based learning." While initially the outcome data might not be used to help support budgeting or operations, the information can be used to help agency personnel figure out what works well and not so well – so it can make future improvements.

If the outcomes of a similar service provided by different jurisdictions can be compared, that information can be used to help identify "best (successful) practices." This generally requires an outside organization to examine the outcome data and identify what it is that the successful jurisdictions are doing to achieve the higher levels of performance – and then disseminate that information to other jurisdictions.

A largely untouched procedure in the public sector is the use of random assignment experimental designs to improve operational procedures. This academic term may be frightening to public employees. However, sometimes the procedure can be used in a relatively simple way to try out different ways of delivering a service. For example, an employment training program might experiment with different media or different amounts of time for major training elements. Such procedures are feasible if customers can be randomly assigned to either the existing procedure or the new procedure – such as by flipping a coin – and if no ethical problems arise by not providing all customers with the same procedure. Subsequently the outcomes would be compared for each of the two procedures to identify if one of the approaches had superior outcomes to the other.

(c.9) Aiding performance partnerships. Outcome data can be used as a glue for establishing performance partnerships. These partnerships are collaborations in which different government agencies (and perhaps non-government organizations) work together to attack a large-scale problem that crosses agency lines. The public partners might be at the same level of government or at different levels.

In such partnerships, the partners would agree on the activities and key outcome indicators, set targets for each indicator, and subsequently report on progress being made against the targets. The indicators would basically represent a pyramid of intermediate and end outcome indicators. Each partner's responsibility relating to each indicator would need to be identified. For example, if the issue is juvenile delinquency, each participating local government would be responsible for tracking the amount and severity of juvenile delinquency within its own jurisdiction. The juvenile delinquency data might be tracked by a criminal justice agency. Educational and social service agencies have also considerable responsibility, such as by working with churches and parents to reduce school absenteeism and dropout rates. Each school district would be responsible for tracking and improving its performance on these indicators. However, as Denhardt and Aristigueta document in Chapter 7, these collaborations can be quite difficult to implement successfully.

(c.10) Marketing/advocacy.   Moynihan believes this is a first use of performance information by agency staff. In the United States, nonprofit agencies have been encouraged by their sponsors, both government agencies and private charitable foundations, to justify their request by presenting outcome information. Nonprofit organizations as well as public organizations can more proactively seek funds based on their outcomes. Even agencies that find they have not been able to produce the outcomes they had hoped for might use that data to help justify their need for funding – in order to improve their services.

(c.11) Communicating with citizens.   Citizens are likely to have considerable interest in outcome information, especially outcomes that relate to their own personal situation, such as their own community, age group, gender, and so on. For example, public officials might use the outcome information as a basis for "State of the Government" reports to their citizens or in meetings with citizens on specific issues to help justify past decisions or new proposed plans.

Limitations of performance measurement information

Unfortunately, key important limitations of performance information have not been sufficiently articulated nor learned by many users. This, among other things, has led to excessive expectations for performance information, leading at the extreme to throwing out the baby with the wash water and giving up on performance measurement and its use. The following is a list of such limitations:

1.   Performance data do not tell WHY performance has been good or bad or what should be done to improve services. However, a well-constructed performance measurement system can help shed light on the why and what should be done. For example, disaggregating out-come data can help pinpoint the cause of the problem, such as possibly showing that the problem primarily has occurred for a particular demo-graphic group. When customer surveys are used, it is good practice to ask respondents to identify reasons for any poor ratings they gave and to provide improvement suggestions.

To obtain a fuller perspective of problem causes, in-depth studies are needed. Performance measurement is intended to be a regular activity that involves reporting on selected key outcome performance indica-tors. More in depth information on causes might be obtained by setting up a special task force to examine the problem or by undertaking an in-depth program evaluation.

2.   For particular issues that arise during the year, public officials will likely need information on more indicators than those included in their ongoing performance measurement process, which inevitably needs to focus on a limited set of indicators being reported. These should be "key" indicators, but for any service, many other service characteristics are likely to be important. At the lower levels of the operating agency each of these indicators might be tracked, but the typical performance measurement system will seldom cover enough of them to provide a full, complete perspective on a particular issue. Thus, during ad hoc program reviews, other outcome information (as well as other information) will likely be needed.

3.   Finally, performance measurement is about the past. It provides data about the past. But, most public decisions are about the future. This includes budget, program and policy choices. The performance data provide a major source of information for decision makers as to what should be done about the future. Data on past performance are used to extrapolate future performance. And they provide the baseline data from which progress can be assessed. However, projecting into the future is fraught with obstacles and difficulties. Even worse, if an agency wants to consider options that are considerably different than the

current ones, past data may be of limited use for projecting the performance of the new options.

The above limitations are substantial and need to be recognized. It also needs to be recognized that the performance information has considerable potential usefulness for purposes such as discussed above. Nevertheless, if the performance information is not or is only barely used for any of these purposes, a government will need to revamp its performance measurement process if not drop it. At present, many, probably most, public officials and managers have limited experience in using performance information.

Crystal-ball gazing: the future of performance measurement and its use

The major shift that appears to be emerging is to transform performance measurement into performance management (see also Bouckaert and Halligan in Chapter 5). Indeed, it is the use of the performance information that is the key element in transforming performance measurement into performance management. More and more scholars and operational public officials are putting more stress on performance management. Performance measurement is a key element of performance management – it is essential to it.

A key indicator of this in the United States is the increasing attention to the "Stat" movement (discussed earlier) by both upper level public officials and operating managers. The phrase "Stat" ("statistics") may frighten off some officials. Some governments are likely to switch terminology to make the terminology more congenial with public officials (such as in the State of Washington's new "Government Management Accountable and Performance" process). These "How Are We Doing?" sessions are characterized by regular meetings between upper level public officials with lower level staff to examine the latest performance information on individual public services and to determine if, and what, actions are needed. This approach appears to be quite promising and to be a natural way to use performance information. It is likely that some governments in other countries will in the future adapt some variation of the approach.

Improved information technology will increase the attractiveness of outcome information. We can expect much greater use of charts and maps and color in performance reports, increasing the information's appeal to, and use by, public officials and the public. Even more important, the technology is making it much easier to disaggregate data by key characteristics of customers or of the workload, such as in road maintenance and environmental protection programs. For example, water quality and air quality data are likely to be mapped in terms of various pollutant levels for particular locations and particular parts of water bodies.

Questions remain about the validity of the outcome information. Outputs and outcomes are still often confused and jumbled together. Key outcome information is not collected. However, in recent years this problem appears to be lessening. A major gap, however, is the considerable resistance to following up outcomes *after* customer program completion, such as to assess whether the client is in good condition six or 12 months after completing the program. For many services, particularly health and human service programs, such follow-ups seem essential for assessing whether outcomes have been successful. Currently such assessments primarily are done only if an ad hoc program evaluation is done. Such studies occur too infrequently to be useful for ongoing performance management. Technology should help in the future to make it easier to reach clients (such as when most citizens have ready access to the internet) so that agencies will become more comfortable in gathering such essential information.

Most of the analytical focus so far has been on examining past performance. Much more attention, if not a real shift, is needed on how such historical data can be used to help make future decisions. The major example that this author knows about occurs in the use of simulation models, such as their use of past relationships to project into the future who and how many citizens would be affected by proposed changes to public assistance program eligibility rules.

Very much needed is exploration into the relationships among costs, outputs and outcomes. The amount of money needed to increase outcomes will likely always be subject to considerable uncertainty. However, more attention to these relationships by both individual governments and across governments is needed, for instance for budgeting and strategic planning. The search for such information has not yet emerged significantly as far as this author can see.

In order to build fully on these various applications and uses of performance information, public officials at all levels will need more exposure to examples of how others have used performance information. Case studies are needed of examples of uses to improve services that have been made by public agencies. Studies are needed that identify the factors leading to use or non-use. The temptation in case studies will be merely to document initial implementation of changes without also seeking information on whether the implementation was sustained and, most importantly, whether the changes actually led to improved outcomes. Such investigations will be a challenge, but are badly needed for use in training and educating public officials.

Final comment

It seems to be just common sense that public officials and other public managers need performance information, especially on outcomes, to properly manage public services. It is hard to believe that performance measurement will not continue far into the future. Many variations will undoubtedly occur, but it seems highly likely that service outcomes will continue to be measured in some form or another and be increasingly used for accountability, budgeting and improving public services.

Bibliography

Aarsæther, N. and Vabo, S. 2002, *Fristilt og Velstyrt? Fokus på Kommune-Norge*, Samlaget, Oslo.

Ammons, D. 1995, *Accountability for Performance. Measurement and Monitoring in Local Government*, International City/County Management Association, Washington.

Ammons, D. 2001, *Municipal Benchmarks. Assessing Local Performance and Establishing Community Standards* (2nd edn). Sage, Thousand Oaks, CA.

Andrews, M. and Moynihan, D. P. 2002, "Why Reforms Don't Always Have to Work to Succeed: A Tale of Two Managed Competition Initiatives", *Public Performance and Management Review*, vol. 25, no. 3, pp. 282–97.

Ansari, S. and Euske, K. 1987, "Rational, Rationalizing, and Reifying Uses of Accounting Data In Organizations", *Accounting, Organizations and Society*, vol. 12, no. 6, pp. 549–70.

Argyris, C. and Schön, D. 1996, *Organizational Learning: A Theory of Action Perspective*, Addison-Wesley, Reading, MA.

Aristigueta, M. P. 1999, *Managing for Results in State Government*, Quorum, Westport, CT.

Aristigueta, M. P., Cooksy, L. J., and Nelson, C. W. 2001, "The Role of Social Indicators in Developing a Managing for Results System", *Public Performance & Management Review*, vol. 24, no. 3, pp. 254–69.

Arndt, C. 2007, *The Politics of Governance Ratings* Maastricht Graduate School of Governance, Maastricht.

Askim, J. 2004, "Performance Management and Organizational Intelligence: Adapting the Balanced Scorecard in Larvik Municipality", *International Public Management Journal*, vol. 7, no. 3, pp. 415–38.

Askim, J. 2007a, "How do Politicians Use Performance Information? An Analysis of the Norwegian Local Government Experience", *International Review of Administrative Sciences*, vol. 73, no. 3, pp. 453–72.

Askim, J. 2007b, *Local Government by Numbers: Who Makes Use of Performance Information, When, and for What Purposes?*, PhD Thesis, University of Oslo.

Askim, J. forthcoming, "The Demand Side of Performance Measurement: Explaining Councillors' Utilization of Performance Information in Policymaking", *International Public Management Journal*.

Askim, J., Johnsen, Å., and Christophersen, K.-A. 2008, "Factors behind Organizational Learning from Benchmarking: Experiences from Norwegian Municipal Benchmarking Networks", *Journal of Public Administration Research and Theory*, vol. 18, no. 2, pp. 297–320.

Aucoin, P. 2001, *Comparative Perspectives on Canadian Public Service Reform in the 1990s*, Office of the Auditor General of Canada, Ottawa.

Australian National Audit Office 2004, *Performance Management in the Australian Public Service, Audit Report No. 6 2004–05*, Commonwealth of Australia, Canberra.

Baker, D. L. 2004, *The Case of Interagency Coordinating Councils: Examining Collaborations in Services for Children with Disabilities*, Institute of Public Policy, Harry S. Truman School of Public Affairs, University of Missouri, Columbia, Report 14.

Baldassare, M. 2000, *California in the New Millennium: The Changing Social and Political Landscape*, University of California Press, Berkeley, CA.

Barber, M. 2007, *Instruction to Deliver: Tony Blair, Public Services and the Challenge of Achieving Targets*, Politico's, London.

Bardach, E. 1998, *Getting Agencies to Work Together: The Practice and Theory of Managerial Craftsmanship*. Brookings Institution Press, Washington, DC.

Bardach, E. and Lesser, C. 1996, "Accountability in Human Services Collaboratives: For What? And to Whom?", *Journal of Public Administration Research and Theory*, vol. 6, no. 2, pp. 197–224.

Barnow, B. S. 1999, "The Effects of Performance Standards on State and Local Programs", in *Evaluating Welfare and Training Programs*, C. F. Manski and I. Garfinkel, eds, Harvard University Press, Harvard, pp. 277–309.

Bauer, R. A. 1966, *Social Indicators*, MIT Press, Cambridge, MA.

Bauman, Z. 1999, *In Search of Politics*, Polity Press, Cambridge.

Baumol, W. 1997, "Health Care, Education and the Cost Disease", in *Baumol's Cost Disease*, R. Towse, ed., Edward Elgar, London, pp. 510–21.

Beck, U. 1992, *Risk Society: Towards a New Modernity*, Sage, London.

Behn, R. D. 2001, *Rethinking Democratic Accountability*, Brookings Institution Press, Washington, DC.

Behn, R. D. 2002, "The Psychological Barriers to Performance Management: Or Why Isn't Everyone Jumping on the Performance-Management Bandwagon", *Public Performance and Management Review*, vol. 26, no. 1, pp. 5–25.

Behn, R. D. 2003, "Why Measure Performance? Different Purposes Require Different Measures", *Public Administration Review*, vol. 63, no. 5, pp. 586–606.

Behn, R. D. 2006, "The Varieties of CitiStat", *Public Administration Review*, vol. 66, no. 3, pp. 332–40.

Bekkers, V. 1994, *Nieuwe Vormen van Sturing en Iinformatisering*, Eburon, Delft.

Bergesen, H. O. 2006, *Kampen om Kunnskapsskolen*, Universitetsforlaget, Oslo.

Berman, E. 1997, "Dealing with Cynical Citizens", in *Local Government Management: Current Issues and Best Practices*, D. J. Watson and W. L. Hassett, eds, ME Sharpe, New York.

Berman, E. and Wang, X. 2000, "Performance Measurement in U.S. Counties: Capacity for Reform", *Public Administration Review*, vol. 60, no. 5, pp. 409–20.

Berry, F. S. 1994, "Innovation in Public Management: The Adoption of Strategic Planning", *Public Administration Review*, vol. 54, no. 4, pp. 322–30.

Bevan, G. and Hood, C. 2006, "What's Measured is what Matters: Targets and Gaming in the English Public Health Care System", *Public Administration*, vol. 84, pp. 517–38.

Beyer, J. M. and Trice, H. M. 1982, "The Utilization Process: A Conceptual Framework and Synthesis of Empirical Findings", *Administrative Science Quarterly*, vol. 27, no. 4, pp. 591–622.

Blair, T. 2004, *Speech to the Labour Party Conference*, Office of the Prime Minister, London.

Blau, P. 1963, *The Dynamics of Bureaucracy: A Study of Interpersonal Relationships in Two Government Agencies*, University of Chicago Press, Chicago.

Bolman, L. G. and Deal, T. E. 1991, *Reframing Organizations: Artistry, Choice, and Leadership*, Jossey-Bass, San Francisco.

Booth, C. (1903), *Life and Labour of the People of London*, Macmillan, London.

Borins, S. 1995, "The New Public Management is Here to Stay", *Canadian Public Administration*, vol. 38, no. 1, pp. 121–32.

Bouckaert, G. 1990, "The History of the Productivity Movement", *Public Productivity & Management Review*, vol. 14, no. 1, pp. 53–89.

Bouckaert, G. and Balk, W. 1991, "Public Productivity Measurement: Diseases and Cures", *Public Productivity and Management Review*, vol. 15, no. 2, pp. 229–35.

Bouckaert, G. and Halligan, J. 2006, "Performance and Performance Management", in *Handbook of Public Policy*, B. G. Peters and J. Pierre, eds, Sage, London, pp. 443–59.

Bouckaert, G. and Halligan, J. 2008, *Managing Performance: International Comparisons*, Routledge, London.

Bouckaert, G. and Peters, B. G. 2002, "Performance Measurement and Management: The Achilles' Heel in Administrative Modernization", *Public Performance and Management Review*, vol. 25, no. 4, pp. 359–62.

Bouckaert, G. and Thijs, N. 2003, *Kwaliteit in de Overheid: Een Handboek voor Kwaliteitsmanagement in de Publieke Sector o.b.v. een Internationaal Comparatieve Studie*, Academia Press, Gent.

Bouckaert, G. and Van Dooren, W. 2003, "Performance Management in Public Sector Organizations", in *Public Management and Governance*, E. Löffler and T. Bovaird, eds, Routledge, London, pp. 127–36.

Bouckaert, G., De Peuter, B., and Van Dooren, W. 2003, *Meten en Vergelijken van Bestuurlijke Ontwikkeling: Een Monitoringsysteem voor het Lokaal Bestuur in Vlaanderen* Die Keure, Brugge.

Boyle, D. 2001, *The Tyranny of Numbers: Why Counting Can't Make us Happy*, Harper Collins, London.

Boyle, R. 2007, *Do Values Inform Comparisons?* Paper presented at the Study Group on Performance in the Public Sector, EGPA Annual conference, 19–21 September Madrid.

Boyne, G. A. and Chen, A. G. 2007, "Performance Targets and Public Service Improvement", *Journal of Public Administration Research and Theory*, vol. 17, no. 3, pp. 455–77.

Boyte, H. C. 2005, "Reframing Democracy: Governance, Civic Agency, and Politics", *Public Administration Review*, vol. 65, no. 5, pp. 536–46.

Bretschneider, S., Wilpen, L. G., Gloria, G., and Earle, K. 1989, "Political and Organizational Influences on the Accuracy of Forecasting State Government Revenues", *International Journal of Forecasting*, vol. 5, no. 3, pp. 307–19.

Breul, J. D. and Moravitz, C. 2007, *Integrating Performance and Budgets: The Budget Office of Tomorrow*. Rowman & Littlefield, Lanham, MD.

Brown, G. 1998, *House of Commons Debate*. Speech 14 July.

Brownstein, R. 2007, *The Second Civil War: How Extreme Partisanship has Paralyzed Washington and Polarized America*, Penguin Press, New York.

Brunsson, N. 1985, *The Irrational Organization: Irrationality as a Basis for Organizational Action and Change*, John Wiley & Sons, Chichester.

Brunsson, N. 1989, *The Organization of Hypocrisy*, John Wiley & Sons, Chichester.

Brunsson, N. and Olsen, J. P. 1990, *Makten att Reformera*. Carlssons Bokförlag, Stockholm.

Bulmer, M. 2001, "Social Measurement: What Stands in Its Way?", *Social Research*, vol. 68, no. 2, pp. 455–80.

Bulmer, M., Bales, K., and Sklar, K. K. 1991, *The Social Survey in Historical Perspective, 1880–1940*, Cambridge University Press, Cambridge.

Burke, B. E. and Costello, B. C. 2005, "The Human Side of Managing For Results", *American Review Of Public Administration*, vol. 35, no. 3, pp. 270–86.

Burnham, P. 2001, "New Labour and the Politics of Depoliticisation", *The British Journal of Politics and International Relations*, vol. 3, no. 2, pp. 127–49.

Carter, N. 1991, "Learning to Measure Performance: The Use of Indicators in Organizations", *Public Administration*, vol. 69, no. 1, pp. 85–101.

Carter, N., Klein, R., and Day, P. 1992, *How Organisations Measure Success. The Use of Performance Indicators in Government*, Routledge, London.

Cavalluzzo, K. S. and Ittner, C. D. 2004, "Implementing Performance Measurement Innovations: Evidence from Government", *Accounting, Organizations and Society*, vol. 29, no. 3–4, pp. 243–67.

Chancellor of the Exchequer 1998a, "Modern Public Services for Britain: Investing in Reform", in *Comprehensive Spending Review: New Public Spending Plans 1999–2002*, Parliament, London.

Chancellor of the Exchequer 1998b, *Modern Public Services for Britain: Modernization, Reform, Accountability: Public Service Agreements 1999–2002*, The Stationery Office, London.

Cherny, A. 2000, *The Next Deal: The Future of Public Life in the Information Age*, Basic Books, New York.

Chetkovich, C. A. 2000, *The NYPD Takes on Crime in New York City.(B) Compstat (Case Study No. CR16-00-1558.3)*, Harvard University Press, Cambridge, MA.

Christensen, J. G. 2001, "Bureaucratic Autonomy as a Political Asset", in *Politicians, Bureaucrats and Administrative Reform*, B. G. Peters and J. Pierre, eds, Routledge, London, pp. 119–31.

Christensen, T. and Lægreid, P. 2006, "Agencification and Regulatory Reforms", in *Autonomy and Regulation. Coping with Agencies in the Modern State*, Cheltenham: Edward Elgar, pp. 8–49.

Christensen, T., Lægreid, P., Roness, P. J., and Røvik, K. A. 2007, *Organization Theory for the Public Sector. Instrument, Culture, Myth*, Routledge, London.

Clark, I. D. and Swain, H. 2005, "Distinguishing the Real from the Surreal in Management Reform: Suggestions for Beleaguered Administrators in the Government of Canada", *Canadian Public Administration*, vol. 48, no. 4, pp. 453–77.

Coe, C. K. and Brunet, J. R. 2006, "Organizational Report Cards: Significant Impact or Much Ado about Nothing?", *Public Administration Review*, vol. 66, no. 1, pp. 90–100.

Commission on the Scrutiny Role of Parliament 2001, *The Challenge for Parliament – Making Government Accountable*, Hansard Society, London.

Committee Office Scrutiny Unit 2007, *Financial Scrutiny Uncovered*, House of Commons, London.

Comptroller and Auditor General 1998, *Benefits Agency: Performance Measurement*, National Audit Office, London.

Comptroller and Auditor General 2000, *Good Practice in Performance Reporting in Executive Agencies and Non-Departmental Public Bodies*, National Audit Office, London.

Comptroller and Auditor General 2001, *Measuring the Performance of Government Departments*, National Audit Office, London.

Comptroller and Auditor General 2005, *Public Service Agreements: Managing Data Quality – Compendium Report (HC 476)*, National Audit Office, London.

Comptroller and Auditor General 2006, *Second Validation Compendium Report*, National Audit Office, London.

Courty, P. and Marschke, G. R. 1997, "Measuring Government Performance: Lessons from a Federal Job-Training Program", *The American Economic Review*, vol. 87, no. 2, p. 383–8.

Cronbach, L. J., Ambron, S. R., Dornbusch, S. M., Hess, R. D., Hornik, R. C., Phillips, D. C., Walker, D. F. and Weiner, S. S. 1980, *Toward Reform of Program Evaluation*, Jossey-Bass, San Francisco, CA.

Crozier, M. 1964, *The Bureaucratic Phenomenon*, University of Chicago Press, Chicago.

Curristine, T. 2005, "Government Performance: Lessons and Challenges", *OECD Journal on Budgeting*, vol. 5, no. 1, pp. 127–51.

Cyert, R. M. and March, J. G. 1963, *A Behavioral Theory of the Firm*, Prentice-Hall, Englewood Cliffs, NJ.

Daft, R. L. and Lengel, R. H. 1990, "Information Richness: A New Approach to Managerial Behavior and Organizational Design", in *Information and Cognition in Organizations*, L. L. Cummings and B. M. Staw, eds, JAI Press, Greenwich, CT, pp. 243–85.

Dahler-Larsen, P. 1998, "Beyond Non-Utilization of Evaluations: An Institutional Perspective", *Knowledge, Technology, and Policy*, vol. 11, no. 1–2, p. 64–90.

Davey, J. A. 2000, "From Birth to Death: A Social Monitoring Framework from New Zealand", *Social Indicators Research*, vol. 49, no. 1, pp. 51–67.

Davidson, P. 1991, "The Social Survey in Historical Perspective: A Governmental Perspective", in *The Social Survey in Historical Perspective: 1880–1940*, M. Bulmer, K. Bales, and K. K. Sklar, eds, Cambridge University Press, Cambridge.

Davies, H. T. O., Nutley, S. M., and Smith, P. C. 2000, *What Works? Evidence-Based Policy and Practice in Public Services*, The Policy Press, London.

Davies, H. T. O., Washington, A. E., and Bindman, A. B. 2002, "Health Care Report Cards: Implications for Vulnerable Patient Groups and the Organizations Providing them Care", *Journal of Health Politics*, vol. 27, no. 3, pp. 379–99.

Dawson, S. and Dargie, C. 2002, *New Public Management*, Routledge, London.

De Bruijn, H. 2002, *Managing Performance in the Public Sector*, Routledge, London.

de Haas, M. and Kleingeld, A. 1998, "Multilevel Design of Performance Measurement Systems: Enhancing Strategic Dialogue Through the Organization", *Management Accounting Research*, vol. 10, no. 3, 223–61.

de Kervasdoué, J. 2007, *Les Prêcheurs de l'Apocalypse*, Plon, Paris.

De Kool, D. 2007, *Monitoring in Beeld: Een Studie naar de Doorwerking van Monitors in Interbestuurlijke Relaties*, Erasmus Universiteit Rotterdam, Rotterdam.

De Kool, D. and van Buuren, A. 2004, "Monitoring: Functional or Fashionable?", *Society and Economy*, vol. 26, no. 2, pp. 173–93.

de Lancer Julnes, P. 2006, "Performance Measurement: An Effective Tool for Government Accountability? The Debate Goes On", *Evaluation*, vol. 12, no. 2, pp. 219–35.

de Lancer Julnes, P. and Holzer, M. 2001, "Promoting the Utilization of Performance Measures in Public Organizations: An Empirical Study of Factors Affecting Adoption and Implementation", *Public Administration Review*, vol. 61, no. 6, pp. 693–708.

de Lancer Julnes, P. and Mixcoatl, G. 2006, "Governors as Agents of Change. A Comparative Study of Performance Measurement Initiatives in Utah and Campeche", *Public Performance & Management Review*, vol. 29, no. 4, pp. 405–32.

De Neufville, J. I. 1975, *Social Indicators and Public Policy: Interactive Processes of Design and Application* Elsevier, New York.

deHaven-Smith, L. and Jenne, K. C. 2006, "Management by Inquiry: A Discursive Accountability System for Large Organizations", *Public Administration Review*, vol. 66, no. 1, pp. 64–76.

Deleon, L. and Deleon, P. 2002, "The Democratic Ethos and Public Management", *Administration & Society*, vol. 34, no. 2, pp. 229–50.

Department for Communities and Local Government 2006, *Local Area Agreements Enabling Measure Requests. Round 2*, Stationary Office, London.

Department of Finance and Administration 2006a, *Australia's Experience in Utilising Performance Information in Budget and Management processes, Report for the 3rd Annual Meeting of the OECD Senior Budget Officials Network on Performance and Results*, DoFa, Canberra.

Department of Finance and Administration 2006b, *Submission to the Senate Finance and Public Administration References Committee, Inquiry into the Transparency and Accountability of Commonwealth Public Funding and Expenditure, 4 August*, DoFa, Canberra.

Desrosières, A. 1998, *The Politics of Large Numbers: A History of Statistical Reasoning* Harvard University Press, Cambridge, MA.

Dixit, A. 2002, "Incentives and Organizations in the Public Sector: An Interpretative Review", *The Journal of Human Resources*, vol. 37, no. 4, p. 696–727.

Downs, A. 1957, *An Economic Theory of Democracy*, Harper Collins, New York.

Dowrick, S. and Quiggin, J. 1998, "Measures of Economic Activity and Welfare: The Uses and Abuses of GDP", in *Measuring Progress: Is Life Getting Better?*, R. Eckersley, ed., CSIRO Publishing, Collinwood, Victoria, pp. 93–107.

Drucker, P. F. 1954, *The Practice of Management*, Harper & Row, New York.

Drucker, P. F. 1976, "What Results Should You Expect? A Users' Guide to MBO", *Public Administration Review*, vol. 36, no. 1, pp. 12–19.

Dubnick, M. 2005, "Accountability and the Promise of Performance: In Search of Mechanisms", *Public Performance and Management Review*, vol. 28, no. 3, pp. 376–417.

Ebdon, C. and Franklin, A. 2004, "Searching for a Role for Citizens in the Budget Process", *Public Budgeting & Finance*, vol. 24, no. 1, pp. 32–49.

Egeberg, M. 1994, "Bridging the Gap Between Theory and Practice: The Case of Administrative Policy", *Governance*, vol. 7, no. 1, pp. 83–98.

Egeberg, M. 2003, "How Bureaucratic Structure Matters: An Organizational Perspective", in *Handbook of Public Administration*, B. G. Peters and J. Pierre, eds, Sage, London, pp. 116–26.

Elmore, R. 2007, *When Good Policies go Bad: Political Accountability and Quality of Service in Education*. Paper presented at the IPMN Workshop on Rating and Ranking Public Services, 7–9 August, Oxford.

Engbersen, R. 1997, *Nederland aan de Monitor: Het Systematisch en Periodiek Volgen van Maatschappelijke Ontwikkelingen* NIZW, Utrecht.

Epstein, P., Coates, P., and Wray, L. 2005, *Results that Matter: Improving Communities by Engaging Citizens, Measuring Performance, and Getting Things Done*, Jossey Bass, San Francisco.

Expertgroep Brinkman 1998, *Verrijkte Steden: Analyse Grotestedenbeleid Rijkszijde*, Expertgroep Zelfanalyse GSB Rijk, Den Haag.

Ezzamel, M., Hyndman, N., Johnsen, Å.., and Lapsley, I. 2008, *Accounting and Politics: Devolution and Democratic Accountability*, Routledge, London.

Feldman, M. S. 1989, *Order Without Design: Information Production and Policy Making* Stanford University Press, Stanford, CA.

Feldman, M. S. and March, J. G. 1981, "Information in Organizations as Signal and Symbol", *Administrative Science Quarterly*, vol. 26, no. 2, pp. 171–86.

Fevolden, T. and Lillejord, S. 2005, *Kvalitetsarbeid i skolen*, Universitetsforlaget: Oslo.

Fidler, L. A. and Johnson, J. D. 1984, "Communication and Innovation Implementation", *The Academy of Management Review*, vol. 9, no. 4, pp. 704–11.

Fisher, J. 1995, "Contingency-Based Research on Management Control Systems", *Journal of Accounting Literature*, vol. 14, pp. 24–53.

Fiol, C. M. and Lyles, M. A. 1985, "Organizational Learning", *The Academy of Management Review*, vol. 10, no. 4, pp. 803–13.

Frederickson, D. G. and Frederickson, H. G. 2006, *Measuring the Performance of the Hollow State*. Georgetown University Press, Washington, DC.

Frederickson, H. G. 2007, "When Accountability Meets Collaboration", *PA Times*, February, p. 11.

Friestad, L. B. H. and Robertsen, K. 1990, *Effektiviseringsmuligheter i grunnskolen*, Agderforskning R&D-Report No. 72, Høyskoleforlaget, Kristiansand.

Garvin, D. 1993, "Building A Learning Organization", *Harvard Business Review*, vol. 71, no. 4, pp. 78–91.

Giddens, A. 1996, *The Consequences of Modernity*, Cambridge University Press, Cambridge.

Gilmour, B. J. 2006, *Implementing OMB's Program Assessment Rating Tool (PART): Meeting the Challenges of Integrating Budget and Performance*, IBM Centre for the Business of Government, Washington, DC.

Gilmour, J. B. and Lewis, D. E. 2006, "Does Performance Budgeting Work? An Examination of the Office of Management and Budget's PART Scores", *Public Administration Review*, vol. 66, no. 5, pp. 742–52.

Goodchild, M. F. and Janelle, D. G. 2004, *Spatially Integrated Social Science*, Oxford University Press, Oxford.

Governmental Accounting Standards Board 2003, *Reporting Performance Information: Suggested Criteria for Effective Communication*, GASB, Norwalk, CT.

Gray, B. 1989, *Collaborating: Finding Common Ground for Multi-Party Problems*, Jossey-Bass, San Francisco.

Greiner, J. M. 1996, "Positioning Performance Measurement for the Twenty-First Century", in *Organizational Performance and Measurement in the Public Sector*, A. Halachmi and G. Bouckaert, eds, Quorum Books, Westport, CT.

Greve, H. 2003, *Organizational Learning from Performance Feedback: A Behavioral Perspective on Innovation and Change.* Cambridge University Press, Cambridge.

Hacker, J. S. 2006, *The Great Risk Shift: The Assault on American Jobs, Families, Health Care, and Retirement, and How You Can Fight Back,* Oxford University Press, Oxford.

Halachmi, A. 2005, "Performance Measurement: Test the Water Before You Dive In", *International Review of Administrative Sciences,* vol. 71, no. 2, pp. 255–66.

Hall, P. A. and Taylor, R. C. R. 1996, "Political Science and the Three New Institutionalisms", *Political Studies,* vol. 44, no. 4, pp. 936–57.

Halligan, J. 2007, "Reform Design and Performance in Australia and New Zealand", in *Transcending New Public Management,* T. Christensen and P. Lægreid, eds, Ashgate, Aldershot.

Hamblin, R. 2007, "Publishing 'Quality' Measures: How it Works and When it Does Not?", *International Journal for Quality in Health Care,* vol. 19, no. 4, pp. 183–6.

Hanney, S. R., Gonzalez-Block, M. A., Buxton, M. J., and Kogan, M. 2004, "The Utilisation of Health Research in Policy-making: Concepts, Examples and Methods of Assessment", *Health Research Policy and Systems,* vol. 1, no. 2, pp. 1–28.

Hansard Society 2001, *The Challenge for Parliament – Making Scrutiny Work,* Hansard Society, London.

Hardin, B. 1999, *The Role of Multisector Collaborations in Strengthening Communities,* Union Institute, Washington, DC.

Hartley, J. and Allison, M. 2002, "Good, Better, Best? Inter-Organizational Learning in a Network of Local Authorities", *Public Management Review,* vol. 4, no. 1, pp. 101–18.

Hatry, H. P. 1999, *Performance Measurement: Getting Results,* Urban Institute Press, Washington, DC.

Hatry, H. P. 2006, *Performance Measurement: Getting Results,* 2nd edn, Urban Institute Press, Washington, DC.

Hatry, H. P. and Fisk, D. 1972, *Improving Productivity and Productivity Measurement in Local Governments,* National Commission on Productivity, Washington, DC.

Hedberg, B. 1981, "How Organizations Learn and Unlearn", in *Handbook of Organizational Design,* P. C. Nystrom and W. H. Starbuck, eds, Oxford University Press, London, pp. 8–27.

Heikkila, T. and Isett, K. R. 2007, "Citizen Involvement and Performance Management in Special-Purpose Governments", *Public Administration Review,* vol. 67, no. 2, pp. 238–48.

Heinrich, C. J. 2003, "Measuring Public Sector Performance and Effectiveness", in *Handbook of Public Administration,* B. G. Peters and J. Pierre, eds, Sage, London, pp. 25–37.

Henderson, L. J. 2005, "The Baltimore Citistat Program: Performance and Accountability", in *Managing for Results 2005,* J. M. Kaminsky and A. Morales, eds, Rowman & Littlefield, Lanham, MD, pp. 465–98.

Hendriks, F. and Tops, P. 2003, "Local Public Management Reforms in the Netherlands: Fads, Fashions and Winds of Change", *Public Administration,* vol. 81, no. 2, pp. 301–23.

Henkel, M. 1991, "The New 'Evaluative State'", *Public Administration,* vol. 69, pp. 121–36.

Hernes, G. (Ed.) 1978, *Forhandlingsøkonomi og blandingsadministrasjon*, Universitetsforlaget, Oslo.

Hernes, T. 2005, "Four Ideal-Types Organizational Responses to New Public Management Reforms and Some Consequences", *International Review of Administrative Sciences*, vol. 71, no. 1, pp. 5–17.

Hibbing, J. R. and Theiss-Morse, E. 2001, "Process Preferences and American Politics: What the People Want Government to Be", *The American Political Science Review*, vol. 95, no. 1, pp. 145–53.

Hibbing, J. R. and Theiss-Morse, E. 2002, *Stealth Democracy: Americans' Beliefs about how Government Should Work*, Cambridge University Press, New York.

Himmelman, A. 1996, *Communities Working Collaboratively for a Change*, The Himmelman Consulting Group, Minneapolis.

Hirschman, A. O. 1970, *Exit, Voice, and Loyalty: Responses to Decline in Firms, Organizations, and States*, Harvard University Press, Cambridge, MA.

HM Treasury 2004, *2004 Spending Review: Public Service Agreements 2005–2008*, Stationary Office, London.

HM Treasury 2006, *Budget 2006*, HM Treasury, London.

HM Treasury 2007, *2007 Budget Report and Comprehensive Spending Review*, Stationary Office, London.

Ho, A. T. K. 2006, "Accounting for the Value of Performance Measurement from the Perspective of Midwestern Mayors", *Journal of Public Administration Research and Theory*, vol. 16, no. 2, pp. 217–37.

Ho, A. T. K. 2007, "The Governance Challenges of the Government Performance and Results Act A Case Study of the Substance Abuse and Mental Health Administration", *Public Performance & Management Review*, vol. 30, no. 3, pp. 369–7.

Holzer, M. and Yang, K. 2004, "Performance Measurement and Improvement: An Assessment of the State of the Art", *International Review of Administrative Sciences*, vol. 70, no. 1, pp. 15–31.

Home Affairs Select Committee 2005, *Home Office Target Setting 2004 (HC 320)*, House of Commons, London.

Hood, C. 1991, "A Public Management for all Seasons?", *Public Administration*, vol. 69, no. 1, pp. 3–19.

Hood, C. 1998, *The Art of the State: Culture, Rhetoric, and Public Management*, Clarendon Press, Oxford.

Hood, C. 2006, "Gaming in Targetworld: The Targets Approach to Managing British Public Services", *Public Administration Review*, vol. 66, no. 4, pp. 515–21.

Hood, C. 2007a, "Public Service Management by Numbers: Why Does it Vary? Where has it Come From? What are the Gaps and the Puzzles?", *Public Money and Management*, vol. 27, no. 2, pp. 95–102.

Hood, C. 2007b, "What Happens when Transparency Meets Blame-Avoidance?", *Public Management Review*, vol. 9, no. 2, pp. 191–210.

Hood, C. and Bevan, G. 2004, *Where Soft Theory Meets Hard Cases: The Limits of Transparency and Proportionality in Health Care Regulation*. Paper presented at the 9th meeting of the European Health Policy Group, at the 5th European Conference on Health Economics (ECHE), 8–11 September, London School of Economics, London.

Hoogerwerf, A. and Herweijer, M. 1998, *Overheidsbeleid: Een Inleiding in de Beleidswetenschap*, Kluwer, Amsterdam.

Horntvedt, G. and Matthiesen, G. 1993, "Riktige og Sammenlignbare Karakterer", *Aftenposten*, 27 September.

Hovik, S. and Stigen, I. M. 2004, *Kommunal Organisering 2004. Redegjørelse for Kommunal- og Regionaldepartementets Organisasjonsdatabase*, Norsk Institutt for By- og Regionforskning, Oslo, no. 124.

Huber, G. P. 1991, "Organizational Learning: The Contributing Processes and the Literatures", *Organization Science*, vol. 2, no. 1, pp. 88–115.

Huxham, C. and Vangen, S. 2000a, "Ambiguity, Complexity and Dynamics in the Membership of Collaboration", *Human Relations*, vol. 53, no. 6, pp. 771–93.

Huxham, C. and Vangen, S. 2000b, "Leadership in the Shaping and Implementation of Collaboration Agendas: How Things Happen in a (Not Quite) Joined-up World", *The Academy of Management Journal*, vol. 43, no. 6, pp. 1159–75.

Inglehart, R. 1997, *Modernization and Postmodernization: Cultural, Economic and Political Change in 43 Societies*, Princeton University Press, Princeton, NJ.

Ingraham, P. W. 2005, "Performance: Promises to Keep and Miles to Go", *Public Administration Review*, vol. 65, no. 4, pp. 390–5.

Ingraham, P. W., Joyce, P. G., and Donahue, A. K. 2003, *Government Performance: Why Management Matters*, John Hopkins University Press, Baltimore, MD.

Jackson, A. 2002, Gaming of Performance Indicators: A Classification Related to Impact", in *PMA 2002 Conference Proceeding*, A. Neely and A. Walters, eds, Performance Management Association, Boston, pp. 723–7.

Jackson, P. 1988, "The Management of Performance in the Public Sector", *Public Money & Management*, vol. 8, no. 4, p. 11.

Jacobsen, D. I. 2003, *Vi har det så Greit: En Studie av Forholdet Mellom Politikk og Administrasjon i 30 Norske Kommuner*. Makt- og demokratiutredningens rapportserie, Oslo, no. 66.

Jacobsen, D. I. 2006, "The Relationship between Politics and Administration: The Importance of Contingency Factors, Formal Structure, Demography, and Time", *Governance*, vol. 19, no. 2, pp. 303–23.

James, O. 2004, "The UK Core Executive's Use of Public Service Agreements as a Tool of Governance", *Public Administration*, vol. 82, no. 2, pp. 397–419.

Jary, D. and Jary, J. 1999, *Unwin Hyman Dictionary of Sociology*, HarperCollins, Glasgow.

Jas, P. and Skelcher, C. 2005, "Performance Decline and Turnaround in Public Organizations: A Theoretical and Empirical Analysis", *British Journal of Management*, vol. 16, pp. 195–210.

Johansson, S. 1995, *Verksamhetsbedömming i Mjuka Organisasjoner. Om Kommunala Ledares Verksamhetsinformation och Forsök att Finna Mått på Effektivitet inom Social Service*. CEFOS, Stockholm.

Johnsen, Å. 1999a, "Implementation Mode and Local Government Performance Measurement: A Norwegian Experience", *Financial Accountability & Management*, vol. 15, no. 1, pp. 41–66.

Johnsen, Å. 1999b, *Performance Measurement in Local Government: Organizational Control in Political Institutions*, Doctoral thesis, Norwegian School of Economics and Business Administration: Bergen.

Johnsen, Å. 2005, "What Does 25 Years of Experience Tell Us About the State of Performance Measurement in Public Policy and Management?", *Public Money and Management*, vol. 25, no. 1, pp. 9–17.

Johnsen, Å. and Vakkuri, J. 2006, "Is there a Nordic Perspective on Public Sector Performance Measurement?", *Financial Accountability and Management*, vol. 22, no. 3, pp. 291–308.

Johnson, C. 2007, "The UK Parliament and Performance: Challenging or Challenged?", *International Review of Administrative Sciences*, vol. 73, no. 1, pp. 113–31.

Johnson, D. J., Donahue, W. A., Atkin, C. K., and Johnson, S. 1995, "A Comprehensive Model of Information Seeking", *Science Communication*, vol. 16, no. 3, pp. 274–313.

Jordan, M. M. and Hackbart, M. M. 1999, "Performance Budgeting and Performance Funding in the States: A States Assessment", *Public Budgeting & Finance*, vol. 19, no. 1, pp. 68–88.

Kaplan, R. S. and Norton, D. P. 1996, *The Balanced Scorecard: Translating Strategy into Action Harvard Business School Press*, Harvard Business School Press, Boston, MA.

Karsten, S., Visscher, A., and De Jong, T. 2001, "Another Side to the Coin: The Unintended Effects of the Publication of School Performance Data in England and France", *Comparative Education*, vol. 37, no. 1, pp. 231–42.

Keegan, W. 2003, *The Prudence of Mr. Gordon Brown*, Wiley, Hoboken, NJ.

Keil, T. 2000, *Strategic Alliances – A Review of the State of the Art*, Helsinki University of Technology, Institute of Strategy and International Business, Espoo, Finland, Working Paper 10.

Kelly, J. M. 2002, "If You Only Knew How Well We Are Performing, You'd Be Highly Satisfied with the Quality of Our Service", *National Civic Review*, vol. 91, no. 3, p. 283.

Kelly, J. M. and Rivenbark, W. C. 2003, *Performance Budgeting for State and Local Government*, ME Sharpe, Armonk, NY.

Kelly, R. 2004, *Modernization: Select Committees – Core Tasks*. House of Commons, London.

Kelman, S. 2007, "The Transformation of Government in the Decade Ahead", in *Reflections on 21st Century Government Management*, F. D. Kettl and S. Kelman, eds, IBM Center for The Business of Government.

Kelman, S. and Friedman, J. N. 2007, *Performance Improvement and Performance Dysfunction: An Empirical Examination of Impacts of the Emergency Room Wait-Time Target in the English National Health Service*, Kennedy School of Government Faculty Research Working Paper Series RWP07-034.

Kettl, F. D. 2002, *The Transformation of Governance*, John Hopkins University Press, Baltimore, MD.

Kickert, W. 2003, "Beyond Public Management", *Public Management Review*, vol. 5, no. 3, pp. 377–99.

King, C. S., Stivers, C., and Box, R. C. 1998, *Government Is Us: Public Administration in an Anti-government Era*, Sage Publications, Thousand Oaks, CA.

King, D. C., Zeckhauser, R. J., and Kim, M. T. 2004, *The Management Performance of the US States,* Research Programs, John F. Kennedy School of Government, Harvard University, Cambridge, MA.

Kingdon, J. 1984, *Agendas, Alternatives, and Public Policies,* Little Brown, Boston, MA.

Kleven, T. 2002, *Målstyring i Skandinaviske Kommuner. Seks Casestudier*, Norsk Institutt for By- og Regionforskning, Oslo, no. 15.

Koontz, T. M. and Thomas, C. W. 2006, "What Do We Know About the Environmental Outcomes of Collaborative Management?", *Public Administration Review*, vol. 66, supp. 1, pp. 111–21.

Koppell, J. G. 2005, "Pathologies of Accountability: ICANN and the Challenge of 'Multiple Accountabilities Disorder'", *Public Administration Review*, vol. 65, no. 1, pp. 94–108.

Koppenjan, J. F. M. and Klijn, E. H. 2004, *Managing Uncertainties in Networks: A Network Approach to Problem Solving and Decision Making*, Routledge, London.

Labovitz, G. and Rosansky, V. 1997, *The Power of Alignment: How Great Companies Stay Centered and Accomplish Extraordinary Things*, John Wiley & Sons, New York.

Lægreid, P. 2000, "Top Civil Servants Under Contract", *Public Administration*, vol. 78, no. 4, pp. 879–96.

Lægreid, P., Opedal, S., and Stigen, I. M. 2005, "The Norwegian Hospital Reform: Balancing Political Control and Enterprise Autonomy", *Journal of Health Politics, Policy & Law*, vol. 30, no. 6, pp. 1027–64.

Lægreid, P., Roness, P. G., and Rubecksen, K. 2006a, "Autonomy and Control in the Norwegian Civil Service: Does Agency Form Matter?", in *Autonomy and Regulation: Coping with Agencies in the Modern State*, T. Christensen and P. Lægreid, eds, Cheltenham: Edward Elgar, pp. 301–27.

Lægreid, P., Roness, P. G., and Rubecksen, K. 2006b, "Performance Management in Practice: The Norwegian Way", *Financial Accountability and Management*, vol. 22, no. 3, pp. 251–70.

Lægreid, P., Roness, P. G., and Rubecksen, K. 2007, "Modern Management Tools in State Agencies: The Case of Norway", *International Public Management Journal*, vol. 10, no. 4, p. 387.

Lægreid, P., Roness, P. G., and Rubecksen, K. 2008, "Controlling Regulatory Agencies?", *Scandinavian Political Studies*, vol. 31, no. 1, pp. 1–27.

Larson, J. R. J. and Callahan, C. 1990, "Performance Monitoring: How It Affects Work Productivity", *Journal of Applied Psychology*, vol. 75, no. 5, pp. 530–8.

Levinthal, D. A. and James, G. M. 1993, "The Myopia of Learning", *Strategic Management Journal*, vol. 14, no. 1, pp. 95–112.

Levitt, B. and March, J. G. 1988, "Chester I. Barnard and the Intelligence of Learning", in *Organization Theory: From Chester Barnard to the Present and Beyond*, O. E. Williamson, ed., Oxford University Press, New York, pp. 11–37.

Liaison Committee 2002, *First Report: The Work of Select Committees 2001 (HC 590)*, House of Commons, London.

Likierman, A. 1993, "Performance Indicators: 20 Early Lessons from Managerial Use", *Public Money & Management*, vol. 13, no. 4, pp. 15–22.

Lindblom, C. E. and Cohen, D. K. 1979, *Usable Knowledge: Social Science and Social Problem Solving*, Yale University Press, New Haven, CT.

Linsley, C. A. and Linsley, C. L. 1993, "Booth, Rowntree, and Llewelyn Smith: A Reassessment of Interwar Poverty", *The Economic History Review*, vol. 46, no. 1, pp. 88–104.

Lipshitz, R., Popper, M., and Oz, S. 1996, "Building Learning Organizations: The Design and Implementation of Organizational Learning Mechanisms", *The Journal of Applied Behavioral Science*, vol. 32, no. 3, pp. 292–305.

Llewellyn, S. and Northcott, D. 2005, "The Average Hospital", *Accounting, Organizations and Society*, vol. 30, no. 6, pp. 555–83.

Loft, A. 1988, *Understanding Accounting in its Social and Historical Context: The Case of Cost Accounting in Britain 1914–1925*, Taylor & Francis, London.

Lomas, J. 2000, "Connecting Research and Policy", *Canadian Journal of Policy Research*, vol. 1, no. 1, pp. 140–4.

Lonti, Z. and Gregory, R. 2007, "Accountability or Countability? Performance Measurement in the New Zealand Public Service, 1992–2002", *Australian Journal of Public Administration*, vol. 66, no. 4, pp. 468–84.

Lowndes, V., Pratchett, L., and Stoker, G. 2001, "Trends In Public Participation: Part 1 – Local Government Perspectives", *Public Administration*, vol. 79, no. 1, p. 205.

Lukensmeyer, C. J. and Torres, L. H. 2006, *Public Deliberation: A Manager's Guide to Citizen Engagement*, IBM Center for the Business of Government, Washington, DC.

Lynn, L. E., Heinrich, C. J., and Hill, C. J. 2001, *Improving Governance: A New Logic for Empirical Research*, Georgetown University Press, Washington, DC.

Macintosh, N. B. 1985, *The Social Software of Accounting and Information Systems*, John Wiley & Sons, London.

Majone, G. 1989, *Evidence, Argument and Persuasion in the Policy Process*, Yale University Press, New Haven, CT.

Mandell, M. and Keast, R. L. 2007, "Evaluating Network Arrangements: Toward Revised Performance Measures", *Public Performance & Management Review*, vol. 30, no. 4, pp. 574–97.

March, J. G. 1987, "Ambiguity and Accounting: The Elusive Link between Information and Decision Making", *Accounting, Organizations and Society*, vol. 12, no. 2, p. 153–87.

March, J. G. and Olsen, J. P. 1976, *Ambiguity and Choice in Organizations*, Universitetsforlaget, Bergen, Norway.

March, J. G. and Olsen, J. P. 1989, *Rediscovering Institutions: The Organizational Basis of Politics*, The Free Press, New York.

March, J. G. and Olsen, J. P. 1995, *Democratic Governance*, The Free Press, New York.

Marshall, M. N., Hiscock, J., and Sibbald, B. 2002, "Attitudes to the Public Release of Comparative Information on the Quality of General Practice Care: Qualitative Study", *BMJ*, vol. 325, pp. 1278–83.

Marshall, M. N., Shekelle, P. G., Brook, R. H., and Leatherman, S. 2000, *Dying to Know: Public Release of Information about Quality of Health Care*, Nuffield Trust and RAND, London.

Marshall, M. N., Shekelle, P. G., Davies, H. T. O., and Smith, P. C. 2003, "Public Reporting On Quality in the United States And The United Kingdom", *Health Affairs*, vol. 22, no. 3, pp. 134–48.

Mason, A. and Street, A. 2006, "Publishing Outcome Data: Is it an Effective Approach?", *Journal of Evaluation in Clinical Practice*, vol. 12, no. 1, pp. 37–48.

Mathews, D. 1999, *Politics for People*, 2 edn, University of Illinois Press, Urbana, IL.

Mayne, J. and Zapico-Goni, E. 1997, *Monitoring Performance in the Public Sector: Future Directions from International Experience*, Transaction Publishers, New Brunswick.

Mayston, D. J. 1985, "Non-Profit Performance Indicators in the Public Sector", *Financial Accountability and Management*, vol. 1, no. 1, pp. 51–74.

McCubbins, M. D. and Schwartz, T. 1984, "Congressional Oversight Overlooked: Police Patrols Versus Fire Alarms", *American Journal of Political Science*, vol. 28, no. 1, pp. 165–79.

McGee, D. 2002, *The Overseers: Public Accounts Committees and Public Spending*, Commonwealth Parliamentary Association with Pluto Press, London.

McGuire, M. 2006, "Collaborative Public Management: Assessing What We Know and How We Know It", *Public Administration Review*, vol. 66, supp. 1. pp. 33–43.

McPhee, I. 2005, *Outcomes and Outputs: Are We Managing Better as a Result?* Paper presented to the CPA National Public Sector Convention, 20 May, Melbourne.

Meijer, A. J. 2007, "Publishing Public Performance Information on the Internet: Do Stakeholder Use the Internet to Hold Dutch Public Service Organizations to Account?", *Government Information Quarterly*, vol. 24, pp. 165–85.

Melkers, J. and Willoughby, K. 2005, "Models of Performance-Measurement Use in Local Governments: Understanding Budgeting, Communication, and Lasting Effects", *Public Administration Review*, vol. 65, no. 2, pp. 180–90.

Melkers, J. E. and Willoughby, K. G. 2001, "Budgeters' Views of State Performance-Budgeting Systems: Distinctions across Branches", *Public Administration Review*, vol. 61, no. 1, pp. 54–64.

Meyer, J. W. and Rowan, B. 1977, "Institutionalized Organizations: Formal Structure as Myth and Ceremony", in *The New Institutionalism in Organizational Analysis*, W. W. Powell and P. J. DiMaggio, eds, University of Chicago Press, Chicago, pp. 41–62.

Meyer, M. W. and Gupta, V. 1994, "The Performance Paradox", *Research in Organizational Behavior*, vol. 16, no. 2, pp. 309–69.

Ministerie van Binnenlandse Zaken en Koninkrijksrelaties 1998, *Grote-Stedenbeleid: Op Zoek Naar de Keer ten Goede*, EIM, Zoetermeer.

Ministerie van Binnenlandse Zaken en Koninkrijksrelaties 2002, *Steden op Stoom: Tussenstand Grotestedenbeleid 1994–2002*, Ministerie van Binnenlandse Zaken en Koninkrijksrelaties, Den Haag.

Ministerie van Binnenlandse Zaken en Koninkrijksrelaties 2004a, *Jaarboek GSB 2003*, Ecorys, Rotterdam.

Ministerie van Binnenlandse Zaken en Koninkrijksrelaties 2004b, *Samenwerken aan de Krachtige Stad*, Ministerie van Binnenlandse Zaken en Koninkrijksrelaties, Den Haag.

Ministry of Education and Religious Affairs 1989, *OECD-vurdering av Norsk Utdanningspolitikk. Norsk Rapport til OECD. Ekspertvurdering fra OECD*, Aschehoug, Oslo.

Mintzberg, H. 1975, *The Nature of Managerial Work*, Harpercollins, New York.

Mintzberg, H. 1993, "The Pitfalls of Strategic Planning", *California Management Review*, vol. 36, no 1, pp. 32–47.

Mintzberg, H. 1994, "The Fall and Rise of Strategic Planning", *Harvard Business Review*, vol. 72, no. 1, pp. 107–14.

Modell, S. and Wiesel, F. 2007, *Marketization and Performance Management In Swedish Central Government: A Comparative Institutionalist Study*, Paper Presented at the European Accounting Association Annual Congress, 25–27 April, Lisbon.

Moore, M. 2002, *Creating Public Value: Strategic Management in Government*, Harvard University Press, Boston, MA.

Moran, M. 2003, *The British Regulatory State: High Modernism and Hyper-Innovation*, Oxford University Press, Oxford.

Mosher, F. C. 1968, *Democracy and the Public Service*, Oxford University Press, New York.

Mouritzen, P. E. and Svara, J. H. 2002, *Leadership at the Apex: Politicians and Administrators in Western Local Governments*, University of Pittsburgh Press, Pittsburgh.

Moynihan, D. P. 2005a, "Goal-Based Learning and the Future of Performance Management", *Public Administration Review*, vol. 65, no. 2, pp. 203–16.

Moynihan, D. P. 2005b, "Why and How do State Governments Adopt and Implement 'Managing for Results' Reforms?", *Journal of Public Administration Research and Theory*, vol. 15, no. 2, pp. 219–43.

Moynihan, D. P. 2008, *The Dynamics of Performance Management: Constructing Information and Reform*, Georgetown University Press, Washington DC.

Moynihan, D. P. and Ingraham, P. W. 2003, "Look for the Silver Lining: When Performance-Based Accountability Systems Work", *Journal of Public Administration Research and Theory*, vol. 13, no. 4, p. 469–90.

Moynihan, D. P. and Ingraham, P. W. 2004, "Integrative Leadership in the Public Sector: A Model of Performance-Information Use", *Administration & Society*, vol. 36, no. 4, pp. 427–53.

Moynihan, D. P. and Landuyt, N. 2008, "How do Public Organizations Learn? Bridging Cultural and Structural Perspectives", forthcoming in *Public Administration Review*.

Murphy, P. J. and Carnevale, J. 2001, *The Challenge of Developing Cross-Agency Measures: A Case Study of the Office of National Drug Control Policy*, The PricewaterhouseCoopers Endowment for The Business of Government (August 2001).

Naschold, F. 1996, *New Frontiers in Public Sector Management. Trends and Issues in State and Local Government in Europe*, Walter de Gruyter, Berlin.

Nathan, R. 2005, "Presidential Address: '*Complexifying*' Government Oversight in America's Government", *Journal of Policy Analysis and Management*, vol. 4, no. 2, pp. 207–15.

National Academy of Public Administration 2007, *A Government to Trust and Respect: Rebuilding Citizen-Government Relations for the 21st Century*, the National Academy of Public Administration, Washington, DC.

National Audit Office 2001a, *Inappropriate Adjustments to NHS Waiting Lists*, Stationary Office, London.

National Audit Office 2001b, *Measuring the Performance of Government Departments*, NAO, London.

Neely, A. (1998), *Measurement Business Performance – Why, What and How*, London, The Economist.

Neely, A. and Micheli, P. 2004, *Performance Measurement in the UK's Public Sector: Linking the National to the Local Agenda*, Paper presented at the British Academy Conference, 30 Aug.–1 Sept., St. Andrews.

Newcomer, K. 2007, "How Does Program Performance Assessment Affect Program Management In The Federal Government?", *Public Performance and Management Review*, vol. 30, no. 3, pp. 332–50.

Newcomer, K. 2008, "Assessing Performance in Nonprofit Service Agencies", in *International Handbook of Practice-Based Performance Management*, P. de Lancer

Julnes, F. Berry, M. Aristigueta and K. Yang, K, eds, Sage, Thousand Oaks, CA, pp. 25–44.

New Zealand Planning Council 1985, *From Birth to Death*, NZPC, Wellington, NZ.

New Zealand Planning Council 1989, *From Birth to Death II*, NZPC, Wellington, NZ.

Nicholson-Crotty, S., Theobald, N. A., and Nicholson-Crotty, J. 2006, "Disparate Measures: Public Managers and Performance-Measurement Strategies", *Public Administration Review*, vol. 66, no. 1, pp. 101–13.

Niven, P. 2003, *Balanced Scorecard Step By Step for Government and Nonprofit Agencies*, John Wiley & Sons, Hoboken, NJ.

Noordegraaf, M. and Abma, T. 2003, "Management by Measurement? Public Management Practices Amidst Ambiguity", *Public Administration*, vol. 81, no. 4, pp. 853–71.

Norman, R. 2002, "Managing through Measurement or Meaning? Lessons from Experience with New Zealand's Public Sector Performance Management Systems", *International Review of Administrative Sciences*, vol. 68, no. 4, pp. 619–28.

Nørreklit, H. 2003, "The Balanced Scorecard: What is the Score? A Rhetorical Analysis of the Balanced Scorecard", *Accounting, Organizations, and Society*, vol. 28, no. 6, pp. 591–619.

Norton, P. 1998, *Parliaments and Governments in Western Europe*, Routledge, London.

NOU 1991, *Mot Bedre Vitende? Effektiviseringsmuligheter i Offentlig Sektor (the Norman Committee)*, Ministry of Labour and Public Administration, Oslo, 28.

O'Neill, O. 2002, *A Question of Trust: The BBC Reith Lectures 2002*, Cambridge University Press, Cambridge.

OECD 2005, *Modernizing Government – The Way Forward*, Organisation for Economic Cooperation and Development, Paris.

OECD 1996, *Responsive Government: Service Quality Initiatives*, Organisation for Economic Cooperation and Development, Paris.

Offerdal, A. and Jacobsen, J. O. 1995, "Auftragstaktik in the Norwegian Armed Forces", *Defense Analysis*, vol. 9, no. 2, pp. 211–23.

Olsen, J. P. 1992, "Analyzing Institutional Dynamics", *Staatswissenschaften und Staatspraxis*, vol. 3, no. 2, pp. 247–71.

Olsen, S. O. 2006, "Krangelen om det Uvesentlige", *Dagbladet*, 30 November.

Osborne, D. and Gaebler, T. 1992, *Reinventing Government: How the Entrepreneurial Spirit is Transforming the Public Sector*, Addison-Wesley, Reading, MA.

Patton, M. Q. 1997, *Utilization-Focused Evaluation*, Sage, Thousand Oaks, CA.

Paulsen, G. E. 2005, "Målstyring, Målforskyvning, Nakkeskudd", *Aftenposten*, 21 January.

Pedler, M., Burgoyne, J., and Boydell, T. 1991, *The Learning Company. A Strategy For Sustainable Development*, McGraw-Hill, London.

Perrin, B. 1998, "Effective Use and Misuse of Performance Measurement", *American Journal of Evaluation*, vol. 19, no. 3, pp. 367–79.

Pew Research Center for the People and the Press 2003, *The 2004 Political Landscape: Part 6: Cynicism, Trust and Participation*, Washington, DC.

Pfadenhauer, M. 2006, "Crisis or Decline? Problems of Legitimation and Loss of Trust in Modern Professionalism", *Current Sociology*, vol. 54, no. 4, pp. 565–78.

Pfeffer, J. 1992, *Managing with Power: Politics and Influence in Organizations*, Harvard Business School Press, Boston, MA.

Pfeffer, J. and Salancik, G. R. 1978, *The External Control of Organizations: A Resource Dependence Perspective*, Stanford University Press, Palo Alto, CA.

Pidd, M. 2005, "Perversity in Public Service Performance Measurement", *International Journal of Productivity and Performance Management*, vol. 54, no. 5/6, pp. 482–93.

Pitches, D., Burls, A. and Fry-Smith, A. 2003, "How to Make a Silk Purse From a Sows Ear – A Comprehensive Review of Strategies to Optimise Data for Corrupt Managers and Incompetent Clinicians", *British Medical Journal*, no. 327, pp. 1436–9.

Poister, T. H. 1983, *Performance Monitoring*, Lexington Books, Lexington, MA.

Poister, T. H. 1992, "Productivity Monitoring: Systems, Indicators, and Analysis", in *Public Productivity Handbook*, M. Holzer, ed., Marcel Dekker, New York, pp. 195–211.

Poister, T. H. and Streib, G. 1999, "Performance Measurement in Municipal Government: Assessing the State of the Practice", *Public Administration Review*, vol. 59, no. 4, pp. 325–35.

Poister, T. H. and Streib, G. 2005, "Elements of Strategic Planning and Management in Municipal Government: Status after Two Decades", *Public Administration Review*, vol. 65, no. 1, pp. 45–56.

Pollitt, C. 1989, "Performance Indicators in the Longer Term", *Public Money and Management*, vol. 9, no. 3, pp. 51–5.

Pollitt, C. 2003, *The Essential Public Manager*, Open University Press, Maidenhead.

Pollitt, C. 2005, "Hospital Performance Indicators: How and Why Neighbours Facing Similar Problems Go Different Ways", in *New Public Management in Europe: Adaptation and Alternatives*, C. Pollitt, S. Van Thiel and V. Homburg, eds, Palgrave Macmillan, Basingstoke, pp. 149–64.

Pollitt, C. 2006a, "Discipline and Punish – or Trust? Contrasting Bases for Performance Management in Executive Agencies", in *Autonomy and Regulation: Coping with Agencies in the Modern State*, T. Christensen and P. Lægreid, eds, Edward Elgar, Cheltenham, pp. 301–27.

Pollitt, C. 2006b, "Performance Information for Democracy – The Missing Link?", *Evaluation*, vol. 1, no. 2, pp. 38–55.

Pollitt, C. 2006c, "Performance Management in Practice: A Comparative Study of Executive Agencies", *Journal of Public Administration Research and Theory*, vol. 16, no. 1, pp. 25–44.

Pollitt, C. 2007a, "New Labour's Re-Disorganization: Hyper-Modernism and Costs of Reform – a Cautionary Tale", *Public Management Review*, vol. 9, no. 4, pp. 529–43.

Pollitt, C. 2007b, "Who Are We, What Are We Doing, Where Are We Going? A Perspective on the Academic Performance Management Community", *Közgazdaság*, no. 1, pp. 73–82.

Pollitt, C. and Bouckaert, G. 2004, *Public Management Reform: A Comparative Analysis*, Oxford University Press, Oxford.

Pollitt, C., Smullen, A., Talbot, C., and Caulfield, J. 2004, *Agencies: How Governments Do Things Through Semi-Autonomous Organizations*, Palgrave Macmillan, Basingstoke.

Popovich, M. G. 1998, *Creating High-Performance Government Organizations*, Jossey-Bass, San Francisco.

Popper, K. R. 1966, *The Open Society and its Enemies*, 5th edn, Routledge, London.

Posner, P. L. and Fantone, D. M. 2007, "Assessing Federal Program Performance: Observations on the US Office of Management and Budget's Program Assessment Rating Tool and Its Use in the Budget Process", *Public Performance & Management Review*, vol. 30, no. 3, pp. 351–68.

Power, M. 1999, *The Audit Society: Rituals of Verification*, Oxford University Press, Oxford.

Previts, G. J. and Merino, B. D. 1979, *A History of Accounting in America: An Historical Interpretation of the Cultural Significance of Accounting*, Wiley, New York.

Pritchett, L. and Woolcock, M. 2002, *Solutions When the Solution is the Problem: Arraying the Disarray in Development*, Centre for Global Development Working Paper no. 10, Washington, DC.

Propper, C. and Wilson, D. 2003, "The Use and Usefulness of Performance Measures in the Public Sector", *Oxford Review of Economic Policy*, vol. 19, no. 2, pp. 250–67.

Public Accounts Committee 2005, *Managing Resources to Develop Better Public Services*, House of Commons, London.

Public Administration Select Committee (PASC) 2003, *On Target? Government by Measurement, Fifth Report of Session 2002–03*, House of Commons, London.

Public Services Productivity Panel 2000, *Public Services Productivity: Meeting the Challenge*, London, HM Treasury, p. 25.

Radin, B. A. 2000, "The Government Performance and Results Act and the Tradition of Federal Management Reform: Square Pegs in Round Holes", *Journal of Public Administration Research and Theory*, vol. 10, no. 1, pp. 111–35.

Radin, A. 2002, *The Accountable Juggler: The Art of Leadership in a Federal Agency*, CQ Press, Washington, DC.

Radin, B. A. 2006, *Challenging the Performance Movement: Accountability, Complexity, and Democratic Values*, Georgetown University Press, Washington, DC.

Radnor Z. J. and Barnes D. 2007, "Historical Analysis of Performance Measurement and Management in Operations Management", *International Journal of Productivity and Performance Management*, vol. 56, no. 5/6, pp. 384–96.

Radnor, Z. J. and McGuire, M. 2004, "Performance Management in the Public Sector: Fact or Fiction?", *International Journal of Productivity and Performance Management*, vol. 53, no. 3, pp. 245–60.

Rich, R. F. and Cheol, H. Oh. 2000, "Rationality and Use of Information in Policy Decisions", *Science Communication*, vol. 22, no. 2, pp. 173–211.

Ridgway, V. F. 1956, "Dysfunctional Consequences of Performance Measurements", *Administrative Science Quarterly*, vol. 1, no. 2, pp. 240–7.

Ridley, C. E. and Herbert, A. S. 1938, *Measuring Municipal Activities. A Survey of Suggested Criteria and Reporting Forms for Appraising Administration*, The International City Managers' Association, Chicago, IL.

Roness, P. G. 2007, "Types of State Organizations: Arguments, Doctrines and Changes Beyond New Public Management", in *Transcending New Public*

Management. The Transformation of Public Sector Reforms, T. Christensen and P. Lægreid, eds, Ashgate, Aldershot, pp. 65–88.

Rosenbaum, W. A. 1978, "Public Involvement as Reform and Ritual", in *Citizen Participation in America*, S. Langton, ed., Lexington Books, Lexington, MA.

Rouse, J. 1993, "Resource and Performance Management in Public Service Organisations", in *Management in the Public Sector: Challenge and Change*, I.-H. Kester, C. Painter and C. Barnes, eds, Chapman & Hall, London, pp. 59–76.

Saltelli, A. 2007, "Composite Indicators Between Analysis and Advocacy", *Social Indicators Research*, vol. 81, pp. 65–77.

Sanderson, I. 2001, "Performance Management, Evaluation and Learning in 'Modern' Local Government", *Public Administration*, vol. 79, no. 2, pp. 297–313.

Sangolt, L. 2003, "Det Statistikkdrevne Samfunn", *Bergens Tidende*, 6 May.

Schachter, H. L. 1989, *Frederick Taylor and the Public Administration Community: A Reevaluation*, State University of New York, New York.

Schedler, K. and Proeller, I. 2002, "The New Public Management: A Perspective from Mainland Europe", in *New Public Management: Current Trends and Future Prospects*, K. McLaughlin, S. Osborne, and E. Ferlie, eds, Routledge, London.

Scheers, B., Sterck, M., and Bouckaert, G. 2005, "Lessons from Australian and British Reforms in Results-oriented Financial Management", *OECD Journal on Budgeting*, vol. 5, no. 2, pp. 133–62.

Schiavo, L. L. 2000, "Quality Standards in the Public Sector: Differences Between Italy and the UK in the Citizen's Charter Initiative", *Public Administration*, vol. 78, no. 3, pp. 679–98.

Schick, A. 1966, "The Road to PPB: The Stages of Budget Reform", *Public Administration Review*, vol. 26, no. 4, pp. 243–58.

Schick, A. 1990, "Budgeting for Results: Recent Developments in Five Industrialized Countries", *Public Administration Review*, vol. 50, no. 1, pp. 26–34.

Schneider, E. C. and Epstein, A. M. 1998, "Use of Public Performance Reports: A Survey of Patients Undergoing Cardiac Surgery", *Journal of the American Medical Association*, vol. 279, no. 20, pp. 1638–42.

Schwartz, B. 2004, *The Paradox of Choice: Why More is Less*, Harper Perennial, New York.

Scott, J. C. 1998, *Seeing Like a State: How Certain Schemes to Improve the Human Condition Have Failed*, Yale University Press, New Haven, CT.

Senge, P. 1990, *The Fifth Discipline*, Doubleday, New York.

Shafritz, J. M. and Hyde, A. C. 2004, *Classics of Public Administration*, 5th edn, Wadsworth/Thomson Learning, Belmont, CA and London.

Simon, H. A. 1976, *Administrative Behavior: A Study of Decision-Making Processes in Administrative Organization*, 3rd edn, Free Press, New York.

Sirianni, C. and Friedland, L. 1995, *Civic Environmentalism*. Available at: http://www.cpn.org/topics/environment/civicenvironA.html. Civic Practices Network, Accessed 9 November, 2007.

Siverbo, S. and Johansson, T. 2006, "Relative Performance Evaluations in Swedish Local Government", *Financial Accountability and Management*, vol. 22, no. 3, pp. 271–90.

Sloan Foundation. 2007, *Program on Making Municipal Governments More Responsive to their Citizens*. Available at: http://www.sloan.org/programs/stndrd_performance.shtml (Accessed 1 November, 2007).

Smith, G. E. and Huntsman, C. A. 1997, "Reframing the Metaphor of the Citizen-Government Relationship: A Value-Centered Perspective", *Public Administration Review*, vol. 57, no. 4.

Smith, P. 1990, "The Use of Performance Indicators in the Public Sector", *Journal of the Royal Statistical Society, Series A*, vol. 153, no. 1, pp. 53–72.

Smith, P. 1995, "On the Unintended Consequences of Publishing Performance Data in the Public Sector", *International Journal of Public Administration*, vol. 18, no. 2/3, pp. 277–310.

Solberg, L. I., Mosser, G., and McDonald, S. 1997, "The Three Faces Of Performance Measurement: Improvement, Accountability, And Research", *Journal of Quality Improvement*, vol. 23, no. 3, pp. 135–47.

Solesbury, W. 2001, *Evidence Based Policy: Whence it Came and Where It's Going*, ESRC UK Centre for Evidence-Based Policy and Practice, London.

St.meld nr. 30 (2003–2004), *Kultur for Læring (Rep. No. 30)*, Ministry of Education and Research, Oslo.

Stewart, J. and Walsh, K. 1994, "Performance Measurement: When Performance Can Never be Finally Defined", *Public Money & Management*, vol. 14, no. 2, pp. 45–9.

Stivers, C. 2000, *Bureau Men, Settlement Women: Constructing Public Administration in the Progressive Era*, University Press of Kansas, Lawrence, KS.

Stone, D. 1997, *Policy Paradox: The Art of Political Decisionmaking*, W. W. Norton, New York.

Talbot, C. 2005, "Performance Management", in *The Oxford Handbook of Public Management*, E. Ferlie, L. E. Lynn, and C. Pollitt, eds, Oxford University Press, Oxford, pp. 491–517.

Telhaug, A. O. 2007a, "Den Bløte Kynismen", *Klassekampen*, 2 January.

Telhaug, A. O. 2007b, "Pedagogikk", *Klassekampen*, 22 January.

ter Bogt, H. J. 2001, "Politicians and Output-Oriented Performance Evaluation in Municipalities", *European Accounting Review*, vol. 10, no. 3, pp. 621–43.

ter Bogt, H. J. 2003, "Performance Evaluation Styles in Governmental Organizations: How Do Professional Managers Facilitate Politicians' Work?", *Management Accounting Research*, vol. 14, no. 4, pp. 311–32.

ter Bogt, H. J. 2004, "Politicians in Search of Performance Information? Survey Research on Dutch Aldermen's Use of Performance Information", *Financial Accountability and Management*, vol. 20, no. 3, pp. 221–52.

Thompson, J. D. (1967), *Organizations in Action: Social Science Bases of Administrative Theory*, New York: McGraw-Hill.

Townley, B. 2002, "Managing with Modernity", *Organization*, vol. 9, no. 4, pp. 549–73.

Treasury Board of Canada 2000, *Results for Canadians: A Management Framework for the Government of Canada*, Montreal.

Treasury Board Secretariat 2003, *Review and Assessment of 2002 Departmental Performance Reports*, Treasury Board Secretariat, Ottowa.

Treasury Committee 1999, *Public Service Agreements*, House of Commons (The Stationary Office), London, Seventh Report.

Treasury Committee 2001, *The Treasury*, House of Commons, London, Third Report.

Tversky, A. and Kahneman, D. 1982, "Judgment under Uncertainty: Heuristics and Biases", in *Judgment under Uncertainty: Heuristics and Biases*, D. Kahneman,

P. Slovic, and A. Tversky, eds, Cambridge University Press, Cambridge, pp. 3–20.

US General Accounting Office 1997, *Managing for Results: Using the Results Act to Address Mission Fragmentation and Program Overlap*, GAO,Washington, DC., p. 146.

US General Accounting Office 2000, *Managing For Results: Barriers to Interagency Coordination*, GAO, Washington, DC., p. 106.

US General Accounting Office 2003, *High Risk Series: Strategic Human Capital Management*, GAO, Washington, D.C., p. 120.

US General Accounting Office 2004, *Performance Budgeting: OMB's Program Assessment Rating Tool Presents Opportunities and Challenges for Budget and Performance Integration. GAO-04-439T*, GAO, Washington, DC.

US Government Accountability Office 2005a, *Performance Budgeting: PART Focuses Attention on Program Performance, but More Can Be Done to Engage Congress. GAO-06-28*, GAO, Washington, DC.

US Government Accountability Office 2005b, *Performance Budgeting: States' Experiences Can Inform Federal Efforts, GAO-05-215*, GAO, Washington, DC.

US Government Accountability Office 2005c, *Program Evaluation: OMB's PART Reviews Increased Agencies' Attention to Improving Evidence of Program Results. GAO-06-07*, GAO, Washington, DC.

Vakkuri, J. and Meklin, P. 2006, "Ambiguity in Performance Measurement: A Theoretical Approach to Organizational Uses of Performance Measurement", *Financial Accountability and Management*, vol. 22, no. 3, pp. 235–50.

Van de Walle, S. and Bovaird, T. 2007, *Making Better Use of Information to Drive Improvement in Local Public Services: A Report for the Audit Commission*, School of Public Policy, Birmingham.

van der Molen, K. and van Rooyen, A. (eds.) 2001, *Outcome-Based Governance: Assessing the Results*, Heinemann, Cape Town.

Van Dooren, W. 2004, "Supply and Demand of Policy Indicators", *Public Management Review*, vol. 6, no. 4, pp. 511–30.

Van Dooren, W. 2006, *Performance Measurement in the Flemish Public Sector: A Supply and Demand Approach*, Faculty of Social Sciences. K.U.Leuven.

Van Dooren, W., Manning, N., Malinska, J., Kraan, D. J., Sterck, M., and Bouckaert, G. 2006, *Issues in Output Measurement for Government at a Glance*, OECD, Paris.

Van Dooren, W. and Sterck, M. 2006, "Financial Management Reforms after a Political Shift: A Transformative Perspective", *International Journal of Productivity and Performance Management*, vol. 55, no. 6, pp. 498–514.

van Helden, G. J. and Johnsen, Å. 2002, "A Comparative Analysis of the Development of Performance-Based Management Systems in Dutch and Norwegian Local Government", *International Public Management Journal*, vol. 5, no. 1, pp. 75–95.

van Helden, G. J., Johnsen, Å., and Vakkuri, J. 2007, *Understanding Public Sector Performance Management: The Life Cycle Approach*, Paper presented at the Study Group on Performance in the Public Sector, EGPA Annual conference, 19–21 September, Madrid.

van Petegem, P., Vanhoof, H., Daems, F., and Mahieu, P. 2005, "Publishing Information on Individual Schools?", *Educational Research and Evaluation*, vol. 11, no. 1, pp. 45–60.

Van Peursem, K. A. and Pratt, M. 2000, "Accountability for Health Sector Performance: What Does the New Zealand Public Want", *International Journal of Business Performance Management*, vol. 2, no. 1/2/3, pp. 30–41.

van Thiel, S., and Leeuw, F. L. 2002, "The Performance Paradox in the Public Sector", *Public Performance and Management Review*, vol. 25, no. 3, pp. 267–81.

Vangen, S. and Huxham, C. 2001, *Enacting Leadership for Collaborative Advantage: Uncovering Activities and Dilemmas of Partnership Managers*. Paper presented at the International Research Symposium on Public Management, April, Barcelona.

Vedung, E. 1997, *Public Policy and Program Evaluation*, Transaction Publishers, New Brunswick.

Verba, S., Kay, L. S., and Brady, H. E. 1995, *Voice and Equality. Civic Voluntarism in American Politics*, Harvard University Press, Cambridge, MA.

Verweij, A. O. and Goezinne, B. 1996, *Jaarboek 1995 Grotestedenbeleid*, ISEO, Rotterdam.

Verweij, A. O., Goezinne, B., and Dijkstra, A. 1995, *Opmaat tot Signalering: Instrumentenontwikkeling voor de Monitor Grotestedenbeleid*. ISEO, Rotterdam.

Vladeck, B. C., Goodwin, E. J., Myers, L. P., and Sinisi, M. 1988, "Consumers and Hospital Use: The HCFA 'Death List'", *Health Affairs*, vol. 7, no. 1, pp. 122–5.

Walters, J. 1998, *Measuring Up: Governing's Guide to Performance Measurement for Geniuses and Other Public Managers*, Governing Boos, Washington.

Walton, D. 1992, *Plausible Reasoning in Everyday Conversation*, SUNY Press, Albany, NY.

Wanna, J. and Bartos, S. 2003, "'Good Practice: Does it Work in Theory?' Australia's Quest for Better Outcomes", in *Controlling Public Expenditure: The Changing Role of Central Budget Agencies – Better Guardians?*, J. Wanna, L. Jensen, and J. de Vries, eds, Edward Elgar, Cheltenham.

Watkins, K. and Marsick, V. 1992, "Building the Learning Organization: A New Role For Human Resource Developers", *Studies in Continuing Education*, vol. 14, no. 2, pp. 115–29.

Webber, D. J. 1991, *The Distribution and Use of Policy Knowledge in the Policy Process*, Transaction Publishers, New York.

Weick, K. E. 1976, "Educational Organizations as Loosely Coupled Systems", *Administrative Science Quarterly*, vol. 21, no. 1, pp. 1–19.

Weick, K. E. 1995, *Sensemaking in Organizations*, Sage Publications, Thousand Oaks, CA.

Weiss, C. H. 1977, *Using Social Research in Public Policy Making*, Lexington Books, Lexington, MA.

Weiss, C. H. 1979, "The Many Meanings of Research Utilization", *Public Administration Review*, vol. 39, no. 5, pp. 426–31.

Weiss, C. H. 1980, "Knowledge Creep and Decision Accretion", *Knowledge: Creation, Diffusion, Utilization*, vol. 1, no. 3, p. 381–404.

Weiss, C. H. 1998, "Have We Learned Anything About the Use of Evaluation?", *American Journal of Evaluation*, vol. 19, no. 1, pp. 21–33.

Weiss, C. H. and Bucuvalas, M. J. 1980, "Truth Tests and Utility Tests: Decision-Makers' Frames of Reference for Social Science Research", *American Sociological Review*, vol. 45, no. 2, pp. 302–13.

Wheatley, M. J. 1999, *Leadership and the New Science: Discovering Order in a Chaotic World*, Berrett-Koehler Publishers, San Francisco.

Wholey, J. S. 1999, "Performance-Based Management: Responding to the Challenges", *Public Productivity and Management Review*, vol. 22, no. 3, pp. 288–307.

Wiggins, A. and Tymms, P. 2002, "Dysfunctional Effects of League Tables: A Comparison Between English and Scottish Primary Schools", *Public Money and Management*, vol. 22, no. 1, pp. 43–8.

Williams, D. W. 2000, "Reinventing the Proverbs of Government", *Public Administration Review*, vol. 60, no. 6, pp. 522–34.

Williams, D. W. 2003, "Measuring Government in the Early Twentieth Century", *Public Administration Review*, vol. 63, no. 6, pp. 643–59.

Wilson, D., Croxson, B., and Atkinson, A. 2006, "What Gets Measured Gets Done: Headteachers' Responses to the English Secondary School Performance Management System", *Policy Studies*, vol. 27, no. 2, pp. 153–71.

Wilson, J. Q. 1989, *Bureaucracy: What Government Agencies Do and Why They Do It*, Basic Books, New York.

Wilson, J. 2004, "Comprehensive Performance Assessment – Springboard or Dead-Weight", *Public Money and Management*, vol. 24, no. 1, 63–8.

Working Party on Performance Monitoring in the Public Services 2005, "Performance Indicators: Good, Bad, and Ugly", *Journal of the Royal Statistical Society A*, vol. 168, no. 1, pp. 1–27.

Yang, K. 2005, "Public Administrators' Trust in Citizens: A Missing Link in Citizen Involvement Efforts", *Public Administration Review*, vol. 65, no. 3, pp. 273–85.

Zifcak, S. 1994, *New Managerialism: Administrative Reform in Whitehall and Canberra* Open University Press, Buckingham.

Index

Introductory Note

References such as "178–9" indicate (not necessarily continuous) discussion of a topic across a range of pages. Because the entire volume is about "performance", "performance information", "performance measurement" and "performance management", the use of these terms as entry points has been minimized. Information will be found under the corresponding detailed topics.